RRR

A Unique Plan for Economic Recovery and Job Creation!

A typical family celebrating a birthday and relying on a good economic plan

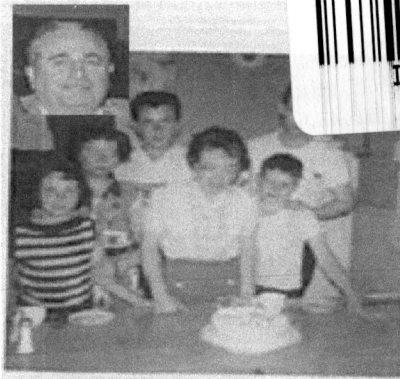

LETS
GO
PUBLISH!

B R I A N   W.   K E L L Y

Published by: LETS GO PUBLISH!
                 Brian P. Kelly, Publisher
                 P.O. Box 621
                 Wilkes-Barre, PA 18503
                 brian@brianpkelly.com
                 www.letsgopublish.com

Library of Congress Copyright Information Pending

Book Cover Design by Michele Thomas

ISBN Information: The International Standard Book Number (ISBN) is a unique machine-readable identification number, which marks any book unmistakably. The ISBN is the clear standard in the book industry. 159 countries and territories are officially ISBN members. The Official ISBN For this book is:

978-0-9841418-7-6

The price for this work is: $11.95 USD

10	9	8	7	6	5	4	3	2

Release Date: January 2012,   September 2016

LETS GO PUBLISH!

Dedication

To My Wonderful Big Brother Ed

We lost Ed last year at Thanksgiving time.

Ed was an inspiration for me in many ways in my life. He was very handsome and he was very bright. He was the number one student at St. Boniface School.
In fact, he was at the top of the class for eight years, and
he graduated valedictorian.
Ed was very bright at Meyers High School also but, at the time, it was tough financially to gain a
college education. He did very well in
High School despite from my
observations, never picking up a book.
Bobby Stanton and Jimmy Malacarne,
his lifelong best friends, could vouch for
that.
I was thrilled that he agreed to be my
sponsor at Confirmation while he was
married and living in New Jersey with
his new family. And, a few years later, I
was just as thrilled that he asked me to
be the Godfather to his first child,
Edward J. Kelly III.
Over time, life removes the age differences
with siblings and Ed became something
for me that he always had been in my
life—a best friend. I miss him
immensely.
He was a fine man and a fine brother.
His counsel on my writing and political
activities was the best and greatly
appreciated. He never lost his gifts and
his perspective on life.
I was a fortunate man to have a brother
like Edward J. Kelly Jr.
Thank you Lord for giving him to me and my whole family until you called him back. I bet
heaven never found a better combo dart and shuffleboard shooter! But, I also bet for fairness, he
has to play on a different team than Dad!

Acknowledgments

I would like to thank many people for helping me in this effort.

I appreciate all the help that I have received in putting this book together as well as all of my other 78 published books.

My printed acknowledgments had become so large that book readers "complained" about going through too many pages to get to page one of the text.

And, so to permit me more flexibility, I put my acknowledgment list online, and it continues to grow. Believe it or not, it once cost about a dollar more to print each book.

Thank you and God bless you all for your help.

Please check out www.letsgopublish.com to read the latest version of my heartfelt acknowledgments updated for this book. Click the bottom of the Main menu!

Thank you all!

Table of Contents

Preface:

I liked the ring of former Presidential candidate Herman Cain's presentation of his 999 plan so much that when I developed my top three bullets for my US Senate campaign against Robert P. Casey Jr. in Pennsylvania in the fall 2011, and all three began with the word *reduce*, the RRR plan was conceived. The full title of this book of course is RRR: A Unique Plan for Economic Recovery and Job Creation. Along the way to a full set of issues that my campaign addresses, there are an additional three sets of 3 R's that are also fleshed out in this book.

Unlike the Herman Cain plan, the RRR focuses on many more areas that need to be addressed for us to turn around our economy and stimulate job creation. Cain's 999 plan addresses a major change in the tax structure. The RRR plan, on the other hand includes taxes but it reaches into critical areas that are impeding economic growth today such as regulations, immigration, and spending. Additionally, the RRR plan suggests that we alter our pure capitalism system into one that is more mercantilist.

Jobs are hard to come by anywhere in the world today including the United States. Even some liberals are starting to say that "you can blame the government for that." In this day and age, you can blame the government for lots more than that, and nobody would think you were kidding.

Despite no jobs for anybody else, the US government is growing in terms of employees at a record pace. This is not part of the solution. This is part of the problem. While government grows, there is less and less real work even for government workers. And, so many agencies, even those that originally did good work in their functionary role as well as their advisory role to the President, have branched into areas that now hurt the economy rather than help it. The more of them there are unfortunately, the greater the drag on private sector jobs and the economy as a whole.

I wrote a book recently about eliminating the EPA as it is the poster child for government agencies gone wild. It really was not too long after its inception that The EPA became a monster in size and in its intrusive tactics. The typical victims of the EPA have been small businesses that do not have the legal staff to withstand the continual onslaught. Everyday people have also been affected indirectly through increased costs, but now with the Light Bulb act, the EPA even terrorizes US households.

This is a serious book. I take leave of a serious tone very rarely because if the serious issues we face are not addressed, and the major changes in philosophies that are necessary to bring our problems under control are not considered, we have little reason to expect improvement.

Why did I write this book?

The quick answer is because it reflects my campaign platform.

Our economy has stopped working. Our financial institutions have been forced to lessen their standards while the taxpayer has become the prop between any of government's favorite businesses and failure. The United States once represented rugged individualism in all we did and only the strong survived. America became the strongest of nations because of that "manly" philosophy. Our government today seems like it is against strength as it attempts, through socialistic, progressive, and Marxist principles to create a society of wimps, in which the American dream can be little more than a handout.

Businesses have obviously decided that the US is not worth it anymore. For PR reasons of course, they are not telling anyone that. They simply don't want to deal with high taxation, oppressive regulations, and a government that is more pro-union than pro-people or pro-industry. Despite government's official stance, it has been more than complicit in helping business execute its destructive plans to rid the US of major industry and suffer no consequences.

The RRR plan addresses all of the sticky areas where corruption reins and corporations have been able to undermine what is good for America and Americans. The RRR plan is good for the economy. It is good for the people. It is good for jobs. And, for those corporations that want to sign up to be American-centric, it is good for corporations. It is the solution balm that offers a gutsy, unique, real, and workable path to get America back on its feet. There is nothing like it anywhere else. All we need is the resolve for the RRR plan to make us successful.

America is under attack from within and from without. Government has one objective and that is to grow so that it can control everything and everybody. Corporations are protecting their assets and their viability from a government that would seize whatever it can get from anybody and that includes corporations and their executives. Government has great ambitions. Dollars are the fuel that permits government to grow and prosper. Our government wants more and more and more from people who make less and less and less. On the outside, we have free trade agreements nipping like piranha at all things American, while our own government accepts trade imbalance without a whimper.

Unions help a small percentage of the population and elevate their life style above all others. If 100% of the population were unionized, we all know that unions would become completely ineffective. The people, who do not work for the government or who do not belong to unions are the ones being squeezed most by this economic malaise with dollars being printed on the presses of the US Mint as fast as the paper can be shipped in. The inflationary effects on the poor are worse than any flat tax system you can imagine.

It is time to say STOP. All of us together must say STOP to save our country. We must say STOP to save our lives. No matter whom we are, it is time to STOP. What good will it be even if our side wins, if there is nothing left. We need to come together, adopt the RRR plan and fight for America and not our own special interests. It is time.

I hope you enjoy this book and I hope that it inspires you to take action to help change the way you think about corporations, unions, government, taxes, spending, immigration, mercantilism and whole host of other items that can help America survive this major recession. I hope you digest the entire RRR plan, be willing to adopt it, and add to it your own positive notions.

You can help make the US a far better country.

I wish you the best

Brian Kelly (For US Senate)

P.S. I have announced a write-in campaign for US Senate v Robert P. Casey Jr. for the 2018 election season. If you like my ideas, and my honesty, feel free to donate to my campaign by going to www.bookhawkers.com. It is one of the sites which sells my books.

God bless America!

About the Author

Brian W. Kelly *is a retired Assistant Professor in the Business Information Technology (BIT) program at Marywood University, where he also served as the IBM i and midrange systems technical advisor to the IT faculty. Kelly developed and taught many college and professional courses in the IT and business areas. He is also a contributing technical editor to IT Jungle's "The Four Hundred" and "Four Hundred Guru" Newsletters.*

A former IBM Senior Systems Engineer, he has an active consultancy in the information technology field, (www.kellyconsulting.com). He is the author of dozens of books and numerous articles about current IT topics. Kelly is a frequent speaker at COMMON, IBM conferences, and other technical conferences and user group meetings across the United States.

Back in 2012, this was the seventh political book Kelly had written and it joins his other great informers: Taxation without Representation, Obama's Seven Deadly Sins, Healthcare Accountability, Jobs! Jobs! Jobs! and Americans Need Not Apply!, Kill the EPA! This is Mr. Kelly's 46th published book. In 2016, when this book was prepared for reprinting, Mr. Kelly had just completed his 78th book.

Chapter 1   Campaigning @ Fish's Barney Inn

Not Exactly Readn, 'Ritn and 'Rithmatic.

RRR is the Kelly jobs plan for American prosperity. This book's subtitle also describes it well: A Unique Plan for Economic Recovery and Job Creation!

On October 18, 2011, I participated in two of the most important events of my early public "political" life. At 11:00 AM, after spending the evening with my sister Ann (Nancy) Flannery, and my life-long best friend Dennis Grimes at the historic Thomas Bond House (Bed & Breakfast extraordinaire) across the street from the historic Philadelphia City Tavern and right outside of Independence Park, all of which are in Pennsylvania, my home state, dual events transpired.

I had been the TEA Party endorsed Democratic candidate for Congressional Representative in District 11 in a five county area in Northeastern Pennsylvania (NEPA) in 2010 against a 13-term incumbent and a very young Country Commissioner from Lackawanna County. I had never run for elected office before. Hoping to gain office with no encumbrances, I took no campaign donations. I surprised everybody, including my wife, by grabbing about seventeen percent of the vote in a three-candidate race. The incumbent received less than 50% and this showed many of us that it was not just us, but a lot of other Democrats that had gotten tired of the incumbent's lack of representation.

I have been a Democrat all my life other than two years as an Independent. I challenged the incumbent because he had become part of bad government in Washington DC and had been way too generous with taxpayer dollars being directed to his family members.

With most Democrats having voted for a change in representation in the primary, I knew the right thing for me to do was to help the Republican challenger to defeat the incumbent in the general election. Lou Barletta was a feisty pro-American Mayor in the small NEPA City of Hazleton. He is a fine man with conservative values like my father and I. He was clearly the best choice for the people of Northeastern PA.

In an area of Pennsylvania that was mostly Democratic, Lou Barletta won the election handily. My father would say, "Brian, always vote for the best man." A ton of Democrats joined me in assuring that Northeastern PA is now represented by the best man after the 2010 general election. That man is Congressman Lou Barletta.

By the way, none of my family, some of whom are actually Republicans, and none of my friends were asked by Congressman Barletta to accept any government positions anywhere as a result of my assistance. There was no quid pro quo. Barletta was simply the best man and we voted him in. No paybacks were expected nor received. That is how America needs to operate. Our collective job is to help the best people get elected as our representatives and then we can smile when they are in a position to help all the people, not just a select few.

I trust that Lou Barletta will continue to bring honesty and integrity to the office in the 11th District.

TEA Party endorsement

On October 18, 2011, long after the elections of 2010, and right about 11:00 AM, I met with the President of the Independence Hall TEA Party, Terri Adams, and the President of the TEA Party PAC, Don Adams. We were positioned directly in front of Independence Hall. I was about to announce my candidacy for the position of United States Senator from Pennsylvania. The position is currently held by Robert. P. Casey, Jr., the son of the famous former Governor of Pennsylvania, Robert P. Casey Sr.

Terri Adams and Don Adams, and their respective organizations had sponsored the event so that, on behalf of the TEA Party, they could personally endorse my candidacy for Senator. They had invited the press and others in the tri-state TEA party organization, which were able to make it at 11:00 AM. Since most TEA Party members hold jobs, none of us expected a phenomenal turnout in the middle of the day in the middle of the week, but it was very nice, nonetheless. So, the two-prongs of the event were the announcement of my candidacy along with the endorsement by the TEA Party of my candidacy. As my sister Nancy summed it up: "And a great day it was!"

Following the Philadelphia event, we journeyed to the State Capitol in Harrisburg for another TEA Party rally announcing my candidacy and a repeat of the TEA Party endorsement. Following the rally, the party of three from Northeastern PA took off again for the Northeast.

My speeches for Philadelphia and Harrisburg were very similar. Knowing that the people in NEPA often come to the Barney Inn in Wilkes-Barre on Fridays, the campaign decided to hold the event outside under their fine pavilion an hour before happy hour so there would be time for a lot of discussion with a lot of Pennsylvanians. The Barney Inn announcement was also covered by the press. The full text of the Barney Inn speech is on my web site, and it is also included as an appendix to this chapter. The web site is:

www.kellyforussenate.com

Look on the left side of the site for press kits, and then pick the Barney Inn Speech.

I must admit that in the weeks before the speech, I was enamored by the 999 taxation plan of Herman Cain, and I admired Herman's tenacity even more as the scum of the earth tried to bring him down (the main stream media). The media showed extreme urgency in attempting to deal Cain a death blow as Obama, who never had a real job, obviously feared the prospects of running against a self-made businessman. The objective of Obama and his media surrogates was to defame Cain so a more beatable Republican candidate would be left to face the American Destroyer in Chief.

Unfortunately, the incessant, tormenting pressure of the media, which was far different from that which President Clinton received from the same press for far more credible accusations, ultimately caused Herman Cain to go back to his family, rather than continue with the campaign. I think this is America's loss.

In the spirit of 999, which is purely a taxation bill but with major positive jobs consequences, I developed a comprehensive Jobs and economic recovery plan that I call RRR. This book is about that plan, which I announced at the Barney Inn on October 21, 2011.

Before we get into the details of the RRR plan let me say that the speeches of October 18 were very similar to the October 21 speech at the Barney. However, at the Barney, my delivery was more relaxed in front of the home town crowd.

I checked out the speeches from Harrisburg and Philadelphia to determine which mix would be best. Though much of the substance was the same, I did reach back to realize that I was in Wilkes-Barre and in Pennsylvania and I had a lot more to say at the Barney about the local venue. The folks related well to the local references in this speech.

I look forward to being out there again in the near future to make my message, the RRR plan, well known in Pennsylvania. Soon, I will be challenging Senator Casey to a debate and that ought to be fun.

By the way, one of my best high school friends, Eugene Aloysius Michael Burke, attended the Barney Event. He had seen the plan for the press conference at the Barney Inn in the Times Leader of Wilkes-Barre, and he decided to show up. When he pranced in, I did not immediately recognize Gene. But, he is unmistakably a Burke, and once I got past the new beard, this guy was a dead ringer for my good friend Gene Burke, and to my delight, he is a conservative.

The first time I mentioned the RRR Jobs Plan for America, was that afternoon at the Barney Inn, Wilkes-Barre on October 21, 2011.

The RRR plan is a way of bringing all of my thinking together in a way that can be remembered easily by all Pennsylvanians. After I had concluded my Barney Inn Speech with the Pledge of Allegiance, including that 60+ year old phrase, "under God," and I waited patiently for the applause of my friends and relatives (they had no choice) to cease, there was a round of questions from the press.

The three R"s traditionally have been about education and how important it is to learn Reading, Writing, and Arithmetic when you are young. But, my three R's are not about education. The three R's are a unique economic and jobs plan for America.

RRR is a simple to understand yet comprehensive solution that can very quickly change the economic and jobs picture into results that include Americans of all ages having the opportunity to go to work again. The three main Rs in this plan are

- **R**educe taxes
- **R**educe immigration
- **R**educe regulations.

There are three other sets of 3 Rs that round out the RRR plan and make it very comprehensive compared to anything else that is circulating. Besides, with all these R's, you can bet this plan will work:

Set 2
- Reduce Spending
- Repeal Obamacare
- Reindustrialize America

Set 3
- Reduce Offshoring
- Raise Tariffs
- Revitalize Energy

Set 4
- Reduce Redistribution
- Reduce / Eliminate Lying
- Reduce Government & Remember Mistakes

The plan is easy to remember, and it will be easy to implement if Congress has the political will to abandon lobbyist and other special interest demands and it chooses to address the needs of American citizens. The RRR plan is all we need to make America successful again.

There are those who suggest that an approach such as the RRR plan will take a long while to be effective as the impetus for tariffs and taxes to cause a change in corporate behavior will

not come overnight. These are the same people, and
Pennsylvania Senator Bob Casey Jr. is among them, who thirty
years ago said it is no use drilling more in the US to solve the
short-term energy problem because it would take more than ten
years to begin seeing results.

We had three times ten years to do the right thing on energy
and we did not because it would take too long. Yet, if we had
addressed the problem thirty years ago, we would not have it
today.

The RRR plan is structured to show positive results
immediately and continue to get better until it is all
implemented. That ten year figure seems to be back however,
by the naysayers.

It is a pretty safe bet for politicians and former politicians to
project negative certainty for any good to happen over the next
ten years, no matter what the issue. For example, former
Secretary of Labor for President Bill Clinton, Robert Reich
offered recently that unemployment in the U.S. will most likely
remain high for the next 10 years.

He backed it with some statistics saying that if the current rate
of job growth (averaging 90,000 new jobs per month over the
last six months), is sustained, then unemployment will remain
constant with 14 million Americans permanently unemployed.
In this case the high unemployment would continue well past
ten years.

Reich then used his Economist hat to opine that if we are to get
back to a normal rate of 200,000 new jobs per month,
unemployment will stay high for at least 10 years before it
eventually corrects itself. Reich ought to know. He is a smart
man. He is a one-time labor secretary and an economist and
now, he is a professor of public policy at the University of
California at Berkeley.

Does that mean we should take action now—implement the RRR plan—so that we affect the number of jobs added per month and shorten the recovery? Or, does it mean that we should sit back like with oil so that ten years from now we can say again that it will take at least ten years for any action to create a positive change? Obviously, my recommendation is that the more prudent approach is to adopt RRR immediately if not sooner; and watch things get better sooner than we would ever think.

Before we move on to the chapters that fully explain the components of the RRR plan, and we flesh out a few more sets of Rs that will also help jobs, let's take a time out so you can see the speech I delivered at 3:00 PM on October 21, 2011,at Fish's Barney Inn in Wilkes-Barre, PA.

Feel free to read any of the other speeches under the title Press Kit on the main page of www.kellyforussenate.com. I will keep the page open for awhile after the election even if I win.

Chapter 1 appendix I
Joe Fisher's Barney Inn speech Oct 21, 2011

Good afternoon—my name is Brian Kelly.

On Tuesday Morning, I was at Independence Hall in Philadelphia where I received the endorsement of the Independence Hall Tea Party. I am a TEA Party member and I love what the TEA Party does for regular Americans like you and I.

There is little doubt that these are tough times.

Nobody really knows how many dips there will be in this recession

But we do know that without controls on spending, our wild deficit and debt will keep us in recession for years to come.

America needs to become like we were before the progressives—Barack Obama, Harry Reid, Nancy Pelosi, and of course Pennsylvania's own Bob Casey Jr. took power from the people.

In this light, I have outlined eight major principles that I will use as a guide in helping our country recover and prosper: These are.

1. *Americans First,*
2. *Fiscal Conservative*
3. *Pro Life*
4. *Restructure Tax system*
5. *Smaller Government*
6. *Transparency*
7. *Pro Israel,*
8. *Strong Defense*

Today, in 2011, JFK, my favorite Democrat, would be considered a conservative!

My views on taxation are very similar to JFK's

His were modeled after those of Andrew Mellon from the 1920's recession.

Both Mellon and JFK knew how to end a recession and so do I.

You all know how Bob Casey and his best friend Barack Obama want to raise everybody's taxes. Kennedy would not approve.

Here's what Kennedy had to say. He offered similar thoughts many times:

"In short, it is a paradoxical truth that ... the soundest way to raise the revenues in the long run is to cut the rates now... And the reason is that only full employment can balance the budget, and tax reduction can pave the way to that employment. The purpose of cutting taxes now is not to incur a budget deficit, but to achieve the more prosperous, expanding economy which can bring a budget surplus."
--- JFK, Nov. 20, 1962, news conference. BTW, that was right after the Cuban Missile Crisis. Kennedy was already on to domestic issues.

If we Democrats had listened to Kennedy, our current recession would be over

By cutting taxes up and down the line and reducing spending, JFK was looking for a big revenue surplus – not a deficit.

By increasing spending and increasing taxes Obama has been creating huge deficits and increasing debt and preparing America for bankruptcy.

Obama is far trickier than even Tricky Dicky Nixon. He's got a new name for this trick now that he is trying to get reelected again. He calls it a Jobs bill. I call it tax and spend.

What does the so called jobs bill have in it?

It's the same porkulus / stimulus stuff with lipstick --increased spending, increased taxes, larger deficits and crippling debt.

Even the Beatles would call out Obama and Casey on this. Remember this tune?-→ "No, No, No, Not a Second Time..."

Obama and Casey used a trillion dollars of stimulus for crony capitalism for their big campaign donors. Americans have smartened up. No more taxpayer money for reelection campaigns.

Senator Bob Casey has been with Obama 98% of the time. That means he has been with Pennsylvanians only 2% of the time. By the way, that Beatles song applies to Casey also—No, No, No, Not a Second Time—

I love the United States of America just as it was founded in 1776.

In those days, Independence Hall, where I was on Tuesday, meant independence for all---

Much revolutionary blood was spilled for our freedom and liberty, and yet, freedom and liberty are at stake again today.

Nobody wanted then or now to be tethered to a corrupt, cowardly, and oppressive federal government in Washington D.C. So let us all tell the Federal Government:

Get off our backs!

It's time to bring all the power we gave away to the feds back to the states – back to the people!

Yes, I love America and I have no problem with citizens of any other country loving their countries more than they love America.

But if you can't come legally, we don't want you here! Stay home!

As an American, I am interested in what is good for Americans first, not foreigners first

If I go to your country, I expect your citizens to be #1 priority. I won't take any of your precious jobs, and I will bring a passport.

I want you to treat me and my country the same.

Americans have nobody to apologize to. Nothing to apologize for. And we are not going to apologize for being Americans.

We are proud to be Americans.

Not all TEA Party members are Republicans. Like me, not all Democrats are hard core progressives.

How would you like to be us?

We woke up one day and found that our Party had been hijacked by a group of people who hate America. You know who they are.

Harry Reid and Nancy Pelosi and Barack Obama, and yes, Bob Casey Jr. Now, there's a crew who show every day; they don't care at all for Americans.

What about my primary opponent, the Unknown Senator Bob Casey?   I have watched him closely during the Obama presidency.

If you like Barack Obama and his progressive policies, you are *"gonna"* love Bob Casey.

Here we are in Wilkes-Barre at the Barney Inn, a wonderful place (now Cris-Nics), which at the time was run by Joe Fisher and Joe Predo, where more blarney has surely been spilled than Youngling Lager. I regret to say that one of the very good ones, Joe Fisher died April 11, 2012—not much more than a half-year later than this event.

Don't you just love it in America! And! How about that Yuengling Lager; brewed in Pottsville Pennsylvania. My dad worked for Stegmaier Brewery for 31 years, and we know the Lion Brewery carries on the tradition of good brew right here in Wilkes-Barre. But we all have to earn our brew.

There are a lot of problems that need to be solved

Like you, I am fed up with the bloated, unresponsive bureaucracy in Washington.

When, with your grace I take a seat in the Senate of the United States, the Washington progressives will get the message.

The days of big government, big regulations, big giveaways, big healthcare takeovers, big healthcare redistribution and big wealth redistribution are over.

Yes, I sure am for helpless people but I am not for making people helpless.

By the way, progressives are the guys that don't like any of us and they probably don't even like Yuengling Lager or Stegmaier Gold Medal Beer.

Don't you think that in America, Americans should come first?

As most Pennsylvanians I too believe in the American Dream.

Quite frankly, I think Pennsylvanians are sick of the progressive's notion that the new American Dream is ... a handout.

With America in the shape that it is, I feel sometimes like I want to scream at the top of my lungs. But because you are all my friends, I won't scream. Nonetheless,

It is OK to love liberty and freedom.
It is OK to love God.
It is OK to love America."

To help restore a limited government and put the people back in charge, today, I offer my candidacy as United States Senator from my state, the great state of Pennsylvania.

I promise to speak out of one side of my mouth and I pledge to represent the people of Pennsylvania honestly and truthfully. My word is my bond.

It is time to heal America and again make her strong.

I pledge allegiance to the flag of the United States of America and to the Republic for which it stands, one nation, under God, with liberty and justice for all.

I wish you all the best. God bless America.

*** End of Barney Inn Speech ***

Chapter 1 appendix II
Eight guiding principles – the detail

The detailed raw ideas for the eight guiding principles are included as a second chapter appendix. When I delivered the speech I did not expand the principles.

1. *Americans First – American Jobs, border security, fence, states' rights, shut down excessive legal and all illegal immigration, BTW, over 2.2 million legal aliens get jobs each year in the US? Let's reduce it to .2 (point 2) Reward businesses that hire Americans. No tax breaks for companies that choose to offshore jobs. Huge unemployment tax on companies found using illegal labor. Import tax on Chinese goods and goods produced overseas by any American corporation. Just watch the jobs come back. Since Americans corporations take American jobs overseas, invite overseas businesses to set up plants in America, and give Americans those jobs in America. Oh, and it is OK when if foreign companies manufacturing in America take the business from so-called American corporations. Let's support corporations that love America and who give Americans Jobs. Let the others sell their stuff overseas.*

2. *Fiscal Conservative--- no bailouts, no takeovers, no porkulus, no government takeover of business. Need balanced budget amendment, reinstitute Glass Steagall, repeal CRA, repeal Dodd / Frank, repeal Obamacare.*

3. *Pro-Life – Human life begins at conception*

4. *Restructure tax system – Reduce taxes to stimulate the economy and spending. Us the John Kennedy style and migrate to the FAIR Tax. The 9, 9, 9 is also a good plan. Reduce or eliminate corporate tax. Introduce tariffs to reindustrialize the US. Offshoring companies get no corporate breaks. Companies that hire illegals get no tax breaks*

5. *Smaller Government – Ron Paul says government agencies are unconstitutional. He's right. Eliminate harmful, costly agencies such as the EPA, FDA, USDA, Interior, Energy, Education, etc. Repeal Obamacare.*

6. *Transparency / accountability – openness, No closed doors. Fire all czars.*

7. *Pro Israel – Israel is our only friend in the Middle East.*

8. *Strong Defense—"Speak softly and carry a big stick," Don't go starting wars. Win all wars in which we engage. Use big drones and micro-drones and few foot soldiers. We have 8000 drones & $5 Billion in budget – use 'em. not American blood. Exit strategy -- get out quickly with a win. Send in the drone dragonflies. It will seem like one of the 10 plagues.*

Chapter 2 Reduce Taxes

The US tax code is a joke

As a starter, please consider that the US tax code is over 75,000
pages of exemptions and exceptions written by lobbyists and
passed into law by our esteemed Congress. Don't forget who
permits this atrocity to continue from one Congress to another.
Vote them out if they choose not to address the use of the tax
code as a political tool. The message here is to get politics and
about 74,900 pages out of the tax code.

Government, regardless of whether the sponsors of legislation
are Republican or Democrat, should not determine who wins
or who loses in any marketplace. It is intrinsically unfair. This
notion extends to the Republican sponsored "Pickens Plan -
House Bill 1380," which was introduced in April 2011.

Republican voters are against crony capitalism for sure.
However, most see it simply as a Democrat thing. But, the
Pickens plan is just as bad as Solyndra. D or R, no subsidies
means no subsidies. There are no home games and away games
that permit us to change that mantra. The only difference in the
Pickens plan is that Republicans like Pickens just as the
Democrats liked Solyndra. Say no to House Bill 1380 and any
other attempt to add more stipulations and more subsidies to
the tax code.

Regardless of how it is restructured and 75,000 pages is
something we all think is a bit much for honest government, the
US tax code should have all subsidies removed. If businesses
cannot make it, then they should not make it. It is that simple.

The taxpayers should not pay for a Boone Pickens boondoggle or anyone else's boondoggle, if you pardon my choice of words.

When things are so good that everybody should want in on the deal, let the people who like the deal and who can afford to risk their capital go for it. Let them become even richer by using their own money. That's OK. That's capitalism.

Rich people should not risk my money in order to become richer. Moreover, they should not think they even have a right to my money and your money for any reason. Use your own money, period. Crony capitalism results from any subsidy. Moreover, there are no regular Americans of which I am aware, in an age when corporations are taking the people's jobs overseas, who would vote to give corporations welfare of any kind. Sorry! No thanks!

Even if after all is said and done, we the people might win by risking our national treasury, it is unfair to all of us to do any favors for any company or any individual. Mr. Pickens and others seeking or enjoying subsidies, if the deal is so sweet, do it yourself. Americans have a lot of reasons to not trust governments, corporations, or unions. Stop playing with us and stop playing with the tax code. It is already too complex to suit my taste. How about yours?

It's time to ship all the wheel barrows loaded with oppressive tax legislation to the scrap heap and do what is right for America. Herman Cain decided to give it a shot, and for that, I applaud him. For honest government, subsidies, which always create crony capitalism, must become a thing of the past.

The 999 plan

Herman Cain sure looked like the real deal. His 999 plan is a tax-only plan that would represent just the first "R" of the RRR Jobs Plan—Reduce Taxes. It would help bring jobs back to

America for sure but the RRR plan is more comprehensive. The intent of Cain's plan is to keep tax collections the same (revenue neutral) and completely restructure the tax code, making it far more simple than today.

[On December 3, 2011 Herman Cain suspended his campaign and thus ended his presidential legacy. The biased media was able to stop Cain because they knew he would beat Obama.]

Eighteen percent of the tax (9 plus 9—sales tax plus corporate tax) brings a lot more taxpayers (unreported tips, druggies, black market action) into the tax game. The "black market" is its own $1 trillion economy if not more.

I like 999 on the surface, but I admit it is not all that easy underneath in terms of how it affects the economy. The unintended consequences, once identified need to be addressed. Cain showed that he was willing to make adjustments. If any other presidential candidate opts for Cain's 999, they too will have to be prepared for some changes. So, let's look at the pieces of this simple, yet highly innovative plan in a little more detail

The 999 plan ends with a nine percent sales tax. So, in Pennsylvania, for example, we would be paying 6% plus the 9%. For the poor, Cain already adjusted one of the 9's by subtracting 9 from it. The plan for the poor is that they pay the sales tax but they pay no social security and no income tax. In fact, nobody in Cain's plan pays a separate Social Security tax, or a separate Medicare Tax. For the poor, no income tax would need to be paid but a form would have to be filed even for those under the poverty line and that is good. If it were my plan, even the poor would pay something, though very minimal.

I think everybody in American needs to be in all parts of the tax contribution game. Anything brought in through withholding, other than perhaps a .25% rate, would be refunded normally. In other words, without working out specifics, I would not make the income tax zero for anybody. It would be .25% instead of zero. I admit, however, that I have not yet learned enough about the Cain plan to know how specifically to modify it to make it work for all.

Cain quipped that this plan version for the poor is really 909. The 9% corporate tax, the first "9" is like a gross receipts tax after investments. Non-capital expenses such as payroll wages would be the big part of the revenue that would be taxed. One of the wishes of Cain in proposing 999 is that seniors are more likely to receive larger dividends as no corporate tax would be extracted on the amount of the dividends provided by corporations to its shareholders.

999 provides a big incentive for corporations to take what would have been tax and return it to shareholders as dividends. Many of these are elderly who may live in government subsidized high rises in major urban areas. Shareholders would then pay 9% tax on the distributed dividend income that they would not have gotten otherwise. Any purchase from another company (non-retail) in the 999 plan would not be taxed so it is not as onerous as a value added tax as in Europe.

Corporate income tax reduction key to job growth

The reduction in the corporate rate is critical for bringing back corporations from overseas. In other words, we need a substantially lower corporate rate to increase jobs in America.

Ireland is now the least expensive country in which a corporation can do business. Its corporate income tax is 12.5% on all corporate bottom-line income. The US deferral corporate rate is 35%. If you add state income taxes, on the average, the corporate income tax (state and federal) totals out on the average to be about 39.3%. That high rate is a big reason why many corporations have taken their jobs overseas.

Nothing is as simple as it first looks. The 39.3% composite rate is a national average of apportioned taxes paid. Pennsylvania for example has a complex corporate tax, in which the major income tax rate is 9.99. To determine the portion of corporate income that is taxable in each state, most multi-state corporations use an apportionment method. This takes three factors into consideration in determining how much income is applicable to each of the 47 states that have corporate income taxes. For income apportionment, it does not matter in which state a corporation is chartered. It matters how much property; how many employees; and how much sales a corporation has in a particular state compared to all other states.

Pennsylvania ranks second in the nation in oppressive corporate tax rates behind Iowa's 12%. In Pennsylvania and other states, once the income is determined, there are other components of taxes which corporations must also pay, making such states very unfriendly towards business. Pennsylvania has about ten of these other considerations.

Congress and the President need to take the combined rate seriously as the US has one of the highest state and federal corporate combined income tax rates in the world. To make the rate more competitive internationally, corporate tax rates will have to be reduced both in Washington and in the state capitals.

Making the federal corporate tax 9% instead of 35% gives corporations a real financial reason to bring jobs back to America. America's competitiveness in the world would increase even more substantially if the states also pitched in with decreases in corporate income tax rates. This is not just speculation. Taxes are more of an incentive for offshoring than lower wage rates. By making corporate tax rate low or non-existent, American corporations will be flocking back to our shores and forcign corporations will be trying to get new plants built as soon as possible. That sure beats "shovel ready."

In any Kelly tax plan, revenue would not be neutral so I differ
with Cain on this one. Revenue would be less than neutral. In
other words, there would be a tax cut at the individual level and
at the corporate level and a good part of the revenue would be
made up by increases in jobs and individual income as well as
by increasing tariffs. In other words, the same that JFK put in
place in the 1960's could take place again. See JFK quotes in
Chapter 1 and information about raising tariffs in Chapter 12.

The Perry plan

Rick Perry has another taxing idea which I also like. I am
normally not so agreeable. His proposal would lower the
corporate tax rate to 20 percent from 35 percent and give
multinational companies a temporary incentive to bring home
foreign-earned income at a far lower rate of 5.25 percent. I
would recommend that Perry set the corporate rate at 12% or
lower so it would be the lowest corporate rate in the world if
the states also cooperated. Lowering the corporate tax rate is
highly desirable and most economists believe it would be a big
factor in helping to bring jobs back.

Lowering the repatriation of cash rate for corporations to 5.25%
will surely bring greenbacks back into the country. When the
corporations give dividends to their stockholders, these
greenbacks will be spent and there will be a temporary surge in
the economy. It will help us get over the hump at least
somewhat.

I like all of that. Additionally, I would like to see incentives for
corporations to hire American workers v. hiring foreigners and
v. offshoring jobs. Members of Congress that are not tightly tied
to lobbyists should agree that those additional criteria are good
for Americans.

What is repatriation?

Many Americans do not know that government for years has permitted multi-national corporations, whose headquarters are in the US and who manufacture or otherwise do business overseas, to keep their overseas profits in overseas banks until they need the cash back home. When it comes back home, the IRS and the states whack the corporations with the 39.3 % plus combined corporate income tax rate minus any amounts that were already paid to the host country.

Most other countries do not tax their home based corporations on overseas income so in these days of globalism it is easy to see why corporations, not loyal to America, would move their headquarters to more tax-friendly countries.

Obviously, multinational companies don't particularly like that they get taxed by two countries so they bring the money back only when absolutely necessary. There is about a trillion, and perhaps two trillion dollars that might come back and be taxed at Perry's 5.25% rate instead of 35%. Since US based corporations must pay a corporate income tax to the foreign countries in which they do business, there is really no free lunch out there for any of these guys.

Let's say corporations earn their dollars in Ireland and they pay the 12.5% Irish corporate income tax. If the corporation is not a US-based corporation; it is the end of their tax obligation. If they are a US based corporation, then they would pay 39.3 % Let's use 40% in the calculations) 40 minus 12.5 gives 27.5 percent additional tax on every dollar they bring back home.

So, you can see that the 5.25% Perry "tax holiday rate," is very favorable and would result in cash immediately coming home. More than likely a share of this corporate windfall would be given out in dividends and the dividends received by John Q. Public, would be spent or invested in US projects or products. Moreover, the fact that the corporation would be banking a lot of the proceeds means that a heck of a lot of money would be hitting the shores of the US. It is a good deal.

The United States bases its jurisdiction to tax international income on residence. As a result, U.S.-chartered corporations are taxed on their worldwide income, but foreign corporations are taxed only on their U.S.-source income. Domestic corporations are taxed on their worldwide income at the federal and state levels.

Corporate income tax is based on net taxable income as defined under Federal or state law. Generally, taxable income for a corporation is gross income (business and possibly non-business receipts less cost of goods sold) less any allowable tax deductions.

US tax laws permit corporations to indefinitely postpone its U.S. tax due from foreign income by operating through a foreign subsidiary. So, that is how most deferrals begin in the first place. U.S. corporate income taxes on foreign profits can be deferred as long as the corporation's foreign earnings remain in the control of its foreign subsidiary and are reinvested abroad. The U.S. firm pays taxes on its overseas earnings only when the subsidiary corporation (wholly owned in almost all cases) pays the income to the U.S. parent corporation in the form of an intra-firm dividend or even as other income.

This is not a tax course. It is simply a book about the fabulous RRR plan devised by yours truly. Though my MBA is in Accounting and Finance, you would not want to hire me as a tax accountant because my area of expertise is operations management and information technology.

It is good to know, however, that the Perry plan for earnings repatriation is almost exactly the same plan as the repatriation provision of the American Jobs Creation Act (P.L. 108-357) which was a 2003 plan to help create more jobs. It did not do that well back then but it surely did help and would help again.

So, I am saying that the 5.25% one-time tax plan has been tried before and it has not worked well for jobs but there is no doubt it would work well for seniors who could use the dividend dollars. I will do my best to figure a way in which the corporate rate can be just 1% or something very negligible so that corporations can have almost no tax owed if they do their business in the US. The 1% means they would still have to file returns, but far simpler forms.

Of course we would want them to all stay US corporations and not become "global" corporations. The US, if my plan passed would ask them to favor US in their policies. Because some CEO's might raise a middle finger to America and do their own thing, I would leave the rate of the corporate income tax at 35% for companies that earn their dollars overseas and I would completely eliminate the deferment of taxes for those that qualify on this negative.

The moral of the story is that if you are a corporation and you want to make a lot of money from Americans purchasing your products, the Kelly plan would insist that you play our American game. Corporations who wish to go rogue will find their competitors, who behave as friends of America, receiving major business advantages in America including good will.

Rate for US companies importing to USA

Any US corporation that chooses to move its corporate HQ as some have done to other countries to avoid taxes would be singled out. All of their goods, whether shipped directly to the US or those goods, which come through intermediaries, would be taxed (via a tariff) at 35% and perhaps more. The message is that Uncle Sam represents the lowliest citizen in America and corporations need to learn that it is not nice to mess with Uncle Sam.

Additionally, any service sector organizations such as call centers or banks or insurance companies or other non-manufacturing organizations that choose to slip off to some other country and establish corporate HQ, the price to do business in the US will be exceedingly high.

Foreign corporations hiring employees in the US will be given the same favorable treatment as those American companies that use American workers, regardless of the business sector. American companies that choose to stiff-arm the United States will be so identified and will be treated by this country as "not a friend." The "not a friend" list will be well published as in the nature of a "most wanted list." This would permit American patriot citizens at their choice, to do business only with companies that are friends of the US. If corporations choose to give Americans the short end of the straw, the tax code under the Kelly plan will make them regret that posture.

The 12-12-0 plan

Michael Busler, writing in his New Jersey Room blog on the Web has yet another idea. Just like Cain's and Perry's plans, his innovative plan is a major restructuring and on balance, it seems like a good plan. The big difference is that Busler is not running for office.

It is all about a 12% single rate tax on all income above the poverty line, with no deductions for anything and no consumption tax? This 12-12-0 plan as Busler calls it would replace the Federal Income Tax only. It leaves the payroll taxes in place. Like the Cain plan it would be revenue neutral. It would also likely encourage significant growth in the economy as the corporate rate (without considering the states in composite form) would be just a hair less than Ireland. And it sure seems like it would be fair since each taxpayer would pay taxes in proportion to her or his income.

As with all these plans, this too would have to be tweaked to assure they are revenue neutral or as I would recommend, less than neutral (tax cut). They must be conceived in a way that GDP increases and thus revenue itself increases while the "neutral" rates remain constant.

Tax code-is not just for Congress

As easy as toying with the tax code may seem, some of the 75,000 pages actually have a noble purpose. For decades on decades, Congress has decided that 75,000 pages were noble and they would never want to find out which were ignoble by wiping out all 75,000. I take a different approach. The 75,000 are killing us since nobody other than Charles Krauthammer can understand them all and we know they are mostly self-serving and the selves served are members of Congress and their corrupt cronies.

So, let's wipe them out in their entirety as Cain, Perry, and Busler suggest, and let's listen to the screamers as long as they are not lobbyists. Then, we can adjust as necessary while the scrupulous people of the US watch closely. The big game right now is for anything that is done—to encourage economic growth which ultimately brings more revenue into the treasury.

Of course as in days past Congress should have to agree or be forced to resign so they would not choose to spend any extra revenue for any purpose. We all must remember that we are 15,000 billion dollars in debt, and Congress is to blame.

Any potential Congressman should be given a simple test with about 20 to 50 questions so that they can be rated as frugal or a big spender. It is time for the big spenders to stay home unless they want to spend their own funds.

Billionaire extra tax provisions

On the Perry tax form and the Cain tax form and the Busler tax form, and anybody else's form, I would like to add a few boxes and lines to permit extra giving to the US treasury. That way folks like Warren Buffet and Jeffrey Immelt or anybody who once was helped by Uncle Sam, and who would like to pay something back, would be able to do so without creating a big public fuss.

Though I find it hard to believe anybody trusts government so much, there may very well be billionaires like Buffet and Immelt, who, rather than give to the American Heart Association or the American Cancer Institute, would prefer to give a few billion to the American Government.

All citizens pay a national $10.00 tax

Under the category of "there is no free lunch," everybody over 18 should be required to file a tax return whether they pay taxes or not. In the Kelly adjunct to any plan, there would also be a required $10 national tax for every non-taxpaying citizen over 18. These make up all the people eligible to vote. I would recommend that any citizen paying no taxes to the federal government shall not vote in any election in which they have not paid taxes within a one calendar year period. The national $10.00 tax would count as payment. Retired seniors, and those on unemployment, and the helpless that are on welfare from the government would also be required to pay the minimum ten dollar tax and submit a very simple income tax form.

Non-citizens pay $250.00 per year

Illegal aliens and any non-citizens living in America for over a year, each year would pay a $250.00 tax to help defray the taxpayer cost of their living in America. Failure to pay the tax would result in a $500.00 fine payable within one month and if the fine is not paid, the freeloader would face immediate deportation.

All remunerations to all are documented

As another thought to help those once helped by John Q. Public to remember who helped them, I would assure that it be written in law that all businesses or federal or state agencies or charitable organizations, who provide any type of earned or unearned remuneration to citizens or non-citizens, provide all recipients with a form such as a 1099, W-2, or a form which acknowledges the type of remuneration they received. The organization, institution, business or government or other, would upload information to a huge database and would not need to mail the documentation. IT analysts can design this to be a smooth operation.

Of course the new element is that even those who did not receive earned income would be required to get a receipt for free services provided by taxpayers, and they would have to file an annual return. Non-citizens would supply all supporting documentation with their $250.00 annual tax. The dollar part of the returns can be done via a source such as PayPal with no paper needing to be filed, though paper would be permitted.

So, that there are no exceptions, all of the following: income, gifts, welfare, cash payments, medical assistance in any program, unemployment compensation, food stamps, SSI, or any other form of remuneration not included in this list would be required to be reported each year to the appropriate federal government agency (Now it is the IRS), by the providing source of service/cash and a copy provided to the recipient (such as a 1099). All of this can be done in machine readable media with no paper required.

The source of the income would also be listed and the receipt would be provided so that there was a match just as with 1099s and W-2's. By the way, this law may help collect from those operating under the radar, if somebody in the government ever decides to find out who they really are.

Depending on the type of service, the electronic form would identify the payment and the purpose if it is government supplied remuneration. As previously noted, everybody over 18 years of age, regardless of whether they are employed or not, would be required to file a "tax" return and submit the documentation provided. If no tax payment is required, the entire form plus the $10.00 national tax may be submitted online including machine readable supporting documentation and something like PayPal. If payment is required, and the taxpayer cannot find a way to submit online, perhaps a surcharge would be required of say, $50.00, if lots of paper must be processed.

As a system designer for many years, I see the key to making this system workable and cost-effective from an IT perspective is that each voucher from any payment source (cash services, or other) needs to contain a unique number which can be entered online so that no postage stamp and no paper would be required for an individual to submit their return once a year with minimal inconvenience. Anybody who receives funds of any kind from government or its surrogate agencies would be required to report it. It will help us all. The IRS or hopefully, a kinder and gentler government agency of another makeup, would thus be able to assemble all of the documentation electronically by key, without inconveniencing the recipient.

Any privacy / data security issues would need to be resolved before such a system were implemented.

Summary: restructure tax system

The United States needs a tax system that helps to grow the economic pie for all to enjoy. There are many recommendations for restructuring the whole code or eliminating it and starting over. All of these notions will take time.

In our time of national need, we cannot wait for a full tax restructuring. The same gain can be realized in the short term through across-the-board cuts in corporate and personal incomes taxes, and shifting towards greater reliance on indirect tax to make up for any shortfall in government revenue while moving towards a FAIR tax.

In the meantime, it is time to dust off the Kennedy tax objectives and implement a plan that JFK would be proud of. With the immediate institution of a tariff on imported goods, which I recommend in later chapters, even more revenue can be achieved while helping American based businesses, and giving those that have offshored a solid reason to come back.

Over all, a growth-oriented tax system is designed to promote economic growth. Faster growth, in turn, means better-paying jobs and higher standards of living for all.

All of the notions in this book (RRR) promote a means of achieving growth for American business in America while Americans also prosper.

Chapter 3   Reduce Immigration

Illegal and legal aliens are a jobs problem

I wrote a book in 2011 titled, <u>Americans Need Not Apply.</u> It is 45 chapters worth of facts about the difficult times Americans are facing while trying to be employed at the same time that illegal foreign nationals are holding jobs in the US. This book also touches on the notion of legal foreign nationals taking American jobs. The statistics on foreigners working in America are really amazing and account for a big reason as to why Americans are unemployed. Illegal foreign nationals have impacted those in lower skilled jobs and manual labor while the influx of legal aliens has taken the best jobs from Americans, especially recent University graduates.

Can you believe that over 2 million legal immigrants begin working each year in the US from green cards and worker visas? Numbers USA statistics suggest that my numbers are high as theirs come in at just 1.5 million. I think I am right but in either case, these represent the people who enter legally each year, and no matter which number is correct, it is a very large number. There are not enough jobs to support such a large number. Another large number comes from those already in the country or relatives, who gain green card status, thereby making them permanent residents.

The huge number of students who come in via student visas are not counted in these statistics, nor are those whose visas have expired long ago, but who are now trying to gain a green card status (permanent resident of the US while an alien). So, if we add the annual green card total each year, the number is more like 2.5 million or better. How are Americans expected to compete in the jobs marketplace when the US government provides such preferential treatment to foreigners?

What if the American government liked Americans?

Let's pretend we were living in a country that actually liked its citizens and its leaders worked for the benefit of its citizens instead of its corporations and special interests. Let's also pretend that this country would tolerate no intrusion that violated that sacred precept. In other words, let's pretend that America was set up for Americans first.

Now, suppose a class of people came into this country with or without invitation and began to take jobs and take sustenance from the citizens for things they should pay for themselves. Citizens in such a country would rightfully believe that their government would deal with the issue immediately upon discovery.

In fact, without the citizens even being aware that such a perpetration was taking place, a government, caring first about its own people, would solve the problem. If you and I were lucky enough to be citizens of such a country, would we not expect that our country would address the problem appropriately and immediately? Since the United States has chosen to purchase the largest sweeper known to mankind so it can sweep this all under the rug undetected, what does that say about our country?

At a minimum, we would expect that no matter what notions our government had about how to make life better for its citizens, it would permit none of us to suffer any pain from a temporary intrusion or infusion of a class of people into our country who were not invited. Unfortunately, we are only pretending that our government would care enough to protect us from such an invasion of uninvited people into our country.

Instead of protecting its citizens, our Congress and our President has instead, through its policies and permissions and demands, invited and incented foreign nationals to take whatever they can get from American citizens, legally and illegally. In so doing, the leaders in America have ended the American dream for many Americans.

With well over two million non-Americans legally taking jobs each year, would it not be prudent, if we were not ready to completely shut off legal immigration, that we would at least reduce it substantially until our economy recovers? I would propose that we shut down the level of foreign nationals who have guaranteed American jobs to about 20% of today's level or perhaps even less.

Can our institutions of higher learning not produce competent replacements for the foreigners deemed necessary in the US business sphere? Or perhaps is the demand based more on the price of labor than on the competency and abundance of labor. Either way, Americans ought to vote for Americans first.

The goal of our national government, elected by the people and for the people, must be to assure that American high tech jobs in America are first filled by American skilled workers. If there are not enough skilled workers available then the next group to gain opportunity should be American fresh college graduates.

If the Universities in America who have benefitted financially from the influx of foreign students want to tell Americans that our children are incompetent compared to the foreign nationals who take our children's jobs, let them go ahead and defend that to the inquirers and the applicants (the mostly high school seniors preparing to apply). Let them produce a document notifying American students that are accepted in their Universities that the University's preference is to admit and teach foreign born students who can easily gain positions in

American companies, and Americans should not expect to succeed after college.

If American Universities want only foreign students, let them tell us all so we can create American Universities that are for Americans only. Only the real dumb Americans think that Americans are dumb and need foreigners to make our country great. The rest of us know that the government and the universities have no problem selling us out so they can gain from placing Americans in an inferior position.

Can an American apply?

Once upon a time, corporations reserved a number of their new hires for American born nationals who were about to graduate from college. Then, those companies started to move operations overseas so hiring a cheap worker with a visa, who was a foreign national in America, no longer is a foreign idea. The fact that the foreign national demands less in wages does not hurt the scenario either.

Illegal aliens take a lot of American jobs

Statistics from various sources including the government agree that illegal aliens are the fastest growing population segment, followed by their anchor babies. In addition, the number of Mexican illegal aliens apprehended is about ten times the combined numbers of all other illegal aliens. So, we do know the source of the problem. The second statistic is not as important for jobs but it shows that there is a large population of OTM, which is code for "Other than Mexican." This group includes aliens who do not necessarily like America.

These statistics are more than likely correct but don't expect most estimates by the government of the number of illegal immigrants to be anything close to the truth. One statistic that is out there in almost all surveys is that the number of foreign born people in the US is 40 to 50 million. I think the number is actually much higher as the illegal population alone is at 50,000,000 and growing, though few statisticians will admit it. Think about the jobs that 50,000,000 illegal foreign nationals take from Americans.

For the last ten years or more the government has been telling us there were less than ten million illegal aliens in the country while they admitted the arrival rate was something like 1 million to two million per year. Does that mean that those who have been here for a while are taking up stakes to make room and are leaving or is it that the numbers are, and have been growing at one to two million per year. Who knows whether the rate is really three million per year? Ask yourself; are there any new people in your neighborhood?

The reason for all the institutional lying is that it is not good for the illegal alien apologists to tell the truth and so they simply do not. For example, the number of illegal aliens is downplayed by the immigration lobby, which we know is a coalition of liberal-radical academics, liberal politicians, federal and state bureaucrats, labor unions, La Raza (The Race, the leading immigrant activist group), other immigrant activists, and even some religious organizations that ought to know how to tell the truth. They do not want you to be concerned that the reason you are not employed in America is because the US government permits others to take jobs that would otherwise be for Americans.

Biased news media is anti-American

Then of course there is the biased news media, which stopped telling the truth years ago about things they do not espouse. These folks do their best to help the immigrant coalition in as many ways as they can. Most of the media live in gated communities so they do not see firsthand the impact of illegal immigration. Yet, many Americans believe the media is reporting facts, instead of the drivel they provide.

A few media lies here and there can go a long way in helping Americans believe there is no issue with immigration. Even while putting the bones back in the soup to get a second batch is becoming a retro means of survival, good Americans do not want to blame others who also are suffering. Yet, Americans well know that the illegal population is partly responsible for their problems.

Nobody wants to think the disenfranchised illegal Hispanics, for example, who are looking for more from a less-than-good situation, should be foodless or homeless. But, maybe so out-of work Americans can eat, as hard as it may be to digest, those from other countries who are here illegally should just go home. Americans who stay home twenty-four / seven and have nothing to provide their families know they cannot honestly buy the flummery that non-Americans have nothing to do with taking their jobs.

Illegal foreign nationals are not all on the government dole. Therefore, they must work to survive. Because many illegals are working, the jobs they now hold would in normal times be held by Americans. Therefore, they are taking jobs from Americans. Illegal foreign nationals get the jobs simply because they will work for pennies on the dollar and they permit their employers to mistreat them without fear of being reported to the authorities. Americans will not put up with abuse.

Still, the media is not interested in anybody getting the true idea of the impact of illegal immigration on Americans. The media in America is a disgrace. Americans should consider turning off all the channels to put these pariahs out of work. The corrupt media simply chooses not to identify anybody as an illegal alien, especially if they have committed crimes. The media agenda is anti-American and pro-progressive and so they have no time to help regular Americans.

When forced to discuss illegal foreign nationals, the media most often chooses to call them out as undocumented persons or unauthorized migrants so that we the people are not as angry as we would be if we were told the real truth.

Despite the falsehoods perpetrated by biased and outright corrupt media outlets, the people are getting smarter. Taxpayers are getting quite annoyed at the sheer numbers of illegal aliens in their states, cities, and communities. More and more we see these uninvited visitors from other countries impacting Americans in many ways—from overcrowded housing, to lowering the prevailing wage, to taking American jobs. Only a fool would believe the government's accounting of the extent of the issue. The actual numbers far exceed the official estimates.

Apologists for illegals have a huge dog in the hunt about downplaying the numbers because the actual costs to federal and state taxpayers are huge and rising each year.

Meanwhile, though America is going bankrupt, progressive legislators keep taking more taxpayer dollars to give to illegal aliens for education, medical and other reasons. Democrats hope one day these people will be permitted to vote so the Democratic Party can be vested in perpetuity. Democrats may not share in the squalor of these people who work for starvation wages. Yet, they cause it.

While we all scourge ourselves that we cannot do something for them, the big money people in the Republican Party also like the status quo. For them, it is not votes; it is profits. They want the illegal foreign nationals to stick around at their own peril to drive the wages even lower, and the profits even higher.

All of us have to be better people to have a better country.

It is smart for biased agencies, including our own government to undercount illegal aliens because that way the increased costs for larger and larger enrollments in schools as well as hospital treatment and other expenses do not have to be explained. It appears a mystery to the general population.

In Rick Perry's Texas, school officials assure that illegal aliens are well taken care of with college in-state tuition paid for by Texans. In K-12 schools, Texas officials are actually recruiting teachers in Mexico so they can have effective bilingual educators teaching the many students who do not know English. Texas school data from six years ago showed over 700,000 students with limited English-speaking skills. If Texas were the United Way that would be a proper way to spend donor money but it is no way to spend dollars confiscated from American taxpayers.

It is not just Texas, unfortunately. Other U.S. school districts are recruiting foreign nationals to come to teach in U.S. schools to accommodate illegal aliens. Besides what we are doing for illegals, these teachers take jobs that could be given to Americans, but nobody in official circles at all levels of government seem to care about that. Why are Americans unemployed? Would a better idea for America not be to teach recent college graduates how to teach in Spanish? Would it not be an even better idea to make sure that all students can be taught in English? Who do we serve teaching somebody in the language of another country? Who are we kidding?

From my vantage point, since I have not given up one part of my Americanism to reap a profit from a foreign country, I still think like an American. From that perspective, think about this: "As long as one American is unemployed, no foreign national, legal or illegal should hold a job desirable to that American." That is my perspective.

The original three R's

When we hear about the three R's, we think of reading, writing and arithmetic. Despite all the dollars we spend on education, the US is not even OK on the traditional three R's, and it has been this way for a long time. The more we spend on education at the federal level, the worse the results. The US wastes over $150 billion per year just on the Department of Education. Since the Education Department began to call the shots, literacy in America has gone down. Logic suggests it is cause and effect. In recent testing, for example, the U.S. has just a 32 percent proficiency rate in math. This places us 32nd out of the 65 tested countries. This is nowhere close to good, and it is expected to have a huge effect on GDP over the next twenty-years.

We need a lot of work but as bad as our education proficiency is, we have the ability to improve that mark far more easily than we can turn the economy around. In my business classes at Marywood University (mostly juniors and seniors), there were few students who had not mastered the traditional three R's. However, thirty-seven percent of the freshmen, on average in the country, never even reach their junior year of college. Clearly the traditional "RRR" problem for most of the students in America begins in K-12.

Just this morning I heard Ben Stein on "Fox and Friends" saying we needed more H-1B visas in the US. This is plain bosh. Stein said that Americans are majoring in music and poetry and not in the hard sciences. In other words, Americans are the reason that Americans are faring so poorly in the workplace. As much as I like Ben Stein, you can do better than that Ben.

Policymakers and consultants and economists like Ben Stein apparently think American high school students, as a group, are not choosing science in college and this is why four years later we need foreigners to take the best jobs we have to offer. If these experts really think this way, why are they not suggesting we solve that problem? How about instead of $535 million for Solyndra-like national rip-offs, we offer substantially more tuition assistance and perhaps work-study internships for

American college and graduate students who engage in the hard sciences?

Boone Pickens has no problem telling Congress that we need to provide every rig-operator in the country $67,000 to convert their rigs to natural gas so he can make his next billion off the American taxpayer. How about instead, we give $67,000 to some bright college students and help them know that we won't let corporations stiff them four years later by giving the Ben Stein best-jobs in America to foreigners and we won't let corporations outsource the jobs for which our American students have trained.

Who are we kidding? If left to their own devices, US corporations would in fact outsource every IT or engineering job they could, even if countless of hard science, A-student graduates were available. If we produced all A-students, Bill Gates and other un-American phonies would be moaning that America needs more B-students to justify his predisposition that American college graduates are worthless. Bill Gates cares about Bill Gates, not Americans. Ben Stein says we have a problem to solve in not having enough qualified graduates to meet the work demands. If we have a problem we need to solve, let's go ahead and solve it. If Bill Gates is the problem, let's solve that one too.

Do you believe that a country that put the first man on the moon needs engineers from Pooh Bear, simply because we have grown incompetent and we don't know how to train good engineers anymore?. Come on! Isn't that really just a lot of baloney that permits the progressives to keep putting America and Americans down?

Why not look around and say it like it is. We are giving our country away to foreign nationals, whether here illegally or legally by invitation. Sorry Ben Stein, I do not think the answer is to invite more in. In fact, it is just the opposite.

I recommend eliminating the Department of Education as it is a local matter anyway and the funding from the federal government has in fact taken results and moved them in the opposite direction. Before we were wasting $150 billion a year on this useless agency, America produced enough engineers to be the top tech country in the world. We can use whatever dollars are saved to prop up the unemployment fund or to give small businesses that choose to expand the loans they need to do so.

College graduates move home

One of the bleakest statistics about the college graduate class of 2011 is the low percentage of new alumni who can afford their own housing. In 2011, I had a number of seniors in my classes. As a professor, I helped prepare students for their future in business. It is hard to believe the statistics on college graduates finding it tough in the marketplace through no fault of their own.

In 2011, in the US, over 85% of the college graduates were forced to go back home to live with Mom and Dad shortly after graduation. They did this mostly for financial reasons. For the 2011 class, there are different income studies about different college groupings from elite schools to below average schools and in no case are the statistics good; and worse than that, they are not improving.

These different studies show some different results based on the type of graduates. For example, some studies show that the average salary for a college graduate was $37,000 in 2011. Just two years earlier in 2009, this same group had an average salary at $47,000. Another study shows the median salary for 2011 at $27,000 and that too is down from the low thirties with the same group in 2009. The point is that no matter which schools are in the sampling, things are bad for college graduates and they are getting worse.

Is it worth going to college?

Salaries of recent college graduates are now so low and the cost of education is so high that some analysts are looking at the economic value of a college education. Is it really worth going to college anymore? Just like listening to government statistics, don't expect to get the truth by reading material produced by the college and university sector as they have a lot to gain by students continuing to attend college even if it is no longer worthwhile.

The huge loans that students need must be paid back, and this puts them at a lifetime disadvantage when they cannot get a job after graduation. Consequently, parents and students need to evaluate the cost / benefit of a college education that prepares students for the unemployment line. If colleges and universities believe they are serving America, then let them put a guarantee on their product. How about if the university pays for half of the loan if after ten years the student is unemployed or underemployed? Watch the statistics get better overnight if our eminent academicians have some skin in the game.

The Occupy Wall Street crowd, the national protest movement that began as anti-Wall Street in late 2011, consisted of a lot of college graduates who may very well typify the results we just discussed. They should not be blaming Wall Street, however. They should not be blaming their huge student loans, which they cannot pay back. Besides themselves, they should be blaming the universities that placed them in the workforce ill prepared for what they needed to know. Maybe they should be blaming Bill Gates for taking all his jobs overseas.

Additionally, and the main thrust of this chapter, is that students should be very upset with our government for bringing in so many top students from other countries and then permitting them to work in the US after graduation thereby taking the jobs of American graduates at the graduate and undergraduate levels.

The raw facts are beginning to show that the economic value of graduating in the middle of the class may just not be there anymore. What does that say to students who have a great time and simply squeak by with a degree? It says borrow less money and have fun for those years but do not add a college loan to the cost of your fun. Those at the bottom of the class will be paying their loans off forever, never having gained what they needed to be successful.

They do have a beef with the educational system but again, not Wall Street per se. Manual laborers such as plumbers, electricians and other skilled laborers, for example, in many cases are doing lots better than today's college graduates. Most skilled plumbers for example are making well over $50,000 per year.

Analysts are suggesting that the average citizen may be better off entering the workforce if they can get a reasonably ok job and forego the four or five year break on earnings and the huge student debt burden. A four or five year college education is now a very expensive proposition without a major return.

The American dream is slipping away from American college graduates and all young people are suffering. Among other factors, the evidence suggests that a big part of this problem is because foreign students / workers take the jobs that Americans would have had. Just as their illegal counterparts, legal foreign nationals also accept substantially lower salaries. Over time, and perhaps sooner than later as the statistics indicate, the average wage declines as the foreign nationals drive wages down and down and down. Corporations are happy, and government is unperturbed, while graduates, who once armed with a degree would have had bright futures, now are finding lights-out on opportunity.

When students graduate from college today, despite what they know, and despite how smart they are, and despite how well they did in all their classes, there are forces in the US that work against their opportunity to gain employment. From the statistics, when they do get a job, it is on the average, not a great job. And so it is very common today to have engineering majors tending bar; social studies majors working in daycares; and IT majors delivering beer and soda. They may be really smart, but these employers do not really care about that.

These jobs are jobs for sure; but, they are not great jobs. Moreover, in addition to not getting good jobs, and having to live at home, the class of 2011 has the highest level of debt than any graduating class ever. More debt and less salary while living at home—what a legacy for our young people? And we wonder why there is a housing crisis. In the past, there was a whole class of graduates to buy these homes. Now, without jobs, the new entrant to the business world often does not have enough to get a beer on Friday night. A home purchase is out of the question.

Go to graduate school?

Ironically, since a college degree and respectable college performance is no longer enough to get a good job, recent undergraduates have been flooding graduate schools in a despairing attempt to avoid the reality of the labor market in its current state. Some look for MBA degrees; others look for the next degree in their field; while still others are prompted to go to Law School to improve their lot. Having two young sons as lawyers who took on that debt and the rigors of the BAR exam, I can say that it is not a picnic route and the competition is very tough for law positions. MBA's and others fare no better.

All graduate students are having trouble getting employed as more and more students try to get more credentials to help assure getting a job. But, unfortunately, there are no real assurances. And, to make matters worse, there are the foreign graduate students who come out with a graduate degree and steal jobs from Americans when our government chooses to give them a six-year visa or a green card.

The numbers

In 2011, about 700,000 graduate degrees were awarded. If all degree holders were able to go out and gain employment in their field at acceptable salaries, then such a large number of master's degree graduates would not be a problem. But it is a problem in these times, nonetheless. The problem is that over the last thirty years, the number of advanced degree graduates has doubled. Moreover, the rate of increase has accelerated substantially in just the last couple of years, and that too is not a good sign. Rather than give up when they cannot get a job, college graduates often try to redeem their mediocre college experiences by excelling in masters' programs. It does not always work.

Eight percent of the people who are 25 and over now have a master's degree. If all were doing well, we would be bragging about that statistic. Unfortunately, that is just about the same percentage that received a bachelor's degree or higher in 1960. Times have changed and just like the price of gold would go down if it were discovered that the whole state of Pennsylvania was a huge gold mine, unfortunately the value of a graduate degree is diminishing each year.

Universities are not doing their part

The only people today who are really benefitting big-time from the rush for advanced degrees are the officials in America's universities. Ironically, despite universities doing so well in these times of dismal economic conditions, from teaching in graduate schools for many years, I know first-hand that more and more institutions of higher learning are adding legal foreign nationals to their employment numbers rather than Americans. And some fire existing professors to take advantage of the excessive numbers of foreign professors who will work for less than American-born professors.

Recent college students see it in the classrooms. Colleges and universities often hire foreign nationals to fill faculty positions. Most foreign nationals who enter the United States for this purpose enter as non-immigrants in temporary status. There are many different types of nonimmigrant visas, each having its own specific rules about length of stay and permissible activities. The most commonly used legal path is a visa called the H-1B and for some reason Congress has decided that the number of H-1B visas permitted for colleges and universities is unlimited. There is no cap on the number who can come in and take American jobs.

I have seen first-hand that Americans are being fired and being replaced by foreign nationals. Nobody wants to talk about it but in order to eventually get a permanent alien status in the US (green card), those wishing never to return to their home countries are happy to work for a lot less money than Americans. Of course this lowers the wage for all Americans as it becomes much more difficult to gain a job as an American, without accepting far less in wages than the degree warrants.

It is tough to be an American today

While more and more young Americans attempt to find jobs, as noted in the beginning of this chapter, our Congress continues to import over 1.5 million new legal foreign workers into the United States each year, while another million or more are granted green card permanent resident alien status after using up their time on their other visas. We really cannot keep this up!

Non-immigrant visas are now turned by trickery into immigrant visas because the lobbyists for foreign students have the ear of our Congress, while there are no lobbyists for the parents of bright American children or displaced faculty.

Therefore those with student visas are most often immediately granted six year worker visas and then when their time is up, they look for green cards so they can stay permanently in the US. Perhaps if Americans were not out of work this would be OK, but while Americans are not working, neither illegal nor legal foreign nationals should be taking jobs and lowering the average wage at the same time. Thank your friendly Congressman and Senator and even good people like Ben Stein for not seeing the whole picture. My pledge is to reduce both types of immigration if elected so that Americans can go back to work.

The verdict on Congress: GUILTY!

This is very unfair to Americans of all ages and all skill levels. If your children, who are college graduates, are finding the workforce unreceptive to their need for a job, I would recommend that you call your Congressman and see why he or she is not taking action on this matter. If you get the wrong answer, make sure you vote next spring and again in November, and let your unresponsive Congressman know that next year, they will be looking for a job. Maybe a less expensive foreign national has the same skills as your congressperson once in industry, and they will work for less.

I have said this before but this is the essence of the issue. Unfortunately, there are no lobbyists for parents and so there is no countervailing power to push Congress into working for Americans. There are many lobbyists for corporations and there are many lobbyists for educational institutions, and there are many lobbyists for foreign students and foreign visa holders. All of these lobbyists make well more than the average wage of a Congressman, and their expense accounts make life much more pleasant for our esteemed representatives.

Since there are no lobbyists for American students or American parents, how should Americans fight the insidious effects of lobbyists brought on by our legislators? It actually would be simple to wage an all-out fight. After you complain and bring the matter to your representative's attention, you can expect them to send you a propaganda sheet via the United States Post Office (USPS). When you get this, make a note that lobbyists don't vote for your representatives; you do. Send it back to them and let them know that you can and you will vote against them. The citizen's vote is always the final word.

Right now we all are outmanned because most of us did not blame Congress originally for the jobs problem caused by foreign nationals. Now, we all know better. Americans can gain back the big edge only by doing the right thing in the voting booth—but first we must believe we can. It is our best source of national strength. Lobbyists may buy a lot of dinners for our representatives, but they cannot add one vote to the victory margin needed by any representative or senator to trek back to Washington. Remember that you and I have the edge. Let's use it.

Is it OK for legal aliens to take your job?

I keep hearing in the media that legal aliens are OK. "Come here legally and all will be well!" But, for whom will it be OK? There has been a lot of attention about the illegal alien community coming in and taking the low and medium skilled jobs, especially in occupations such as meat packing and construction. I estimate there are 50 million illegal aliens in the country and that substantially more than about 10 million of these have jobs that American high school graduates and even those who have not graduated could easily fill.

In 1980, meatpackers, who were organized at the time, enjoyed an average wage of $19.00 an hour. Today in many cases, the wage is less than $9.00 per hour. What has changed? You know the answer. Corporate moguls can now join even finer country clubs.

Though George Bush said there are jobs Americans won't do, the fact is that illegal aliens work so cheaply that it is tough for Americans to compete and still feed a family. In America's farms it is estimated that well over 1 million illegal foreign nationals are employed. Americans need not apply on the farms because the farmers have figured out how to pay dirt cheap wages to illegals and they do not have to worry about government interference because the illegals are happy to be quietly employed in this country. Do you really think illegal aliens are paid well compared to the US minimum wage?

Americans for all the years we have been a country harvested crops and picked berries and American stores were filled with produce. Then, the farmers realized others in the underground community would get the job done for less. Sorry George (Bush) Americans are not only willing to do the work; nobody but Americans has been doing the work for many, many, years. The corporate farmers decided to play wage games with illegals and that changed the whole game. Americans will not do hard work for less than the proper wage.

It is an economic problem, not a philosophical issue. To repeat; it is not caused by Americans not willing to work; it is caused by the willingness of illegal foreign nationals to work for substandard wages with no benefits and no protection that is afforded by US industry laws.

NLRB is not for Americans either

Obama's National Labor Relations Board should be busy making sure the minimum wage law is defended on all farms rather than engaging in unconstitutional acts such as prohibiting Boeing from building and operating a non-union plant in South Carolina. What is that all about?

Then, let the farmers hire cheap labor but at no less than the minimum wage. What illegal foreign national would complain about a pay raise? So, let's say we permit these one million plus people to work in the US with impunity with a six month temporary guest worker status and they must agree to go home at the end of the season. Well, if we choose to do this, we still must be concerned about the other 49 million who have no growing season to end.

By the way, regarding all forms of immigration, George Bush was not pro-American at all. He was pro Bush and pro-business-barbecue attendee; he was anything but pro-American. Most Republicans like legal and illegal immigration because it helps keep wages way down. Has anybody considered that houses cannot be afforded and purchases cannot be made as in the American past in this country because the wage scale is now so low nobody can afford anything nice?

Conservatives, who may be members of any political party, are for Americans first. Democratic leaders of my Party, choose to ignore the atrocities of the grist mills that hire illegals. They pretend to be beneficent and munificent and then the notion of quid pro quo is expected to compel the lowly poor illegal immigrant to vote Democratic if ever elevated to citizenship. It is all very dirty.

Foreign nationals receive most of the publicity because they are mostly illegal. Yet, it is well documented that for many years our U.S. Congress has also been importing high-skilled workers. As noted, these people compete directly with graduates from our colleges and universities. I think it is simply because the media and our politicians choose not to pay attention.

Of course they may get payoffs; but I would rather not go there now—at least not today. The downward pressure on high skilled wages comes about because corporations know they can get a skilled legal worker for 45 % to 65% less wages than an American would demand. And, Congress does not take the time to assure that Americans come first. As hard as it is to believe it is not politically correct to suggest that anybody should be for America and Americans first!

Americans have been forgotten by our own government. The progressives love to take taxpayer money to use it against the taxpayers. These leaders keep giving more and more to non-citizens while they put a masquerade on what is wrong with the economy. These percentage wage losses are harmful and the fact that corporations are permitted to do this hurts not only the prospects of the return of the American dream; it is a harbinger of a continual American nightmare. Can American parents handle this nightmare as an ongoing reality as their children consume more and more of the family pie and government does not permit them to have a good job? I sure hope not.

When elected, I will **R**educe immigration and assure that Americans come first.

Chapter 4   Reduce Regulations.

Reduce regulations.

I just completed a book called <u>Kill the EPA</u>, which outlines in very specific detail what the US Congress and the new President must do so that American companies can hire more and more and more and even more Americans—young and old. The major maxim is to reduce harmful regulations. The book is at the printers and I have yet to receive a copy as I write this new book, but it will be available for all for free online at www.kellyforussenate .com. A hard copy of it with a nifty cover will be available at www.itjungle.com/store.html for their going rate. IT Jungle carries all of my recent books, including this one in hard copy.

The bearer of the most bad news on the regulatory front is the EPA. They are simply bad actors. Few would argue that we need *commonsense* regulations to protect workers, families and the environment. The part the EPA missed and keeps on missing is the notion of common sense. As in all things in life, we must pursue a balanced approach to the environment.

Unfortunately, way too much regulation is the modus operandi of the EPA and other major government regulators.

The EPA is not the only sinner in the government, however. The team, headed by the Regulation Czar—Cass Sunstein, have been driving business nuts with new regulations on a continual basis. The results of overregulation are well demonstrated today with our dismal economy and poor prospects for recovery.

While the US is searching for a jobs solution and an economic solution, excessive government regulations continue to force American companies to send their operations to foreign countries, taking much-needed jobs with them. These companies and those jobs are not going to be easy to get back.

According to the Small Business Administration (SBA), since 2005, just a few years ago, the number of federal regulations has increased by over 60 percent. Many of us in our own lives have considered going into business for ourselves. Those of us who took a shot at it know first-hand how difficult it is to get started. Instead of doing all it can to help, government is always the biggest obstacle.

Instead of facilitating new business startups, the government is a major impediment. We face many local, county, and state obstacles to be able to fire up something with a chance of success. It is not just a matter of conceiving the best idea in the spirit of Edison and then charging forth. Bureaucrat upon bureaucrat extorts the entrepreneur and the innovator so that today, most regular people with great ideas would prefer to operate in the underground economy and never really try to be known to the "regulators" and the inspectors.

Regulations must be agnostic

These regulations cost our economy an awful lot of money and a lot of unproductive work in compliance and the paperwork to prove compliance. In addition to the cost of compliance, the latest green initiative about to go into effect is supposed to add over 200,000 new federal employees to the EPA at a cost of over $22 billion per year. Can any country afford such a burden? If elected Senator, I will vote against this measure for sure. You can count on that.

Big companies that ship jobs overseas have a good way of avoiding the EPA and other regulatory consequences. They move overseas and with good reason. They are out of reach from US regulators.

The US must stop punishing its businesses. Yes, corporations are knaves and if they were really persons, they would be unseemly and arrogant and self-indulging, and they would not care who they hurt. Even not being persons, other than in a fictitious nature, they are able to carry the same characteristics as we just defined for an ignoramus.

Small companies, more and more are looking at the 60% new federal regulations, which are designed to kill capitalism, and they conclude quite appropriately, "why bother?" If they are successful after working 20 hour days for years, this government will then try to take the fruits of their hard work— their earnings and capital, and redistribute it to others who choose to stay home and collect a government stipend.

It is upside down and it will stay there until again it is respected in the US for people to work hard and for them to keep the fruits of their labor while employing tons and tons of other people. I don't know of any man who was ever employed by a poor person. So, let's not denigrate the rich so much. The rich are the reason why all of us have a shot at doing so well. I may not like to be in their company but they have helped America more than Obama can imagine.

On the statistical side, the reports we have been discussing also show that compliance with federal environmental regulations costs small firms 364 percent more than large firms based on revenue. It is simply outrageous and it must stop.

All of us like to go outside and after a length of time; we need to wash the outside from our clothing. We call that doing the laundry. Long before we were created, God permitted wind and rain to be prevalent on the planet. Since wind and rain carry dirt and grime, is it possible that these natural forces will soon become banned by the EPA or some other agency – perhaps the Department of Energy?

The EPA can decree that wind and rain are banned simply because they do not like these natural forces and the damage they may cause. But, they do not do so—because this would cause the EPA to look as fools to all of their subjects. Wind and rain seem to have a secret—an EPA unapproved energy supply behind them. It is called God. Perhaps the EPA does not like God either but they do love Mother Nature, who last time I checked reported to God. Regardless, they cannot control God or Mother Nature, but they can sure be annoying.

Rather than let this agency run rampant, the US must rein in the EPA along with all other job killing agencies and become realistic about our current abilities and technologies, and while at it, become pro-American. If one of the by-laws of the EPA was that it had to hold a pro-American posture, I would suspect it would be devastating to the loyalist environmentalists in the EPA. Mass resignations would already be underway.

I am surely not suggesting that US corporations be given a free rein, but it helps to know there are 50 EPA like agencies run by the individual states. The difference between the 50 Departments of Environmental Protection (the DEPs) in the states and the EPA is that the former cares about the environment while the latter has a socialist / Marxist progressive agenda as its guiding light. State agencies are so close to the people they care about the environment and their state and they are not about to place the environment in front of the needs of the human beings in their states.

US states have environments!

I have promoted the notion that the states need to be the focal point for handling the environment. The Feds (EPA) are ready to put us all in jail for missing the basket when we simply shoot a crunched up candy wrapper trying to score a fictitious goal. A miss is litter. A goal is compliance. We must mount a defense against such intrusion in our lives.

There is no real environment for the federal government. Other than Washington D.C., the feds own none of America. Environments therefore exist only in the states. Since each state has its own environment and the federal government has no environment per se, the states should be in control, not the feds. It would appear logical—even for Spock.

The term "red tape" was invented to describe the perception of government intrusion in our lives. We need to cut all the red tape and look for free-market solutions to increase private-sector job growth. One way to begin is to get the federal regulators off the backs of businesses. That would be a great start. States actually understand what is needed. The feds are seemingly locked up in a university lab looking for a place to try out their next experiment. Please stay out of Pennsylvania.

Regulators can de-certify regulations

Always trying to influence perception above reality, President Obama, the regulator in chief, issued Executive Order 13563, on January 18, 2011 calling on every federal agency to review their regulations to ensure they "promote predictability and reduce uncertainty; take into account benefits and costs; and identify and use the best, most innovative, and least burdensome tools for achieving regulatory ends." Obama is the master of rhetoric and spin. You and I both know he did not mean it.

Despite the press opportunity and photo ops, and despite the hoopla of these major pronouncements, there was a catch. Independent federal agencies were not subjected to the executive order. Well, who was subjected then? Obama does not lie. He simply uses deceit or chicanery to get his work done.

You have to pay attention to catch him. Since most Americans simply want government to work, Obama rarely gets caught.

Quite strangely, the EPA, the biggest violator of American rights ever to be permitted to exist in our country, chose to answer the Obama optional call. I would have thought the EPA would have abstained because they are really being watched today as they are hurting all Americans. On top of the big watch, our mostly useless Congress is now evaluating the usefulness of the EPA. That is amusing to a point.

Nonetheless, the EPA chose to conduct its own review of Obama's decree on its own agency. This did surprise me. But, as I think about it; it is like the farmer comes in and suggests to the fox, which has been hired to watch the henhouse that the number of hens disappearing has been increasing. The fox tells the farmer he will check it out but he intimates there must have been a weasel in the neighborhood. What kind of review would the EPA conduct on its own regulation?

If you talked to some CEOs that are in the energy industry, you would not even know the EPA went through the charade. Should the fox be the one responsible for an accurate count of the chickens? In my recent book, <u>Kill the EPA</u>, I identified the EPA as an agency that continually puts out regulations that are oppressive to American industry. The conclusion is that it needs to be dismantled and quickly.

Dodd-Frank: second graders respond to the need for experts.

The Dodd-Frank financial reform bill is another regulatory killer. It only looks good to Barney Frank and Chris Dodd. Dodd was out in 2010 and in early December 2011, Frank announced he was leaving Congress. Dodd-Frank adds many more financial regulations on businesses and community banks. In this case the perpetrator is the Treasury Department.

You may remember when the economy almost fell apart in fall 2008. It was really an unparalleled financial disaster in our Nation's history. The Wall Street monster separated trillions in wealth from investors whose only fault was that they believed in the system. Everybody that I know suffered a large reduction in the value of their retirement savings. Some say a generation's worth of retirement was destroyed.

Neighborhoods, cities, and counties were crushed with foreclosures during this period and it was mostly because the government had demanded banks to stop making prudent loans. Credit checks on people who could not afford a mortgage were not permitted by the unofficial cadre of neighborhood police known as community organizers. And, yes, Acorn was one of the major perpetrators in the fiasco. Barack Obama's *"What me worry?"* face somehow disassociated him from the reality of the financial collapse.

Dodd-Frank was Congress's feeble attempt to make it so that such national trauma could never happen again. Many of us blame Dodd, who got one of those special deal mortgages from Countrywide. Countrywide called it a VIP mortgage discount but some regular Joe's would call it simple corruption. Frank of course is to blame as he is almost personally responsible for the debacle with Fannie and Freddie. But, true to form, of course, he never saw the need to admit to any of it. Hey, why go to jail if you don't have to?

The Dodd-Frank financial reform bill has been law for almost two years now. Like many laws passed by our Congress, the original idea behind the bill—to help avoid another economic crisis—and how it turned out, are two different things altogether. The bill was to reform or eliminate Freddie Mac and Fannie May and it was to simplify and add clarity to the banking system. It did neither. Instead it was another paper monstrosity put together by the Nancy Pelosi led 111th Congress. It consisted of about 400 new rules and when printed it took more than 2300 sheets of paper.

Ironically one of the worst parts of the Dodd-Frank law is something called the "Durbin Amendment." Every time you swiped your debit card at a store in the last two years or so, Dick Durbin, Democratic Senator from Illinois took a bow. His tiny amendment capped bank card interchange fees to help consumers. This stopped the banks from charging as much as they once did for a credit or debit transaction.

On the surface, this all seems good. But in reality it is not. Our Congress too often performs for political reasons and not for the good of the people. Surely, with all of the expert advice, Congress should understand the law of unintended consequences, which is what Dodd-Frank is really about. Just because it looks good at first does not mean it is any good at all.

If banks feel they need an extra dollar per transaction to remain profitable, the Dodd-Frank bill prevents them from increasing their fees. Though perhaps well-intentioned, Dodd and Frank and Durbin per the Constitution, cannot stop banks from making money. So, by stripping them of the ability to charge the fees they felt were right to assure their normal profit, the banks needed to come up with another way to make up for those lost revenues by instituting other fees.

You may remember one of the most public displays of a major bank's response to Dodd-Frank in fall 2011when banks were trying to catch up on lost revenue. Bank America began to charge a $5.00 debit card fee. That is $60.00 per year whether you use the card or not. There was no legislation preventing them from doing it. It just proves that it is not really nice to fool with the mother of all banks!

Even if Bank America gets rid of this fee, they will figure out another way to gain back their profit margin. Dodd-Frank might just as well have required every neighbor to give every other neighbor $5.00 per month forever. You give $5.00 and you get $5.00 so is that really a good deal for anybody? It does, however, make the government look very powerful.

Dodd Frank contains over 400 rules that were supposed to be in place by summer, 2011. Most of the work on the regulations is still undone, the uncertainty of when the hatchet will fall and how severe the regulations will be is adding to the malaise instead of the recovery.

There are a lot of bad things in the banking system today. Have you noticed that nobody is loaning anything to anybody today. I could not get a car loan this past week for a high mileage mini-van for my daughter from a bank that I have been doing business with for years. They would give me a loan but they wanted it secured by cash. No wonder nobody is buying anything—especially homes.

The best thing in Dodd-Frank is that they raised the $100,000 limit on deposit insurance to $250,000.00. There are also major restrictions for banks when they go to casinos or use risky investment contraptions. They can no longer put your money at risk for their profits. This is good but overall Dodd Frank is a big regulation loser.

Regulations—a huge burden on business

Overall, since Obama took office, over $38 billion in new major regulations came into being and $14 billion more are scheduled in the short term and even more after that. This is a big burden on an economy fighting for survival.

It is therefore tougher and tougher to conduct business in the US. This overly-regulated environment creates more uncertainty than any other factor, causing businesses to either sit on their cash-hordes or do business overseas. Analysts suggest that the notion of uncertainty is the greatest obstacle for investing and hiring

There had been some good bills in the past such as the Glass
Steagall Bill which was put in place to stop the abuses that
contributed to the Great Depression. To put the Dodd Frank
bill in perspective, at 2300 pages, it is fifty-five times larger in
terms of pages than Glass Steagall (42 pages), which was
introduced in 1933 and repealed in 1999. Its repeal is why
banks were able to go rogue and create havoc until 2008 when
they just about all crashed along with the whole US economy.
Yet, for the past four years, Congress has not reinstated the
protections of Glass Steagall. They too often forget they work
for us.

Dodd-Frank is 34 times the length of the Gramm-Leach-Bliley
Act (145 pages. In 1999, this Act is what repealed the most
protective and beneficial parts of Glass-Steagall. The 1933 bill
provided protective barriers in the market among banking
companies, securities companies and insurance companies that
prohibited any one institution from acting as any combination
of an investment bank, a commercial bank, and an insurance
company.

The Gramm–Leach–Bliley Act undid all the good that helped
us recover from the depression. In other words, commercial
banks, investment banks, securities firms, and insurance
companies are again permitted to consolidate. The legislation
was signed into law by President Bill Clinton to satisfy
Republican demands for looser regulations while the
Democrats agreed for their own selfish purposes. Acorn and
Obama really came to life at this time. By doing a quid pro quo,
Republicans agreed to looser credit with the Community
Reinvestment Act, which is another doozer of a Congressional
Act that ultimately helped bring the US down in 2008.

There have been other bad financial bills to which Barney
Frank and Chris Dodd conspired and upon which other leading
Democrats had their grimy fingerprints. The major sins of
Dodd-Frank unfortunately are in trifecta form. 1. It did not

undo Gramm–Leach–Bliley and bring back Glass-Steagall. 2. It did not undo the problems with the Community Reinvestment Act permitting Acorn to determine who got a home loan. 3. It left Fannie and Freddie to continue to strangle the American taxpayer whenever they needed a buck from the mismanagement of national assets.

Yes, a moderate level of regulation is necessary in large and vital sectors of the economy such as finance, housing, and healthcare. But, 2300 pages permit too many agenda items to be filled long before any real help to the country is proposed. Huge legislation and regulation is surely not the solution to the current economic problems that face the United States. In fact it is quite the contrary. Bankers actually know a lot more about banking and how banks and people can be mutually successful than does Barney Frank and Chris Dodd. Soon both of these poor Americans will be out of public office.

Banks are not model children but they are necessary for our modern society. It would help for the President to stop demonizing banks—as if they are not vital to the credit needs of our country. Banks are needed for new business formation and many other reasons. Why the banks and the country need to be at odds on everything cannot be helpful to either. It is time for regulations to take a back seat to the potential for economic prosperity.

Nobody can run as fast with a full grown human being on their back as they can if running free. The same goes for a business trying to survive while having to carry a huge pack of regulators along with every move. We need businesses to be allocating their capital towards expansion, which would call for the hiring of new people. We need businesses to be allocating their resources to invest in new facilities and technologies.

Unfortunately, just to stay even, business are now spending dollar after dollar just to figure out how the latest government regulation can hurt their business. Then they must spend more dollars to assure they can survive. It may be a great day for lawyers but not for regular Americans. As little as I trust the government, I see its big hammer appears always cocked to end any of my personal aspirations. Moreover, the hammer of regulation is ready to whack the opportunities identified by business. This regulatory hammer is feared more than perhaps anything else by businesses trying to move forward and trying to get to where they can hire people. Government today is not the solution. It is the problem.

It would behoove Treasury to address overly burdensome financial regulations that slow job growth and fail to improve consumer protections. I do not expect that they will cross Barack Obama and the will of his puppet, the former Congressman Barney Frank so this problem more than likely will be with us until a new Congress steps in with a big broom.

Obama gave over thirty speeches in a few months after he announced the infamous stimulus 3, a.k.a the "2011 jobs bill." He used it as a campaign gimmick to gain a lot of press in late 2011. I sure hope Americans reject it for the fraud which it is.

Don't you wonder why Congress and / or the President choose to place labels on legislation that does not really describe its intent? Why do they purposely try to deceive the American people? The Obama jobs bill is simply a porkulus bill and it will feed crony capitalism in time for the next election. I hope it does not work. It is plain and simple bunk? Will Americans buy it? I sure hope we are all smarter this time around.

No name generic bills

A suggestion I heard recently is that the bills should have no names, just the numbers they already have or perhaps an amalgam of their sponsors. It is obvious to many of us looking at what is going on that Obama's jobs bill is not really an honest jobs bill. People, including Obama, should simply be honest. Why won't Obama and the Congress simply say what they really mean? Would America not be better off if this were the case? Why can elected officials not simply tell the truth? Don't hold your breath, but it is a nice idea.

Shall we ask for common sense?

Hard as it is to believe, doctors and others in the medical industry are also complaining about the massive amount of paperwork necessary to run their businesses and to receive proper remuneration for services under government provided healthcare—Medicare and Medicaid.

Who would not agree that unnecessary paperwork—overly burdensome to home health care providers and consumers, should be eliminated? The problem of course is that government bureaucrats love regulations and the paper that regulations consume. It gives them something to do. If only we required our legislators to take a course in common sense before they voted on their first bill. Would we be able to improve their efficacy?

In that light, it would not be a bad idea to have continuing education credits offered for members of Congress so that they can sign up for graded seminars on all matters of government. As a side benefit, their constituents could then learn their grades? Would it not be nice to know how well they did when tested on the matters of the day?

Additionally, the both houses of Congress should also attend required educational seminars about their Party's perspective on various topics. Again, all of these seminars should be graded so that Party members can really know the real abilities of those they have placed into the highest offices of the land. Maybe we would have less chance of incompetent lawmakers gaining such important positions if we knew more of the truth about them before they were permitted by law to mess up the country.

New regulations on limiting regulations

Who are the bad guys? The answer is that they are everywhere in the Federal Government and for the most part, much of the work that is appropriate work should be handled by the states. At the top of everyone's list, however, is Harvard Professor Cass Sunstein, Obama's Regulation Czar.

His real title is Director of the White House Office of Information and Regulatory Affairs (OIRA). Sunstein is overall responsible for regulations in the Obama regime and to say the least, he does not think like regular Americans. He is a brilliant man but his thoughts and my thoughts rarely line up together. I have concluded that sometimes brilliance can be deadly to the person who does not have control of the situation.

Sunstein's major responsibility is supposedly to examine the many regulations that exist and get rid of the bad ones. Some say that progressives, such as Sunstein, have never met a freedom-limiting regulation that they do not like. The news of nixed regulations from the Sunstein camp is actually not much news. In other words, there are substantially more re-approvals.

The major accomplishment so far, after several years of work from the Sunstein camp is that milk is no longer classified as "oil." I kid you not and since it is no longer a type of oil, dairy farmers are now exempted from the burdens of the 1970's EPA-era law that declared that milk was an oil. Would that mean if you cozy up tonight for some great sleep, and some kind soul brings you some warm milk, and you have not heard it is no longer oil, will your constitutional sitting in the AM be or not be appropriate. Will it foster the proper leaving? Think about that one for awhile!

At the country level, that should mean that costly rules designed to prevent oil spills that are really milk spills no longer need to be strictly followed by the dairy industry. Well, even though it is forty years late, at least it is something. Thank you Cass!

Sunstein has actively defended the work of his regulators as you might expect and he has taken issue with the popular notion that regulations are being produced more rapidly by the Obama Administration than under previous administrations.

Sunstein says that the "costs [of his regulations] are not out of line by historical standards. And he notes that "the annual cost of regulations has not increased during the Obama administration."

The obvious reason that Sunstein is not being heralded by the conservative press for limiting regulations is because it isn't true. Obama has imposed regulations on America at a much faster clip than any of his predecessors and thus Sunstein's perspective, as sharp a guy as he is, can be graded as *False*.

Despite all the liberal media hype that his department was going to root out obsolete rules, the cost of regulations continues to rise.

Who writes legislation / regulations?

We can blame the staffers in the many costly and mostly unconstitutional US agencies as well as lobbyists for writing legislation and regulations. They write more stuff than all of Congress combined. Yet the role of writing legislation was not given to staffers and lobbyists by the founders; it was given to Congress. Over the years, our Congress has made its job softer and sweeter while others drafted the laws for our country.

When you look at the hundreds of thousands of pages of laws and rules put out every year, some like Obamacare, which approaches 3000 pages of legalese, it is clear that all members of Congress, not only have not written the bills; the Congress, whose signatures are on the bills, have not even read them.

Environmentalists and lobbyists from anti-business non-governmental organizations write the laws for our politicians more often than not, and then they influence the agencies that fine tune the laws into regulations so their pet requirements are included in the acts. This is a real crime and it must end.

To assure that this does not happen in the future, I would propose that a Congressional watchdog group be hired to capture the proper statistics on who writes what and then publish a monthly report. Regular Americans should know if their Congress is doing its job or whether the lobbyists are doing it for them. Additionally, some legislation, prohibiting lobbyists from writing legislation would certainly help.

Do regulations really hurt business?

Bernie Marcus, who is now over 80 years old decries the fact that nobody today would be able to get past the government regulations to be able to form a company like his baby, "The Home Depot." Though retired for some time, Marcus knows why nobody today wants to start the next Home Depot. He says that it is because of the restrictions imposed by obscene government regulations. In his own words, Marcus says:

"They've maligned the word capitalism so bad, that no one has any touch with business."

Marcus feels guilty that after living through his own great success in building Home Depot, other entrepreneurs are held back by the simple fact that "It can't be done any more." Marcus cites environmental regulations and constant lawsuits which make creating new businesses almost impossible.

I hope that like I do, you do not feel good about this. I know there are a few radicals on the leftist cause that would prefer to shoot all successful capitalists so those who have no idea of running a business can be enabled to take over.

Can we not say that without a shot, we are now experiencing what this warning idea put forth? The President of this United States has no idea of what running a business might be, and it surely seems that he has no concern for those who must produce, to be able to produce.

Though many economists see government uncertainty regarding taxation and regulatory policy as reasons why businesses are holding on to their capital and not investing in the US, Marcus sees it differently. He does not suggest this is not true but he thinks that certainty, rather than uncertainty is the real jobs and economic killer.

Marcus believes that businesses know for sure that they can expect the worst from government. It is a certainty that government is going to raise the cost of doing business. He cites Obamacare, EPA regulations, and many other government rules and regulations and notes that such certainty of impending doom leads businesses to shut down rather than expand.

David Park is the new chief at the Job Creators Alliance (JCA). He offers a killer statistic that shows how tough it is for businesses to get started in the US today. The initial public offerings (IPOs) for companies under a million dollars have decreased by 77% since the beginning of the Regulation Age, which he notes began with Sarbanes Oxley legislation. That places new small business startups at less than 23% of the number when times were not so tough.

Consequently, thousands of small businesses have been frustrated or destroyed by the anti-business atmosphere that the government continues to push in the US.

The EPA: the prince agency of regulators

I have called for the elimination of the EPA, Commerce, Interior, Energy, Education and a number of other bloated nasty federal agencies at least until such time as we can reset our economy without such constraints and move on to solving the problem of what is actually killing us. The Environmental protection Agency (EPA) is the worst offender. Yet, somehow, it has been able to get more powerful each year under Obama.

For example when the EPA issued a new regulation in April 2010 requiring housing contractors to take extra precautions around hazardous lead paint, it had a big impact on legitimate contractors. Those small contractors that took the law seriously had a tough time complying. In fact, Kathy Faia's little construction company followed the new regulation to the letter of the law because she felt the competition had to do the same also.

She invested many dollars to comply. Among the costs, she sent one of her workers to attend formal classes to become government-certified in the paint removal procedures. The company bought expensive coveralls, special goggles, gloves, hoods, rubber boots and anything suggested in the law for such workers. The company developed new methods for the remodeling crews to enshroud houses with plastic bubble wrap to prevent lead paint flakes, which potentially can cause damage to the brain and nervous system, from escaping into the atmosphere. Faia was not sure of the risk of such damaging results as she had never observed such health hazards in her prior work but she complied nonetheless. Feel free to read more at:

http://articles.businessinsider.com/2011-11-
13/markets/30393392_1_epa-lead-paint-paint-
flakes#ixzz1f1uXDmEK

The bottom line is that after such hard work, her costs were
raised so much just a little more than a year later; Faia's small,
family-owned construction business became financially ruined.
The new cost of doing business made it much harder for her to
compete for remodeling contracts.

You see, the EPA does not have the resources to check to
assure everybody is complying so when Faia competed with
companies that chose not to add the EPA burden to their costs,
she lost. Additionally, contractors with illegal alien workers
were able to get more and more business in the US as they
rarely comply with any regulations. Against these contractors,
Faia also lost.

EPA rulemaking is destroying jobs and harming the economic
recovery all across the country. The Hippie types at the EPA
have no idea about how to run a business so they press forward
with regulations that may permit an extra iota of cleaner air
while they put real live Americans, such as Kathy Faia, in the
bread lines.

Republicans are taking the impact of regulations far more
seriously than Democrats. Since January 2011, with the 112th
Congress, the GOP-controlled House has taken at least 160
votes on environmental issues, including over 80 that targeted
the EPA. There is a list compiled by Democrats on the House
Energy and Commerce Committee, which has all of the
particulars.

Congressional review

It is time for Congress to step in to help reverse the regulatory
tide. As a first step, it should bar regulators from imposing

major new burdens without the expressed signed approval of Congress. Congress should also demand that there be an automatic sun-setting of old regulations and there needs to be a pool of experts, who work for Congress, to help enhance Congress's own ability to assess regulatory costs.

It is not just Obama; though he is the worst ever. The rise in regulatory burdens began long before Obama. Right now, however, it has reached the overflow stage under his watch. Rather than ignore the danger, our lawmakers must immediately address it. That really means that the do-nothing Senate, of which Bob Casey Jr. is a proud member, need to bring up the legislation already introduced in the House, and pass it for the good of America.

The balance between federal regulation and job creation is a very fine line and it is now overwhelmingly controlled by the regulators. The President is not looking for compromise on that one. If we pay attention, however, and we insist that Congress do its job, we all can win.

Chapter 5   The RRR Jobs Plan Summary

It All Started at Fish's Barney

As you know, the saga of the three R's began as I was telling you all about my speech at the Barney Inn on October 21, 2011. I did not share all of the information with the Barney Inn crowd in the speech. As we continue to explore the positions that I had already painted, new notions are sure to pop up. Perhaps this is quite obvious.

I have a great number of friends and I love them all. Many of them chose to come to the Barney Inn, run by Joe Fisher, and Joe Predo for my October 21, speech. My friends and family came simply because they love me and that is what keeps me going in life. I can tell you this. Whether they came to the Barney or not; whether they ever choose to hear a speech of mine ever, I am so lucky to have these wonderful people in my life. I love them all immensely.

The secretive side of me says my cohorts and even some Wilkes-Barre strangers wanted to see if I could give a speech and remember all my lines. The audience members were all old enough to remember the immortal words of Jackie Gleason. Have you ever heard these three words right in a row? You would remember these if you had: Humma! Humma Humma! Every time I recall these words and Ralph Cramdon stumbling to get out a coherent sentence, I smile. If it ever does happen to me, I know exactly what I will say.

I surprised these potential constituents, who came on my behalf, with not one Humma—not even one. But, my message was still confusing until the crowd tuned in to the fact that this first RRR speech was not a speech about academic achievement or Jackie Gleason. It was a speech about the economy and jobs, and how jobs could be made available to ordinary American citizens in this country. A few good R's can make America a much better place.

Let me say it here before you begin to think I am promoting job creation by government. I do not think government can create one job on its best day. Government thinks its job is to aggregate confiscated wealth in something called the National Treasury so that it can pillage it from the treasury for its own purposes. It also thinks it can provide it for those who choose not to work or take care of themselves. The type of plan, where nobody is expected to work, creates zero jobs. That is not my plan.

If the "solution bird" landed on the doorstep of our government, a minister with a big US label on his or her lapel, would quickly stomp on the solution bird, as if it were simply a rat. Governments are not trained to recognize solutions as solutions. So, there is little hope that any solution will ever come from our government, as they choose not to recognize anything that can help America.

The reason this seems like a recent phenomenon is that for more than seventy years, things have not been so tough. Few remember the great depression. Over the last seventy years, things overall have gotten pretty good. There was so much wealth to be confiscated by the government that even those giving it up did not care as much as today and those that received it stopped appreciating it until finally those on the receiving end of pure welfare believed they were entitled to it.

Today, many Americans are simply broke and America is so broke if it could not print money, it would be bankrupt. So, maybe we would all feel better if we were to shout at the top of our lungs: "We're broke!" Say it again if need be: "We're broke. We're stinking broke. There is no more left for government to take." Dear Congress: stop spending! Please stop spending and please stop giving our contributions away to those who have not contributed.

This government is failing because with so little coming out of the economy, everybody wants to keep what they have and what they earn. Americans begrudge anything today that is taken from their wallets or purses because most of us are running on "E." Americans especially hate having to satisfy a government that is greedy, and whose appetite for other people's meager possessions and limited wealth cannot be satisfied.

The economy is in bad shape, and no business savvy people are being called on to offer advice to a very "suggestion-needy" government. Therefore, unless the RRR plan and other R's coming up are followed, it is apparent that the economy will stay sick for a long time to come. Robert Reich, as noted previously thinks the economy will take about ten years to recover, and his estimate is not based on any cause and effect policies. "Sick" is a good way to explain where we are today, and the people know it is from gross government incompetence.

Americans have learned from experience to balance their own checkbooks and so we can offer fine solutions to a government that could work if it were directed to do the right thing. Unfortunately, this government does not accept solutions. One could easily conclude, based on the behavior of this government that it intentionally wants to fail.

Now that we have worked our way through learning about the first set of R's in the RRR plan, if we adopt them all—in other words, if the three R's are heeded, soon, more and more Americans will be working and the economy will make a big positive turn.

So, let's make sure we get the first set of R's done while we are learning about the second set and a third set of R's and a few stray R's after that. In fact, let's go ahead and pretend we have already solved the problems outlined by the first three R's. What would we do next?

Thank you for asking. There is a lot to do and it all begins with the first R of the second set of R's. The good news for all of us is that there is a three by three set of R's coming up. If implemented, these too would do wonders for the economy and the character of our country, the land that we love. No, this is not the Cain 999 Plan, even though Cain is a good man. Overall, there are 9 more R's and maybe some surprises arranged in three more sets of three. The complete RRR Jobs Plan gets a lot of help when the other sets in Chapters 6 through Chapter 17 and the separate "R" pieces are also implemented.

Let's go to Chapter 6 and begin fishing for some more R's.

Chapter 6   Reduce Spending

If you no got it, you should not spend it!

With all the fuss put up in the Summer 2011 battle over raising the debt limit, if Congress and the President were not lying, one would have believed that something good would have come out of it. Conservatives, Democrats and Republicans alike, were watching the Republicans in Congress since they had established themselves as the only group of people who believed as I do that we cannot continue spending like drunken sailors, no matter how good the rum tastes.

As predicted in the debt ceiling battle, the Republicans who were supposedly representing conservatives caved under pressure. They forgot their roots. It is much easier to do easy things than difficult things. So, under that set of rules, with weak Republicans representing conservative interests, the conservatives were destined to lose.

The master wins all battles against an inferior team. Obama is a master of all things that can be shaped like a campaign. He is really impressive when nothing important is on the table. Obama is the master of all things political, though he fails miserably on substance. The debt ceiling was a political battle with an aroma just like a campaign battle. Obama does not lose campaign battles because he is the master of deceit.

In fact, in the sordid world of Obama, the President was concerned more about the photo ops as the savior of America, which can be used for his campaign, rather than the actual substance of the debt ceiling battle.

The campaigner in chief is always just one teleprompter away from his next victory. In August 2011, He needed to show just how presidential he was in scaring the elderly into submission during the debt crisis. At sixty-three I was not affected but there were some in my age group who felt like they were affected and they were intimidated by Obama. Most of my cohorts, however, Democrat though they may be, blamed Obama for the scare tactics and they blamed Democrats for the spending that is crippling the country.

Unfortunately, there were also many who believed the spender in chief was being truthful. When he cannot spend, Obama creates one scenario uglier than the next threatening whoever he can in whatever way he can. All the while he does this, his split tongue blames Bush, the Republicans, or the Congress. Obama is never to blame as he is faultless to a fault.

He'd be blaming Herman Cain if it would help him; even now that Herman Cain has been pushed out by the Obamaguard. Obama never said a bad word about Cain because he knew that type of spin would come back to bite him. Yet, Obama sent his "best men" out to destroy Cain, who would have beaten him in a clean race, and they did exactly that. The master attempts to victimize anybody who he thinks needs his magic; but he first assures himself that they won't bite back. Cain's teeth are gone.

The elderly, who are convinced they need government to assure their rights to collect their due, did not know they were being used but nonetheless they acted as if trained according to Obama's plan. They became part of the Obama stage and when he mentioned the fly in the ointment, as predicted, they immediately went for the swatter. Obama then called out the flies one by one and they all had Republican sounding names. Telling the truth is really tough when your name is Obama.

On the debt crisis, the President, the liberals in Congress, and the main stream media scared the heck out of the elderly—at least those whose relatives could not help them sort it out. Shame on Obama et al!.

You may recall that the new Rambo in chief, after his big military wins actually tried to scare the military. He said it would be the military and the elderly that would not be paid if the debt ceiling were not increased. Shame on Obama again!

The military recognized that he was not Rambo. Instead, he was the ole prevaricator in chief and he was unsuccessful on that count as hard as Obama tried to intimidate the US military. No matter what he does, he will not get the votes of our patriots in the military, because they are smarter than a president who has decided to be a liar in chief.

When trying to create a solution to the debt ceiling. there were the usual Democrat threats of no social security or military checks and other assorted Obama campaign notions from his all-purpose campaign grab-bag. In the panic, Republicans, who need a lot more training in defending their allies from Democratic psychological warfare inflicted on them by the Obama minions, gave into a deal that does not even begin to address the government spending problem at all.

Yet, the American public, guided by a corrupt media, thought the Republicans had won a victory. That is how good Obama is at campaigning. People who know he lies get convinced that he is telling the truth. When will we ever learn?

The point as I view it is that Americans lost again as Obama won the debt ceiling victory and he is prepared to win all battles with the very weak Republicans. Obama will be taking bows for a long time as if he saved the day when the debt clock almost ran out. But, if you are a judge of character, you already know he is a phony. If you can't judge character, go to somebody you really trust and gain their perspective. It will help in the long haul as Obama tries to undermine all Americans to suit his progressive / socialist / Marxist agenda.

Obama is the best at hiding the truth. When it was all over, it appeared with the help of the corrupt press that Obama had rescued the American people and he had extracted another compromise from the Republicans, apparently to benefit America. Yet, the opposite occurs each time Obama dons the winners cap. . When looking at the details of this deal, four large concerns rise to the top. None benefit regular Americans. Here is the deal:

1. The debt limit rises by as much as $2.4 trillion. It permits the debt to grow by $7 trillion over the next decade. One must ask, which brainiac Republican signed up for that deal?

2. A new, 12-member "super-committee" with the power to force major tax increases through Congress came into being. The risk for conservatives is that dangerous national security cuts may be unavoidable. For Democrats, they will probably just hand over the Bush Tax cuts again. They like keeping the tax cuts in limbo so they can use them again and again and again to win the day from the not-too-astute Republican "fighters." Before this book went to press, the Super Committee took its bows and claimed victory. Meanwhile the country lost an opportunity.

For Democrats the one-year extensions of the Bush Tax cuts, have been the gift that keeps on giving. Republicans appear first as dumb, and then when we see the movie, they appear "*dummer.*" The continual prize is the retention of the Bush Tax cuts. Now, is that not a good reason for nothing to ever be labeled as temporary?

Newsline Dec. 2011: The committee could not come up with one law or one recommendation because they think they have Americans by the wallakers. Congress failed miserably again.

3. Supposedly if Republicans signed onto the Obama deal, the AAA bond rating would continue and the Republicans bought that argument or at least could not defend themselves. Don't forget they came to meetings unarmed and they were dueling with the guiltless prevaricator in chief. In just days after the debt deal, Republicans learned that they were buffaloed again. S & P downgraded the AAA rating anyway. Maybe Obama was only kidding! Surely, it was not a lie!

4. As hard as they tried (not hard enough) the conservatives also lost on the promise to balance the budget. I almost don't want to explain it since it is so childish. The best I can say is that it was mentioned in the negotiations. However, the staunch Republican negotiators representing the conservative faction forgot that it was important enough to make part of the agreement.

The best explanation I heard of how dumb the Republicans are when supposedly fighting for America is that they insisted on a dollar of spending cuts for each dollar of debt ceiling increase.

This really sounded like a good deal but when the Democrats signed up so quickly, the play could not be reviewed in the booth. Since the spending cuts are over ten years and the debt increases are immediate, in essence for each dollar on the national debt clock, Republicans settled for ten cents. Is it possible that American Citizens can field a new team of conservatives for the next negotiations?

OK, so big deal, the conservatives looking to keep America solvent lost a battle against the elderly, the media, the Congress, and Obama. Now what? Unless, Republicans can begin to think while on duty, or at least listen to bright conservatives, many lost battles loom in the future.

Monty Pellerin, writing for American Thinker offers exactly the words I would have used if I had not seen this first hand and then seen his words before I offered my own thoughts. Please listen to Monty:

"There will soon be a crisis affecting US citizens beyond any experienced since the Great Depression. And it may happen within the year…Unlike the Great Depression, however, we will enter such a shock in a weakened state, with few producers among us and record mountains of debt. More cataclysmic is the specter of inadequate food, as less than 4% of us farm …"

The best I can say is that even though I do farm with 40 beautiful tomato plants, at this time of year, I only have my seventy-five bottles of homemade V-6 juice to keep me going. This Congress and the last Congress sold us out to the lobbyists but Obama claims he is not for sale. He already sold his soul to the progressive / Marxist store years and years and years ago. Try to get an audience with anybody who is not progressive / Marxist!

The sixteen tons of Obama would be regulated by his rules as all farm by-products are regulated. Since it would be the regulations put forth by the EPA, and / or the FDA, Obama knows he would be the winner in charge. Unlike in the tradition in which Alfred E. Neuman ran for President; Obama actually got elected. He sure is the president. The similarities, unfortunately for America, are alarming.

Maybe, for Americans, no government agency at all should regulate what is the best for America! But, people, ordinary citizens of the Republic must also have to decide to be honest.

The bottom line is that Obama and the Congress must stop spending. The raw truth is that neither wants to stop spending. They can't even agree to slow the growth in spending from one year to another. The Senate has decided that it knows that

Obama is right. The House knows Obama is wrong. And, Obama knows Obama is right.

Since Obama is so wrong about the damage that his excess spending is doing to America, there is no other way to solve the problem than for the United States to become a country whose main leader is not Obama. While we are at it, we can also flush out the ~~toilet,~~ -whoops! Senate—but that is the right verb. Don't you think?

Make a flush sound as often as you can.

Chapter 7   Repeal Obamacare

The worst legislation in American history

Before I begin the facts of this chapter, it is time to remind all
that this is the RRR book and its purpose is to outline things to
add and things to subtract and things to change so that the
economy improves and job growth becomes the order of the
day.

Do you think that the CEOs of large businesses are kidding us,
time and time again, when they say that Obamacare is
discouraging their operations from hiring? I know of a scant
few businesses and even fewer American people who see an
advantage in paying more for less.

The U.S. Chamber of Commerce conducted a survey to see if
this thinking was also prevalent in the small business sector.
Thirty-nine percent of small business owners say the
Obamacare law is either their greatest or second-greatest
obstacle to new hiring. Should we believe Obama or should we
believe the small business owners? Look at the economy and
you know that nobody is hiring. Look at Obama and you know
that when he says things are good and getting better, he is not
telling the truth. Obamacare is his finest lie.

The Heritage Foundation and the Cato Institute are
conservative think tanks. Both have been analyzing the
economy and the effect of policies and laws like Obamacare.

James Sherk of The Heritage Foundation, for example,
compared the rate of job growth before and after the health law

was enacted in March of 2010. His work shows that job creation came to a screeching halt in the month after Obamacare was enacted. That is all that it took.

Before April, jobs were being added at a pace of about 67,000 jobs per month. Though 67,000 per month for the whole country is not necessarily very good, the fact that it was not zero or negative before Obamacare passed is a stark contrast to the numbers post passage.

Obamacare is like a big Al Capone extortion racket. In fact, Obama runs the Presidency like he is Capone, and extortion is a legitimate tool to get things done. This administration actually threatened insurance companies that explained their recent massive premium increases on Obamacare. It is not that it is not true. Obama simply did not want the negative PR.

When Obamacare passed, we the people won nothing but large increases in insurance rates. A big thank you goes to Obama and the dirty rotten 111th Congress. I hope there is a company like Terminix or Orkin, whose mission is to clean out the stink of corrupt administrations. The scent in Washington would improve with a good dose of their remedies.

Insurance companies are not suicidal. No business is in business to please Obama or the Democratic Congress. They are in business to make a profit and to return something to the shareholders, many of whom are regular Americans with pensions tied up in these companies. Damn them as he may, Obama is the biggest hurt to business in my lifetime and thus he is a big hurt to the prosperity and the lifetime savings and the retirement of many Americans.

Insurance companies are businesses that compete with each other. The only way to assure that the price for their service is fair is to assure that there is competition. Instead, government blocks insurance companies from competing across state lines. Who does that help? It surely does not help the people that government represents or is at least supposed to represent. Obama cannot impose his will on any business legally. This is not the USSR. This is not a totalitarian state. Try as he may, Obama's threats may create angst but no company is going to willingly go out of business to please any president.

When insurance companies cannot make a profit and return some wealth back to the stockholders, with or without Obama's help, they simply increase the premiums based on their cost projections and profit expectations. They do not complain but their customers—you and I—demand explanations for their rationale in raising their prices. It is called the customer relationship.

Has your insurance gone up? Mine has gone up big time since Obamacare was passed. Will insurance rates go up again this year? You can bet your socks they will. Healthcare insurance in the US is going up and that is because Obama wants to push it up so high that you will tell him to get rid of all those pesky insurance companies and go with a single provider plan run by guess who—Obama! You can then let the trusty Obama government handle all of your life needs and concerns. Yes, that includes whether you are permitted to live or die. Do you trust Obama with your life? I don't!

Soon, there will be an Obama Medical School and an Obama Dental School, and miniature Obama's will be working on us all. When the Obama Insurance Company fires up, will life really be better than we ever could have imagined? Can Obama possibly be frantically searching through all the people in America named Kevorkian to find the right people to staff all those new companies?

Government Cost Cutting?

The mission of the Patient Protection and Affordable Care Act, commonly referred to as Obamacare is noble to the extent it is intended to keep costs down. Unfortunately, no government knows how to keep costs down. If the US government were actually good at keeping costs down and keeping service up, the cost would not be so high (15 trillion in debt) and the quality of service would be through the roof. For our health care, many of us would like to see government completely out of the picture. Health is a doctor / patient matter. But, that is not how Obamacare sees it.

Its objective is not to improve health care. It is over 2700 pages long and yet nothing addresses improving care. Egalitarian progressives in government want to make sure that all health care is equal, not better and the most important part is that government is in charge of it all. The United States Preventive Services Task Force (USPSTF), formed in 1984 with little power, now has a new life. It is the agency to decide which health care services Americans can access and which we cannot. Remember, their big mission is to cut costs.

Those of us paying the freight know that Obamacare has already raised health insurance costs, and it is reducing the number of covered services. Doctor surveys conclude there will be lots more free patients, fewer hospitals and fewer physicians, meaning less health care. Many believe the plan is to make the elderly feel guilty for living long lives.

Before government takes over all of healthcare, insurance companies are raising rates while they can. They are worried the President will put them out of business, making them pay more for claims than they collect in premiums. So, until something like an Obama Insurance Company takes everything over, insurance rates must rise to cover the extras that Obamacare has added to the insurance cost picture. When government takes over all of health care (a scary thought for many), rates will continue to rise as you will be paying for yourself and your neighbor's insurance. That's how a progressive government works.

So, to say again, the law has forced insurance companies to raise their rates while gripping for the full impact of Obamacare. No matter what we were promised, there is no free lunch. The Obama plan is eating more and more of our lunch every day. That reminds me of an important lesson about government run rackets. President Gerald Ford once warned, "A government big enough to give you everything you want, is big enough to take away everything you have."

We all get great emails from time to time. Some are worth keeping. Some give you a picture so clearly that you are compelled to share. While I was editing this part of this chapter, I received an email that fits in here someplace. I will not modify the contents so it comes off as it was received. Somebody went through a lot of trouble to tell us all that we cannot trust the government with something so important as our health care. Whether you agree with everything in the note is not as important as understanding the message:

"Do not trust the government with your healthcare." Here it is in a tone as if the writer was speaking to the US government:
----

a. The U.S.Postal Service was established in 1775. You have had 234 years to get it right and it is broke.

b. Social Security was established in 1935. You have had 74 years to get it right and it is broke.

c. Fannie Mae was established in 1938. You have had 71 years to get it right and it is broke.

d. War on Poverty started in 1964. You have had 45 years to get it right; $1 trillion of our money is confiscated each year and transferred to "the poor" and they only want more.

e. Medicare and Medicaid were established in 1965. You have had 44 years to get it right and they are broke.

f. Freddie Mac was established in 1970. You have had 39 years to get it right and it is broke.

g. The Department of Energy was created in 1977 to lessen our dependence on foreign oil. It has ballooned to 16,000 employees with a budget of $24 billion a year and we import more oil than ever before. You had 32 years to get it right and it is an abysmal failure.

You have FAILED in every "government service" you have shoved down our throats while overspending our tax dollars.

AND YOU WANT AMERICANS TO BELIEVE YOU CAN BE TRUSTED WITH A GOVERNMENT-RUN HEALTH CARE SYSTEM ??

End of email----

How about some truth?

When interviewed by Fox News, Verizon Wireless CEO Dennis Strigl called the members on President Obama's "Jobs Council" campaign bundlers, meaning they were on the council because they are good campaigners for Obama. "Politicians and lobbyists and crony capitalists are not going to help America survive but, while feathering their own nests, they can surely cause total failure sooner."

The real stinking part of the Obama "Jobs Council" that demonstrates the lack of sincerity of the people involved is that their companies have eliminated about 100,000 jobs in America while continuing to increase their presence overseas. Obama does not even demand that they show pro-American tendencies to sit on what should be an American "Jobs Council," not a reward for bundling campaign cash. Should Obama be trusted with your health and the health of your families?

The Cato Institute has openly discussed projections that Obamacare will permanently eliminate 800,000 jobs by 2020 if not sooner—not to mention any temporary job losses.

"If the President and the Administration were really serious about creating jobs in this country, they would listen to what people have been telling them over, and over, and over again. Cut corporate taxes, eliminate the regulatory morass that we have in this country, and by the way, repeal Obamacare. How many times do people have to say it?" Strigl told FOX News. The message seems quite clear yet Obama has no plans to give it up, no matter whether you lose your job or not. That's why many are calling for Obama to lose his job as soon as possible for the health of America.

The Heritage Foundation asks the question that the liberal media have continually avoided: *Why* will Obamacare hurt small businesses? An Indiana franchisee of IHOP chose to answer the question. The manager explained that the costs will outstrip profits per employee, which means layoffs, cutting benefits, and an end to expansion plans.

Obamacare is simply bad medicine and must be repealed for the country to survive.

Chapter 8   Reindustrialize America

Post Industrial United States

"The United States is rapidly becoming the very first "post-industrial" nation on the globe. All great economic empires eventually become fat and lazy and squander the great wealth that their forefathers have left them, but the pace at which America is accomplishing this is absolutely amazing. It was America that was at the forefront of the industrial revolution. It was America that showed the world how to mass produce everything from automobiles to televisions to airplanes. It was the great American manufacturing base that crushed Germany and Japan in World War II.

But now we are witnessing the deindustrialization of America. Tens of thousands of factories have left the United States in the past decade alone. Millions upon millions of manufacturing jobs have been lost in the same time period. The United States has become a nation that consumes everything in sight and yet produces increasingly little.

Do you know what our biggest export is today? *Waste paper.* Yes, trash is the number one thing that we ship out to the rest of the world as we voraciously blow our money on whatever the rest of the world wants to sell to us. The United States has become bloated and spoiled and our economy is now just a shadow of what it once was. Once upon a time America could literally out produce the rest of the world combined. Today that is no longer true, but Americans sure do consume more than anyone else in the world. If the deindustrialization of America continues at this current pace, what possible kind of a future are we going to be leaving to our children?

Citation: The above quote is from "19 Facts About The Deindustrialization Of America That Will Blow Your Mind," at http://theeconomiccollapseblog.com/archives/19-facts-about-the-deindustrialization-of-america-that-will-blow-your-mind. I included it to help get the juices flowing as we are in trouble as a nation.

Where did all the industrial plants go?

This last "R" in this second set of Rs is also very important and perhaps it is just as important as the three R's in the first set in terms of creating jobs and making the economy run better.

Reindustrialize

Tax policy will help welcome back the industrialized firms from their hiatus offshore. It is the carrot for American businesses to come back to reindustrialize the United States of America.

Welcome to America! There is another word besides carrot to describe why American companies will come back. The word is *stick.* The proverbial stick can also be used by our government once we take it back to help American companies that have gone astray to choose to come back to America. The stick is a really simple notion called protectionist tariffs. Tariffs are good for the people; good for unions; and they are good for American corporations operating in America. They will not be good at all for the corporations that took their jobs out of town.

Tariffs are a prerequisite for reindustrialization

Tariffs can also help foreign companies who choose to operate in America. No matter how this word (tariff) looks to you right now, it is a big word, and a big deal, and it is exactly what America needs right now.

Tariffs should be levied first against American companies as a stick, no matter where they operate offshore. Tariffs would not be levied against American companies or foreign companies on their operations in America.

American companies must begin to pay tariffs

The target against American companies is for the tariff to be levied against that portion of their product or services manufactured or performed in a foreign country and imported or used in America. Services to which tariffs would apply would include call center support and computer software, Internet wares, and all types of phone, email, mail, Internet or other support.

The message to American companies that choose to offshore all these functions is that the people they left behind will have their unemployment paid "forever" until the companies choose to operate in America in a manner in which Americans prefer. If American corporations do not like it, they can opt to sell the products they make to other countries and ignore the US market. We'll do fine without you!

Tariffs bring revenue and incentives to operate in America

The tariff rate on products and services sold to American companies (including cash transfers or sales to their home company) will be at least the same as the American corporate income tax (approximately 39.3%) on all products or services. Unfortunately, there will be no deductions for cost of goods sold or anything else permitted because this is not a tax. It is a tariff. Right now this tax is 39.3%, an average composite of the federal and state portions.

American firms will also be required to pay the American corporate income tax for all profits created overseas. There will be no repatriation needed as the shelter will be eliminated. Domestic organizations may consider this the privilege of being an American Corporation. Since the federal law does not permit states to collect tariffs, I would recommend the additional 4.3% be apportioned equally to the states regardless of their corporate income tax rate.

This amount would be provided to the states to help their losses from unemployment compensation for lost jobs. Of course in all cases, both the tariff and the foreign income tax would be collected.

The tariff rate for mostly all imported products and services from all companies from all foreign countries and their companies would be 20%. With total imports from all countries at about 1.5 trillion dollars, a 20% tax would bring in $300 billion in revenue on goods plus the 15% additional factor (35% tariff) only for American based corporations. Let's use a WAG of 33% of the total revenue for the taxes that would be paid at the 35% rate. This would provide an additional 15% X 33% X $1.5 trillion = about $80 billion. Thank you American corporations that forgot you were American.

Now, let's take a WAG on another $500 billion in revenue on services. A 20% tax would bring in about $100 billion in gross tariff revenue plus the 15% factor (35% tariff) only for American based corporations. To further explain, this would be for services provided offshore in some way by US based companies for US consumption. Let's use the same WAG of 33% of the total revenue for the taxes that would be paid at the 35% rate. This would provide an additional 15% X 33% X $500 billion = about $27 billion.

So, with grossly optimistic ballpark numbers what we are looking at if we choose to implement tariffs in the way I have prescribed above is a little math that can make a big difference in our economy. Let's Add it up:

20% tariff on all goods:	$300 billion
35% tariff on goods from	
--American based companies	$80 billion
20% tariff on all services	$100 billion
35% tariff on all services from	
--American based companies	$27 billion
Total estimated US revenue—new	
reindustrialization tariffs	$507 billion

Why would anybody do this?

No more free trade encumbrances

The days of free trade are gone until we the people of the US can rebuild our industrial base. We surely cannot count on this government or the current American corporations to do this for us. As a sovereign nation, as Senator, I would propose that the US withdraw from the WTO club of worldwide corporate shylocks for at least 20 years and then, if we are ever to join again, I would recommend that we make sure we are well represented the next time we go to the bargaining table.

To better explain the last sentence, please let me continue. All agreements that US trade negotiators have ever given US are bargains for every other nation but US. For the US, all such propositions have been killers for small businesses and for the people of the US.

Considering that we consume 25% of the world's everything, the industries of the world want to do business in the US. Our negotiators should have been able to gain favorable treatment from the world but they did not. Whoever they are, these dummies or traitors will be the first to go if I have any say.

In a fair market, US companies will do fine. My program creates a fair market in the US, and quite frankly if the rest of the world does not like it, after they have been huckstering us for the last forty years, *Frankly my dear I don't give a damn*!

This is not a book on trade or free trade or anything of the kind. But, the reindustrialization of America is a key element in anybody's strategy when the objective is to save America. Nobody in America, including me really wants to talk about the trade imbalance and how we have gotten victimized by past trade agreements. If you do, Pat Buchanan is probably your best source on the topic. If we really wanted to save America, we would draft Pat Buchanan as the man for the job for the conservatives today—the Republican Party. My party, the Democrats needs a lot of reform first.

Before you run out and grab a Buchanan book, try this on. It is free and it is just one paragraph and it gives a sense of all the terms that enter into the debate of whether we can ever reindustrialize America or not. When you read it, please continue in this chapter.

Facets of the trade game

Stephen Spruill, a graduate student in public policy at the U of Texas, http://www.globalenvision.org/library/15/1211 offers an extremely succinct and pithy explanation of the notion of trade tariffs, etc. It is required reading to understand the basics of free trade. The good news is that it is just one paragraph and it has much merit:

"Examples of trade barriers include tariffs, which are high taxes on imported goods that make them less competitive with domestic products, and subsidies, which are monies paid to domestic producers that allow them to sell goods more cheaply than their foreign competitors. Both policies keep foreign producers from selling very much in domestic markets, because when given the choice most people will buy what is cheapest. Trade policy is extremely simple: it boils down to what tariffs or subsidies a government chooses to implement to keep its country's markets closed to other countries (of course there are other policies governments can use, such as quotas on imported goods, expensive licenses for importers, and sometimes outright bans on foreign goods, but tariffs and subsidies are the main ones). A policy agenda that seeks to maximize the number of tariffs and subsidies a government employs is usually called protectionism."

The way to really understand Spruill's short tutorial with respect to the jobs problems in America today is to take it one step further—through the notion of mercantilism. This trading system is practiced by just about every other government leader in the world who cares about the country which they govern, except one—Barack Hussein Obama. The US is consumed in the notion of free trade today, which is a major reason why nobody in America has a job.

Mercantilism will feed reindustrialization

Please keep this important fact in mind. The object of mercantilism is always to minimize imports that cost money to the country (US) and maximize exports and the trade that brings money into the nation (US).

England declined switching Mercantilism to Free Trade

When England ruled the world it was a successful mercantilist nation, and when it fell from grace, it was a free-trade nation. If this were a TV ad, somebody would scream out, "Any questions?"

All things being equal, the US should be as mercantilist as it was when it grew the industrial base. Some may argue that we should be for free trade because the Clinton/Bush Menagerie would like that. Free trade is the policy we employed when we lost its industrial base. Why would we insist on a do-over just because Clinton/Bush thought it was a good idea? By the way, we beat England as the # 1 industrial force early on in our history as England switched from mercantilism to pure capitalism.

Why did I have to discover this? Why was it not our Congress saying we cannot go on like this as the debt sponge of the world? Help me understand how anybody caring about America should not be screaming about this in an effective way?

The US has only been around for two hundred plus years. England was the master of everything in the colonial days. Eventually, the colonists had offspring who had the same type of mettle and the newness of the country invited even more tough and self-sustaining individuals through immigration to help make the United States become the exceptional country which it is today. There is no room for American wimps in policy positions!

The people who came to early America endured many hardships and those who thrived were tough and resilient individuals. Once in America, they learned to care about this country and the freedom and liberty, which they began to enjoy. For many, America was tough but overall it was more than anything that they would have believed before experiencing its bounty. Americans made America what it is. As time went by, the people of the United States knew what had to be done in order to become one of the largest industrial powers in the world. And, we did it!

For a review, it helps to recall that England operated on a mercantilist system in which everything was structured for the good of the mother land. In fact, Americans were forced to survive England's mercantilist trading system for many years.

Americans learned well from the English and we learned that mercantilism was a practice of protectionism for a country. It announced to all others in the world: "My country is number one. When you come here; your country is at best number two."

Redistribution of strength

While America was becoming strong and especially after we became strong, other countries wanted us to redistribute our strength to them. As silly as this may sound, there were elites in our own country who, without our explicit permission—our leaders—began to sign up for globalism as if it was good for America. Globalism is another word for *redistribution of strength*. We have been giving our strength away for too many years.

As we have experienced, globalism did not bring with it prosperity for Americans. Between 1980 and 2011, the United States lost about 8 million manufacturing jobs, about 40 percent of its manufacturing base. Service sector jobs are beginning to disappear rapidly. Estimates are between 2 million and ten million service jobs have been offshored and many more are to about to leave town. The offshoring of all these jobs under the mantra of globalization benefits large corporations and governments and elite world citizens. However, their gains come from the body of people that the representatives were elected to serve. That would be US.

The growth of a globally-interconnected economy has permitted U.S. companies to now be able to move more and more aspects of domestic business operations abroad. The receiving country is typically a developing country with lower labor costs. This "offshore outsourcing" trend cuts across all industries and occupations, ranging from lower-skilled manufacturing jobs to those requiring higher levels of skill and education. During this period, the Chinese have become the most popular country for US manufacturing and other countries, such as India excel in the services sector. India has

become very adept at taking over call centers, accounting, and information technology functions.
http://www.americanthinker.com/2010/07/the_reindustrializ ation_of_ame.html

But, does all of this corporate success help Americans. A flippant Latino American might suggest, "No way, Jose!"

Jane Birnbaum offers the union point of view on offshoring in the lead article on the www.aflcio.org web site. It is titled: "American Jobs Going Going..." Thank you, Jane.

Birnbaum rightfully notes that corporations are escalating efforts to ship out jobs that pay well and build the middle class—and she adds that corporations are also aiming their axes at workers in the nation's fast-growing white-collar sector. I could not agree more with Ms. Birnbaum on this point.

You see, unions are necessary to keep corporations in check so that labor arbitrage is not the order of the day for all Americans. Even those Americans who are not unionized benefit from the fact that there are unions in these United States.

If unions did not employ thug tactics, perhaps more Americans would understand the value of unions in the "game" as a countervailing force against corporations.

Ironically, in her article on the 2011 AFL-CIO web page, Ms Birnbaum blames George Bush for unemployment. I guess that helped her getting her article accepted on this site. The fact is that the day George Bush lost his power as chief executive was the day Nancy Pelosi and the 110th Congress came into office—January 2007. The Democrats fully controlled Congress until January 2011 when they were ousted by the people in a popular revolt. Barack Obama did not assume the presidency until 2009.

Yet, in 2007, the Democratic Party run by Nancy Pelosi claimed they had a major mandate. This was two years before the infamous 111th Congress, which was also run by Ms. Pelosi. The 111th Congress will go down as the least competent, and the most corrupt in American History. It brought us the mega-thousand page bills including the infamous Obamacare.

This Congress made George Bush's years seem like a third Camelot. Why the media never defended poor George Bush on the economy and has yet to this day chosen to tell the truth about political happenings, can only be attributed to the fact that the main press no longer thinks the people matter. The media thinks that all Americans are dumb. I would suggest a revolt against the media but which media organization would really support us? That is a conundrum. So, maybe we need to create our own media.

Which media organization has yet to inform the public that when the Democrats took over in the first week of January 2007 in the 110th Congress, while Bush was still president, the Bush statistics for his first six years were already well published; George Bush, with a Republican Congress had brought the employment and other economic numbers in just fine. They would not stay fine under Nancy Pelosi and the media would "blame Bush."

It took just two years for Nancy Pelosi and Chris Dodd and Barney Frank to shoot the golden goose and the sacred cow so the gold was gone and all the milk in the jobs fountain was tainted for the next four years. At the end of 2006, when the people said that Republicans can no longer be trusted in Congress, the official labor statistics show that the U.S. Unemployment Rate had averaged 4.6%.

Let me let that hang out there for awhile. Now, let me repeat it:

4.6% unemployment. In December, 2011, Obama and company were singing their own praises as the numbers went to 8.6% from having been over 9% and almost 10% for all of the

Obama years. So, why is a retired George Bush punished and blamed when his numbers were good until Nancy Pelosi and Harry Reid took over Congress?

Amazing! But, who remembers this 4.6 rate was just in 2006/2007. This also was the year in which Bob Casey became a US Senator representing Pennsylvania? Now so few years later, all of the years which mark the Casey term and his accomplishments, unemployment now averages over 9% and it has gotten as high as 10%. Will the Senator claim that the changes in percentage were because of cause and effect? I would expect some good spin coming from the Casey camp on this one. Will it work in Pennsylvania?

To repeat for effect, unemployment is now averaging between 9 and 10 percent. Who in the media has written a story about that recently? The truth is the truth, no matter whether you are a Republican or a Democrat. At the end of 2006, contactomagazine.com enjoyed publishing these bright-eyed statistics.

"Americans are working, inflation is under control and wages are increasing with December unemployment rate at 4.5%, according to the U.S. Department of Labor.

"The wages surge was 4.2% in 2006 and the annual unemployment rate came in at 4.6%. " To put this number in perspective, from October 2010 to October 2011, average wages decreased 1.6% Maybe the "miss me yet" billboard reflects the truth, which the media hides?

Figure 8-1 Miss Me Yet?

So, help me out now if you understand why the US media cannot tell the truth? Will the media help in the reindustrialization of America? I see no signs that they would as they promote the redistributive mentality which is not what is needed to bring prosperity to America. Once reindustrialization is on its way, workers, not welfare recipients will be needed and hopefully, unions will cooperate with government and industry to assure that we can get the job done. Reindustrialization will make a bigger pie while redistribution takes pie slices from those who earned it.

I do think the modern media lies for agenda purposes. I think government lies. I think unions lie. And I think corporations lie. If you don't think so, then please do us all a favor and do not vote this time so we can get the situation straightened out without you.

Why won't this recession end?

In July 2011, a total of 15 million U.S. workers were unemployed, underemployed or too discouraged to job hunt, according to the Labor Department. Some estimates have this # as high as 26 million. Who really knows?

Why will this recession not end? There are big differences with this recession and those from the past. Companies today are sending well-paying manufacturing and service jobs to countries with few, if any, protections for workers and the environment. And unless we use tariffs and a mantra of reindustrialization to change America, these jobs are probably not coming back.

"The movement of jobs and production overseas is handcuffing the recovery." This is according to Mark Xandi, chief economist at Economy.com, as quoted in the New York Times.

"With NAFTA, the World Trade Organization and other trade deals of the last decade, American corporations are now tapping into a global supply of workers who can be trained to do everything from design to production, maintenance to marketing," says Jeff Faux, economist and founding president of the Economic Policy Institute.

"And while these workers become more productive, their pay doesn't rise, because in many of these countries, to be a labor organizer means you risk winding up in a ditch with a bullet in your head."

American jobs sent out of the country aren't likely to return anytime soon. "As long as employers can take advantage of much lower labor costs in other countries, there's no compelling reason to bring back many of these well-paying jobs," says Ron Hira, an engineer and assistant professor of public policy at Rochester Institute of Technology. "Policymakers seem to be at a loss as to what to do about this problem."

African American workers have been hit particularly hard. Because of manufacturing job losses, the unemployment rate among African Americans is rising twice as fast as it is for whites and faster than in any downturn since the mid-1970s.

"The number of jobs and the types of jobs that have been lost
has severely diminished the standing of many blacks in the
middle class," says William Lucy, president of the Coalition of
Black Trade Unionists and AFSCME secretary-treasurer.

Corporations are now winning against unions but neither play
fairly. The most powerful most often win. Unions have
overplayed their hands in many scenarios and have hurt not
just union workers, but also non union American workers. We
need to care about both.

My fear is that even if the R R R plan is adopted, the unions
won't accept it and they will go nuts even if American jobs
begin to come back to America. My fear is that unions will see
this as a capitulation by corporations and the unions will
become as nasty to regular Americans as the corporations have
been with offshoring. But, maybe it will not be so. If it is,
however, America's long awaited recovery will have to wait
some more.

People choose to unionize. Unions tend to people-ize. If neither
do either then a certain group of people have no power and the
unions have no power. If nobody will talk to anybody then
even if we can bring all the jobs back, the unions still have a
chance to mess it all up. So, let's be honest about the country
we really want to have.

Summary and Conclusions

Nothing is straight forward. Even simple solutions become
complex as other factors intercede. Reindustrialization is a
simple notion and if it were a goal of a country that could send
a man to the moon, you can bet factories would be in some
process of being built wherever you might go in these glorious
United States. I don't care a bit if the factories are owned by
foreign countries, foreign corporations, or American
corporations. What I care about is that they employ Americans
who can buy goods in this country and support a bustling
economy.

Of course, in order for smart business people to want to make America their beachhead for future profits, America must be ready. We thus need a tariff system as explained in this chapter and amplified in Chapter 12. We also need to have a union mentality that permits business to flourish rather than force businesses into bankruptcy.

Overall, we need an America with clean smokestacks all across this great land, built with concern for the environment but not built with demands that the new industrial revolution in America must come with cost prohibitions to deploy environmental notions that are financially unfeasible.

A great balance is needed eventually but the need today is to gain industry, not to send it away. So while we are gearing up for the next industrial revolution, let's not forget that corporations and companies can only implement technology that is available and affordable. Then, when we see the smoke coming from the stacks in the newly industrialized US of A, it will simply be steam vapors or perhaps steam with a small but bearable bit of pollution that will eventually be high priority for elimination.

Either way, if we all cooperate we can all enjoy the profits of America for the long haul.

Chapter 9   Reduce Offshoring

How many US jobs could be outsourced offshore?

Ironically, there still are no official sources of reliable comprehensive statistics that precisely count the number of jobs outsourced offshore by U.S. businesses. In fact, there are no publicly or privately funded national surveys that would collect information on the number of jobs that have moved offshore. The US Economics Census, which is taken by law every five years, makes a feeble attempt at making this determination by linking various data bases but its attempt is as feeble as the non-attempts by official government agencies to come up with the real numbers.

The bottom line is that no company wants to be called out for being the # 1 outsourcer in the US because it would be bad for business. When firms are asked about outsourcing offshore, they enter into a protective spin-zone. They have no interest in disclosing their reasons for closure or transfer of specific operations. It can only hurt them if the truth were known and so, not having suicidal interests, firms which practice pure capitalism, choose to hide their dirty little secrets.

Small or incremental relocations of jobs offshore may naturally go unnoticed by the media, but since we are talking about as many as 13 million jobs or more that are lost for good to American employees, the only rational explanation for non-reporting is that the media is owned by corporate America. And, of course it is. So, now tell me who is telling the truth?

When a business offshores and it is continually successful as is the case with Apple for example, their increased volumes and increased overseas jobs are frequently overlooked by the media. Some suggest that it is because these new jobs somehow do not involve the displacement of existing workers, even though the new workers would have been Americans if the company had not moved its operations. As an aside, companies like Apple and Microsoft and HP and Dell make just about nothing (no products) in the US anymore. Why does our government not ask them why, and why does our government not publish their answers?

When there is a void of something, it typically means that there is an opportunity for an entrepreneurial organization. So, in the absence of data that accurately reflect the full extent of offshore outsourcing activity, several analysts and research organizations have stepped in to fill the opportunity void and they have developed estimates.

They do admit the estimates for service offshoring are not fully accurate but they are better than raw guesstimates. There is little need to study the offshoring effects today on manufacturing as there is very little left in the US. The stats are in and we have lost over 50,000 plants with many employees, but which media giant is telling us about that?

In the future some analysts who know how to fill data gaps have suggested that legislation be created that assures the following will be collected so as white collar jobs are given up to the overseas merchants, we will at least be able to count them:

1. More and better data on services trade must be collected.
2. More information should be extracted and published from existing data resources.
3. Quantitative research methods must be combined with qualitative methods to provide a better view of the context and character of services offshoring.

Based on all the studies and the guesstimates, and the few facts in the mix, I have my own estimate about the total service jobs that have been lost. It is as much as 5 million jobs and perhaps more. The service element in offshoring is surely now the fastest growing.

When the Census Bureau performed its last survey in 2007 (next one scheduled in 2012), they discovered that the majority of establishments in the US do not offshore. Of course this is correct. But it is spin. For example, I have a several contractor firm myself and I do not offshore but I have been involved in the process. In other words, my company lost business to companies who offshored IT jobs. Those that do offshore are likely to belong to a grouping of larger firms as small firms do not even try to get involved in the charade.

Considering that all businesses that can be located for the Census Bureau Economic Survey, are in fact surveyed, it is already well known that only the larger organizations, which could afford to engage in offshore outsourcing and for whom it pays off in decreased costs of doing business, would be those engaged in the practice. Small businesses, the bulk of those surveyed, have about zero interest in offshoring.

If you think that your friendly large corporations, many of which have sent more than ¾ of their jobs overseas in the past twenty years, are about to tell dirt on themselves, think again. Now, think about whom their best business friends in life are and ask yourself whether these other folks would be more forthright if asked. Their friends of course are paid by us. We call them the Congress of the United States of America. Judging from their record, we would be better off without them if we could only get a President we could trust.

For years from Reagan to Bush through Clinton to Bush to Obama, politicians have signed onto the globalization train and the free trade train. Corporations never would have been part of this if our friendly representatives had not sold out all

Americans to give the corporations the bone that they wanted more than anything else.

You see, in the past it was the corporations who were afraid that they would lose out to the foreign traders. It was corporations demanding high protective tariffs. Now, ordinary Americans need protective tariffs to be levied on the American corporations who now import products to the US.

It was always the corporations who demanded protectionism from the government. With offshoring, corporations need no such protections and in fact count on our government wringing its hands "oh woe is me" while doing nothing. I say whack their imported products with stiff tariff and watch tm come back quickly.

In the 1980's and beyond the notion of globalism was the mantra of all administrations from Reagan to Bush through Clinton to Bush to Obama. It was not a Republican thing. It was an elitist thing. Through this period, corporations learned that if they no longer had to act American, they could succeed in offshoring. Our representatives in Congress decided that it was more important for corporations to make money than for Americans to hold jobs. Ironically corporations cannot vote but they do have a lot of money to buy politicians.

Eearly on, when globalists were looking for any excuse to ram offshoring down the throats of Americans as if it were a good thing, they called offshore outsourcing " the *alleged* migration of American jobs overseas."

Buoyed by the indifference of Americans who had not caught on yet that the government was not acting in their interests, Gregory Mankiw, the head of President George W. Bush's Council of Economic Advisers offered some reality that Americans paying attention had hoped Bush would reject. Bush, however, was not for the little guy. If the opposition party got him right on anything, it was that Bush could give a crap about regular Americans, and Laura Bush, a fine lady otherwise admitted they were not even pro-life during their time in the White House—but they could not tell the truth about that either.

The consensus of the elite was that no economist really had disputed Mankiw's observation that "outsourcing is just a new way of doing international trade," which by definition made it a good thing. Despite how convinced the globalist elites were that they could actually be frank about putting the hose on Americans, the depth of alarm that the government would sell out Americans was viewed as an unexpected firestorm. What did they expect?

All of the insincere politicians chimed in. For example, Mr. Insincerity, a global political opportunist, John Kerry was ahead of his day. He blamed Bush for wanting "to export more of our jobs overseas." Yet, Kerry's Heinz industries conducts most business overseas. Senate Minority Leader Tom Daschle, who got thrown out in the next election demanded that "Bush apologize to every worker in America."

If it were two other Senators at the time making the complaints, perhaps conservatives would have joined with liberals against Bush and the globalist elites, and we would already be working on the reindustrialization of America rather than waiting until the economy actually collapses. When average income is substantially reduced and the average price increases, less is purchased and fewer workers are needed to build the products no matter where they are built. Neither Bush nor Obama ever cared about that "inconvenient truth."

Most of the middle class jobs in the early days of offshore outsourcing were not in jeopardy. The big successes came in less skilled manufacturing jobs. When computer chips and subassemblies took the hit, though the US employees were well educated and very smart, it was still perceived to be a blue collar job necessary for manufacturing so there was concern but not much action.

It was only when the white collar knowledge worker, "thinking jobs" began to be offshored that concern was raised in a big way across America. But, even then it was mostly the IT crowd and many saw this group as having done too well perhaps in the dot com explosion and maybe it was OK they had a few setbacks. Nothing seemed to be affecting all Americans at once and so the offshoring divide and conquer in small pieces strategy was working like clockwork for corporations that were recklessly determined to sneak their operations off to foreign lands.

Now, everybody knows that the only place a large US corporation wants to hire an employee is someplace other than America. Finally, that is not setting well with Americans. But, perhaps we Americans are so "on the take" that it no longer matters. Obama and company have made it more and more comfortable to not hold a job in America. Why else would regular out-of-work Americans not be staging protests against corporations all across the country? Do we have too much pride?

The apologists for outsourcing offshore like to rant that protectionism is not going to solve today's economic employment problems. But, how do they know? They claim that protecting Americans would succeed in providing massive subsidies to special interest groups. If I may interject here, those special interests do have a name—"Americans."

The big point is that if regular American employees can become special interest groups, then, let the subsidies for the special interests roll. In open markets, they claim that greater competition spurs the reallocation of labor and capital to more profitable sectors of the economy. In other words, to the apologists, it does not matter where the product is made or the service is performed as long as the consumers and the producers gain. Unfortunately, if the consumers have no jobs, the wealth equation computes to zero.

So, the apologists say no to protectionism as it may be better to lie humbly prostrate before representatives from the People's Republic of China than demand fair and equitable treatment from US representatives. They say that cushioning this process for displaced workers makes sense as long as they do not complain about being displaced. They hate the notion of protectionism as they think it will halt the process of offshoring every possible American job to a country more worthwhile. They are right and that is why we need a mercantilist perspective for our economy.

Their idea is an open economy as long as the people who vote have no power. I think they are all wet. We as voters should help them all get a big shower next time around.

Quick Stats

Many different states, who are closer to the voice of the people than the federal government, have heard the voices of the unemployed, especially those in the high tech areas. Additionally, those who have lost their manufacturing jobs to China are outraged but probably not as outraged as they are when their children lose their computer programming jobs to India.

Cataloging this issue, in a September 2010 State of New York report, Princeton economist Alan Blinder estimated that 42 million to 56 million jobs are *potentially at risk* of being offshored over the next 10 to 20 years. For those of us prone to count, this is the equivalent of roughly 30-40 percent of all current U.S. jobs.

Where are the apologists now? When no facts were in, they assured the continuation of policies that permitted US corporations to do whatever they wanted. Now, the verdict is in, the economy is in quagmire, and the apologists have gone on to anonymity!

There is nobody of whom I am aware that thinks the companies who offshore do not have strong financial incentives to do so. Now that manufacturing and IT is solid offshore, the real question for a number of different companies that once thought they needed Americans is, "how quickly can we too get on the offshoring wagon?"

Financial Institutions are ready to offshore

For example according to the FDIC, the financial institutions of today who have been saved from bankruptcy by untold contributions from US taxpayers believe they can make a big buck by forgetting that they owe anything to America. Estimates are that they can achieve significant cost savings—as much as 40 percent) by moving non-core functions (including IT) offshore as soon as they can get the contracts in place.

Nobody ever accused a financial institution of not understanding the power of a buck. So, as long as their bonuses are assured, these pimps have felt no need to be loyal to America and they are preparing their next move against the nation that saved their collective bippies.

Their plan is to move 15% of their cost base (approximately $400 billion) overseas over the next five years. The IT successes of the last twenty years have given them the surety that they can make it since the IT operations, expected to move, represent about 70 percent of the offshore job activity.

In addition to reduced labor costs, those who claim to be U.S. companies may also be drawn to developing nations by less stringent environmental and safety and health regulations. Today, these other notions, mostly required by government regulations, are very important. They are as important as the

American corporations who offshore manufacturing, that also know they must work as hard as they can to get from under the grips of the union stranglehold on their operations. We have already been there.

So, we can see that offshoring is a scourge on all Americans, whether it is noticed or not. There are no advantages to losing a high tech job or a fine skilled manufacturing job and being able to take advantage of the fast food wave in America by being a flipper at one of the nation's many fast food manufacturers.

Perhaps George Bush was an idiot. Perhaps Barack Obama is an idiot. Nobody knows for sure. What we do know is neither of these two presidents cares much about real Americans. The results of their independent collective efforts surely indicate that is the case.

Enjoy the commercial burger grill

Bill Press was the guy I bristled against most on *Crossfire* when he appeared on the scene. I admit that I liked Pat Buchanan the best on that show. One thing that always came from that show was controversy and unlike the trite Hannity and Colmes, it was a quality hour in which everybody learned a lot as all of the participants were well into the issues of the day.

So, at the time, while I had been writing a lot of tech books, I never thought I would find it necessary to quote Bill Press in anything I ever wrote. But, this is the exception, and here it is:

This is from page 94 of the non-famous non-seller *Bush Must Go* book by Bill Press.

Here's the quote:

"Declaring that 'outsourcing' was good for America was not the only anti-labor provision of 'The Economic Report of the

President,' which Bush signed and sent to Congress in February 2004. The same report seriously suggested reclassifying fast-food jobs as manufacturing jobs. That was one way Bush could boast of 'new manufacturing jobs created by my administration'—even though there was no guarantee that former steelworkers or autoworkers would be happy flipping burgers at McDonald's."

I have to admit that when I recall the old spy v spy notions from MAD Magazine, I think of things like this. There are a few differences; however as # 1, I am not a teenager. # 2, I expect that those elected officials that we put in charge of our OK-ness in America would be more interested in keeping us OK than they would be in winning the next oral championship at the Bush barbecue series.

It may have been the game that beat out horseshoes as the most important at the barbecue but so what? Of course, to make it more challenging, they tell me the Bush's played horseshoes while the horses were wearing the shoes.

Offshoring's second wave

There was actually what some call a second wave of offshoring. Having watched the first wave, to me, this just seemed like a continuation of a bad deal for America. The "second wave" started in the early 1990s, and it was different from the first wave in that it basically declared victory on the selling of all blue collar jobs. Its focus had become the movement of white-collar service industry type jobs overseas.

Just like when offshoring manufacturing began, long before whole plants were moved, the types of service jobs that were moved offshore were relatively low-skill and low-wage. The early white collar departments were back-office. The initial area of choice was the call center, which was a natural operation to send offshore because it was a separated business function. The

secret to success in this area of course continues to be to have a staff with a solid command of the English language.
Regardless, the jobs are not held by Americans in America.

Y2K – Anything goes!

As the year 2000 approached another key task in the late 20th century facing all firms was the notion of Y2K date conversions in IT and embedded systems. It was not an idle threat. Computer programs could stop working or produce erroneous results or even shut down services and even buildings. It involved the coding of the year 2000 in databases in a shortened form that permitted it to be interpreted by software as the year 1900. Many Y2K projects were accomplished by in-house programmers as well as the nation's best retired gurus.

However, those systems and programs that could be segregated from the pack and which were not quite as important that the firm or the nation were at risk, could be shipped overseas to India or other IT centers for verification and modification. In other words, these segregated application could be offshored. The fine success that the overseas IT experts had in the Y2K mission prompted the determination that more and more IT work could be performed overseas at substantially less cost to the firm in many other IT areas.

A 2006 report from the Government Accountability Office determined that "in the 2000s, firms further expanded their [white collar] offshoring operations, based on the low-cost and high-quality work from the off-shored services undertaken in the late 1990s."

All problems cannot be laid at the feat of offshoring. However, with about 13,000,000 blue and white collar jobs displaced by offshoring over the last thirty years, it sure would be nice to have those jobs back. Joe Biden says those jobs are not coming back and because of Obama and Biden policies, Biden is right.

They have not come back, and as long as guys like Biden and Obama get to say those jobs are not coming back and nobody challenges them on that, they are right.

The number of unemployed Americans is listed consistently at 14,000,000. It is obvious that offshoring is the major reason why the jobs picture is so bad. We cannot accept Joe Biden's opinion that there is nothing we can do. We can start solving the problem by firing Obama and Biden.

As you know the second R in the RRR plan is reduced immigration. This was covered fully in Chapter 3. When companies cannot offshore because the nature of their industry means their production must be close by their markets, such as farming, construction, meatpacking, etc. they use the best next thing to offshoring to keep their labor costs down – illegal and legal immigrant workers.

What they do not do is hire Americans and that is the problem. Instead, they hire foreign labor in America to do these jobs. They use illegal labor for non-skilled jobs and they use legal labor from H-1B visas and other visas for the highly skilled jobs. Our immigration policy and our policies of babying illegal immigrants are killing jobs in America. If you add the effects of offshoring to the foreign invasion, Americans in the workplace have little chance.

So, when we solve offshoring as a national illness, there will be enough jobs for everybody. However, since nobody in the Obama Administration is working on making the problem go away, it is actually getting worse; not better. From the 2006 GAO report referenced above, companies have become even more emboldened to move white collar operations offshore as technology and network bandwidths have grown to meet the demand.

For the first time in a year, in August 2011, the US economy showed no job growth. With no new jobs, the unemployment

rate hovered around 9.1 percent and it has been over 9 percent
since May 2009.

If we add those who are underemployed, the statistics look even
bleaker. Adding them up, almost 26 million Americans are
either unemployed, marginally attached to the labor force, or
involuntarily working part-time. The experts see this as
unprecedented. Patrick O'Keefe, director of economic research
at accounting firm J.H. Cohn and former deputy assistant
secretary in the U.S. Department of Labor made the rounds in
the news organizations in late October 2011. He hit the nail on
the head: "The labor force is substantially underutilized relative
to what we experienced in most of the post-World War II
period."

There have been periods over the time since May 2009 when
the actual raw number of job losses seemed to be improving but
economists note that the real troubling sign is discovered when
you dig deeper in the data. Nothing highlights the changing job
complexion more than Wal-Mart announcing that it is
expanding with plans to hire ten or twenty thousand new
employees while Whirlpool, the largest appliance maker in the
country announces major cutbacks and immediate layoffs.
Moreover Cisco cut back its workforce and Borders declared
bankruptcy and laid off about 11,000 workers. Topping the list
of cutbacks for 2011 was BankAmerica who are set to fire about
30,000 employees.

I am the last to suggest Wal-Mart jobs are not jobs. They surely
are jobs but they do not come close to putting the same amount
of earnings in an employee's pocket as the others listed above.
What this shows is that the US is shifting to retail low wage
work while destroying higher paying manufacturing work and
that is why reduced offshoring and the reindustrialization is so
necessary.

Peter Paul and Mary once asked: "Where have all the flowers
gone?" Today we can ask "where have all the jobs gone?"

There are two answers today and together both are responsible for the jobs mess we are in

"gone to offshoring everyone."
"gone to foreign nationals everyone"

In the future, when we solve the problem, and since we have the will, we will solve the problem, there will be just one answer to the question of where the jobs have gone:

"gone back to America everyone."

When will we ever learn that in order to solve a problem, jawboning will not help? You have to examine the options, make a plan, and go for it. The RRR plan does it all. Getting everybody back to work in America is my objective. I believe we can get this done as a nation as soon as we decide to move forward on the plan.

Protectionism / reindustrialization is the answer

The solution for offshoring is reindustrialization. The solution for reindustrialization is protectionism and reduced corporate taxes. We are in control of our own destiny. If our leaders take bold steps, we can be back on top again.

Of course, the ideal solution without the government making any demands and without people changing their buying habits like, say boycotting the products of those companies, would be for companies to choose to come back to America on their own. Hah! If they were going to do that, they would have already begun the process instead of continuing the flow of jobs overseas.

So, other than through government action in the form of tax reductions and tariffs, and people buying American brands made in America, there is one other way. Let us recall that the so-called American companies have abandoned American workers and have taken what should be American jobs overseas. So, we can begin as a nation by identifying these companies and not considering them to be American. As the Irish like to say, "and we shall know them by their limp."

Once we know who the bad guys are, we can begin to invite good guys into the country to compete against the bad guys. In other words, instead of American companies hiring illegal and legal foreign nationals, the American government creates ideal circumstances for the good guys, companies from other countries who want to be friends of America.

We invite foreign companies to come in and take the business that was once the privy of American firms. Just as there is the notion of outsourcing, there is an opposite trend as seen from China and India's perspective called insourcing. The US needs to become a target for insourcing. As you would expect, *insourcing* refers to foreign direct investment (FDI). This phenomenon occurs when foreign-headquartered multinational companies make direct investment in the U.S. and they hire workers in this country to handle their business operations.

Though this is not the typical way reindustrialization occurs, the battle is typically not against firms from the nation trying to reindustrialize. Insourcing is something the US should immediately do. If our American companies want to be global companies then let's let other global companies that act more American than their American counterparts gain the benefits of selling in a preferred environment to American consumers.

The more typical way of reindustrializing or in the case of the US, since it has been so long, industrializing the first time is by using protectionist tactics. In this way, American firms that operate in America have the advantage. The big difference today is that I for one no longer care if the firms are "American," just as they do not care if they hire American. I want companies to hire Americans in America. Whether those companies want to be American companies or not is moot as long as their operations are in this country.

Summary

Offshoring is a big problem for Americans. To solve the problem America needs to become a mercantilist country again. In Chapter 8, we introduce the notion of reindustrialization, and in Chapter 12, we hit on mercantilism and protectionism via tariffs, especially on domestic corporations that bring their products now built overseas back to America to sell. My suggestion is that we hammer these products with big tariffs and those who build in America using American labor reap the benefits of a country that protects its own.

Two chapter break in the "R" Action

Because the history of the industrialization of America (Chapter 10) and the notion of insourcing (Chapter 11) are relevant now as we are studying three highly related R's, we will take a two-chapter break and squeeze these two chapters in before we continue with Raising Tariffs. The three related R's of course are as follows:

Chapter 8 Reindustrialization of America
Chapter 9 Reduce Offshoring
Chapter 12 Raise Tariffs

Chapter 10   A History of the Industrialization of America

Early US gained from protectionism

Without protecting the fledgling poorly capitalized firms in America against the British and others, the US would never have become the industrial power that it was by the 1920's when our government decided free trade was more important than a successful America. Let's retrace some history so we can learn again how we built up our industrial complex the first time. We surely can do it again.

History – The first Industrial Revolution

The period in US history known as the First Industrial Revolution came about between 1820 and 1870. This was a time when the country changed from "hand and home" production to machine and factory. This industrial revolution was important as inventions permitted massive outputs to be produced in factories.

For example, one of the most important industrial inventions that predate the revolution was Eli Whitney's cotton gin. He built the first one in 1794 to split out the cotton seeds from the cotton crop. Additionally, during the same time, huge spinning and weaving machines were developed that could be operated by water power even before electricity was readily available. Later the water powered units were often replaced by steam, and then finally electricity. These inventions and the risks taken by American entrepreneurs helped spur on America's growth, making the country a modern and more urban industrial state. Protective tariffs were used by government to assure the American companies were successful.

The Second Industrial Revolution occurred approximately from 1867–1914 though some see a combination of the first and second industrial revolution occurring in the 1850 time period and beyond. Some may have slightly different dates for this period, but they are all in the same vicinity.

The ability to produce clean steel is often given as the first of several new areas for industrial mass-production, which are said to have brought on the second industrial revolution even though the major method for mass producing steel was not invented until the 1860s, when Sir Henry Bessemer developed what was known as the Bessemer Process.

Most of the great American innovations were brought forth during this time. Instead of using vision, trial and error, and tinkering, the inventions and innovations of the Second Industrial Revolution were science based. During this period, there was the development of steam-powered ships, railways, and later in the 19th century came the internal combustion engine and of course electrical power generation. Again, protective tariffs were used by government to assure the American companies were successful.

From the 1890's to the 1920's, the time period is given the name the Progressive Age. By this time, a middle class had formed in the US and this group was not trusting of the business elite or the radical political movements of farmers and laborers in the Midwest and West. These people took on the label of "progressives." Like the progressives of today, these people favored government regulation of business practices. Their pet peeve back then was monopolies as opposed to the environment, but their zeal for regulations matched the zeal of today for environmental regulations.

The progressives were not quite as socialist back then though the socialist and communist movements were well underway in other countries at the time so they were much influenced shall we say.

Some good came during this period such as laws regulating railroads in 1887 (the Interstate Commerce Act), and laws preventing large firms from controlling a single industry in 1890 (the Sherman Antitrust Act). Though they looked good on paper, it took Teddy Roosevelt to begin enforcing the laws for them to become effective for America. Roosevelt was the bane of the robber barons and he characterized them as "malefactors of great wealth."

When President Woodrow Wilson (1913–1921) came into office, the progressives gained in popularity for awhile as he was very sympathetic to their views. Many of today's U.S. regulatory agencies were created during these years, including the Interstate Commerce Commission and the Federal Trade Commission. With the US suffering under excessive paperwork and paper forms and regulatory burdens today, it is easy to understand that again the progressives are responsible.

From the progressive era, the country moved through the roaring twenties and through the great depression. Of course there were substantial contrasts with the periods. The twenties were full of mirth and prosperity as the auto industry brought along the oil and gas and road construction industries. Good jobs were plentiful. Telephones and electricity spread even to the countryside. Then in 1929 the Stock Market crashed and the great depression took hold of the country.

Many credit World War II (1941 to 1945) with getting the US out of the depression. When the war was over, the US enjoyed a long period of prosperity from 1945 to 1973. It was the golden era of US capitalism. The US could do nothing wrong with major companies like IBM leading the way with technology innovation after innovation.

The US was doing so well that Congress kept playing with the tax code and had upped the top tax rate to 90% before JFK said, "Enough!" There was so much money in the Social Security fund that after Kennedy, President Johnson stole it to finance the Vietnam War in the late 1960's.

In addition to the war spending, President Johnson was the first president that spent all he could waiting until the hogs came home to stop spending. Most hogs never, never, came home and the few that did got barbecued at the LBJ Ranch. Johnson began one social program after another truly believing the pot had no bottom. For example, Johnson began both Medicaid and Medicare and his administration financed some of private industry's research and development throughout these decades.

A number of the projects were visionary and successful while others were merely redistribution efforts. One of the greatest achievements from all of this was the ARPANET, which would eventually become the Internet in the late 1980's.

From the mid-1970's to the early 1990's was a period that some call deregulation and Reaganomics. Because of poor productivity growth and increasing operation and capital costs in several key sectors, presidents in this period turned back the spigot on regulations.

Many conservatives see Barack Obama as the worst president of all time. However, there is one president who many recall that in the pre-Obama era had carried the title well. Like Obama, President Jimmy Carter put forth a huge fiscal stimulus package in 1977 in order to boost the economy but like the Stimulus I of 2008, and the little stimulus of 2010, and the projected jobs bill stimulus of 2011, the Carter stimulus failed miserably. In fact, inflation was never so bad in the country. It began a steep rise beginning in late 1978, and it jumped into double digits and hit 20% with the 1979 energy crisis.

In the Reaganomics era, there were no stimulus packages as they had proven not to work. Dr. Arthur Laffer became a major economic adviser to Reagan for Supply Side Economics which was Reagan's Answer to the failed Keynesian theory practiced by Carter and now Obama. Reaganomics brought a, fiscally-expansive economic set of policies. Like Kennedy, Reagan cut taxes to promote economic growth. In fact, he cut marginal federal income tax rates by 25%. Inflation then dropped dramatically from 13.5% annually in 1980 to just 3% annually.

Unfortunately, at the same time that mostly positive massive deregulation began under Reagan, so also did the offshoring of manufacturing jobs. Reagan did not do everything right. At the time, there were many that did not really think that offshoring would work while some pioneers chose to give it a try?

Long before Reagan, almost right after World War II, the US was doing so well that it stopped protecting its own industry base with tariffs. The removal of tariffs began in the Wilson years but like a slippery slope, the US gave up more and more of this revenue and the associated protection it gave American industries.

The country began to embrace the notion of free trade but an analysis of the work our negotiators did in these agreements has proven that Alfred E. Neuman as president would have done a better job. There was no trade deal from which the US benefitted.

The US trade negotiators were outflanked and out-tricked and outsmarted and every deal was bad for the US. In addition to the fiscal deficits that came with one president after another adding to the pile, the U.S. started to have large trade deficits. Nobody seemed to connect the dots that the two were related. Free trade policies were undermining the US economy and we all just stood by and watched as other countries became successful at our expense. At one point, you may recall Americans thought that Japan was about to buy all the real estate in the US.

Too big to fail

The problems with the too big to fail rescues of the banks in 2008, when the banks began to fail, began during the Clinton years as this liberal President undid some regulations that even Reagan would not touch. Some say Clinton's action did more to repeal FDR's New Deal than Reagan ever did. Clinton dismantled the Glass Steagall Act. This action permitted the creation of mega banks like the rescued Citibank and now after the bailout, banks like J.P. Morgan Chase, an amalgam of some of a number of Wall Street's formerly famous institutions, Bank of America, taken back by its own acquisition of Merrill Lynch, and Wells Fargo, the biggest West Coast bank. Together, these banks now issue one of every two mortgages and about two of every three credit cards. On November 29, 2011, it was announced that these banks were given unsecured loans over $7 trillion by the Fed in 2008 to avoid their potential failures.

In addition to Glass Steagall, Clinton removed oversight on derivatives and he got on the free-trade bandwagon just like Reagan and continued gutting American jobs through NAFTA and his permissive attitude towards offshoring.

Bush / Clinton – free traders!

Bill Clinton was a romantic regarding free trade and offshoring, both of which were killing the country during his presidency. In his 1992 presidential debate with George Bush and Ross Perot, it was not Bush or Perot who made the big statement of offshoring and its effects on jobs. It was Bill Clinton, himself. Regarding offshoring Clinton said it "will, on the whole, do more good than bad... if [the US] has a genuine commitment to educate and retrain American workers who lose their jobs."

That is how either naïve our leaders were / are or how much they simply had sold out to corporate America.

In March, 2006, buoyed by his reelection after a very aggressive first term regarding free trade and offshoring, George Bush took his message to India, a fine country, but one which consistently defeats the US in any trade negotiations. The Indian people are the sharpest in the world in putting together offshoring deals and the US is India's # 1 victim. Yet, despite how miserably the US performs in trade deals compared to India, Bush II did not see it that way any time throughout his eight years in office.

When he went to India in March 2006, President George W. Bush addressed offshore outsourcing (offshoring) to India. He surprised me at how little he cared for Americans jobs.

Bush stated that outsourcing offshore needs to be accepted as a natural part of the global world. He said it should not be feared but embraced. Bush noted that he felt that offshore outsourcing will assist the U.S. in the long run in many ways. According to him, globalization facilitates great opportunities and offers new ways to any country for future growth.

Bush admitted that "several people" do lose their jobs as a result of the full globalization procedure, and he acknowledged it was painful for those losing their jobs (the losing side). Despite the loss of jobs and the personal tragedy it brings, Bush concluded that the offshore development process is really a very fruitful process and would definitely help both India and the United States in the near future.

If we fast forward to the end of the Bush era and into the Obama years, if this were a Burger King ad, somebody would be asking, "Where is the beef?" Since we not only export jobs to India, the US gives lots of hi-tech visas to Indian people so they can come to America to take American jobs. Bush was right. It is a great deal. Unfortunately, it is only a great deal if you are Indian, or Chinese, or Indonesian. If you are American, it is a personal tragedy. Obama, who seemingly hated everything Bush did, continued these policies.

George Bush also said that the US sells lots of air conditioners to India from GE and Whirlpool. He felt that made up for all the jobs they took from US. As of 2008, though it so far has been unsuccessful as GE has been trying to unload its appliance division completely and Whirlpool has been in so many joint ventures with the Chinese that you know it is just a matter of time before Whirlpool can ship those fine air conditioners from their plant of origin in China to India and save a few miles on freight.

No matter how you look at it, the point is that offshoring does not help US jobs one bit. Whether George Bush was lying about that is something that the history books will have to sort out.

So, now in this historical trip, we enter the Obama Administration and its response or shall we say non-response to offshoring. In November 2010 after he had two years to think about it, the President reshaped the notion of offshoring simply as a part of international trade. As a globalist with a number of free trade agreements to his recent credit, the new Obama position on offshoring is to ignore the impact on American jobs. Instead of complaining about American jobs moving to Bangalore, just like George Bush before him, the President soothed India's leaders by suggesting that trade works both ways.

In his own words: "I want to be able to say to the American people when they ask me, 'Well, why are you spending time with India? Aren't they taking our jobs?' I want to be able to say, 'Actually, you know what? They just created 50,000 jobs.' And that's why we shouldn't be resorting to protectionist measures; we shouldn't be thinking that it's just a one-way street. I want both the citizens in the United States and citizens in India to understand the benefits of commercial ties between the two countries." Thanks for the pep talk Mr. President but it is not trade deals that are needed. It is protection from trade deals. One year later, in 2011, and there have been no results—but it was a good speech! There are no 50,000 jobs. There are none.

Under Republican Administrations and the Clinton Administration, the US has been going global. When Democrats took over in 2007, they said no more trade deals. They were right. Yet, in October 2011 Congress passed three long-awaited free trade agreements. South Korea, Colombia, and Panama are the beneficiaries of these agreements. I see it as US, 0—trade partners, 3.

Despite protectionist sentiment, which is the appropriate medicine and long overdue, President Obama, the new globalist on the US team, claimed victory by getting the three agreements passed. For Obama, it makes him appear politically strong while he is in campaign mode, though the benefits to Americans at best will be minimal and if it comes down like every other trade agreement, the US will lose more jobs.

As a sweetener, to show confidence in a plan that should need no sweeteners, House Republicans agreed to approve an expansion of benefits for displaced workers. So, who is to benefit? Word is that banks and law firms should gain but manufacturers, and the ailing textile industry, which likes to operate in America, in particular, are expected to get another whack right on the chin.

The US is becoming a banana republic

Our esteemed corporations and their incessant outsourcing of what were once American jobs from the 1980's on have created major economic woes in America. This great recession, which continues into 2012, is replete with runaway spending and corruption galore. It is so bad that some predict that we are becoming a banana republic, if we have not already arrived.

O. Henry created the term "banana republic" in his 1904 book *Cabbages and Kings*. It is about the fictional Republic of Anchuria—a servile dictatorship engaging in the large-scale production of bananas. Today, the definition has expanded to mean the collusion and even the melding of government and private enterprise. When government and private enterprise collude, who wins and who loses?

One can see many similarities of O. Henry's vision with a modern government that encourages its corporations to offshore jobs. In this scenario, the taxpayers incur the expenses, (unemployment compensation etc.), while the profits are taken in by the corporations. I'd say that about explains how the United States got to where we are today.

Chapter 11   Insourcing Our Way Back to Prosperity

By-by Banana Republic

So, as we become more of a banana republic and we begin to behave in many ways as a dictatorship of bananas, perhaps the correct solution for America to get back on its feet is the solution the United States, when we were at the top of our game, would recommend to smaller nations that were suffering through banana republic regimes.

One such solution is called *Import substitution industrialization. It is also known as Import-substituting Industrialization."* (ISI).

Businessdictionary.com defines import substituting industrialization as a theory of economics which is utilized by developing market nations that are looking to increase their self-sufficiency and decrease their dependency on goods from developed countries. To implement the theory, there must be a focus on protecting the domestic infant industries so they can compete with imported goods thereby making their economy more self-sustaining. Investopedia.com has a similar definition.

The term primarily refers to 20th century development economics policies, though it has been around since the 18th century. As we discuss the reindustrialization of America, we must examine a modified version of ISI as a fitting solution, as the unholy alliance of our government and our corporations have in effect de-industrialized the people's America.

Sometimes you need a slap in the face to wake up. This intentional and uncomplimentary slap in the face goes to my country's leadership that has permitted us to be in a position that it would be good for us to begin again to industrialize.

Is there a difference in the countries for which the United States in prior years would have recommended ISI and the condition of the US today? The only difference I see is that America is not yet fully denuded of its industry but then again, the offshoring process is not finished yet. So far, politics has prevented any response to the destruction of American industry. Instead, we see the US giving more and more of our white collar jobs to overseas concerns.

So, I recommend an approach that pretends that we have nothing at all. This can be very effective in bringing us back as right now, we are on the road to economic perdition for sure.

The basic tenet of ISI therefore is to replace imports with domestic production. If we treat all American industries (those that build products or conduct business in the US using American employees) as infant industries and we incubate those industries from the outside world that is unfriendly to America, we can again succeed as we did in the two industrial revolutions which ended in the 1920's. It is time for the US to enter the third industrial age, just ninety years after we ended our second and adopted free trade principles instead of advocating America first.

In addition to protecting the interests of the American people by protecting American home country firms, government must also embark on a public relations campaign that positions our interests above those of the faux American interests.

The false prophets in this case are the corporations who have abandoned us. Regardless of whether Apple or IBM or Microsoft or HP wants us to believe they make American products, they do not. They import products from other countries where they pay workers from those countries to produce the products. So, when we talk about avoiding imports, it is a larger term than some might initially conclude.

The ISI idea is simple. By making products themselves, small countries create jobs and rely less on other nations. The ISI thus is based primarily on the internal market. The product is sold to the home market. The USA is a huge market. In fact, it is the largest market in the world. It represents 25% of the total world market. Therefore, products built in the US through efficient means should be able to sell in the US, unless, of course there is unfair competition from other countries as there is now.

In truly developing countries, ISI is a total package. It works by having the state lead economic development through nationalization, subsidization of vital industries (including agriculture, power generation, etc.), increased taxation to fund the above, and highly protectionist trade policy. I would look towards a modified ISI approach for our reindustrialization.

For example, nationalization of American home based industries is very important. However, it is not the kind of nationalization in which private industry becomes controlled by the government. Instead it is the second definition of nationalization, "To make national in character, scope, or notoriety." For our rebuilding it would be an exaggerated form of "buy American." Yet, the producers of goods and services do not have to be American companies. Any company with an American-first attitude regarding site locations and employment would benefit from the new notion of nationalization. Products made in America would be known as American products no matter who made them. Products made in other countries would be imports regardless of whether they were made by corporations chartered in the US or in other countries. But, they would pay no income tax.

Government-induced industrialization through governmental spending was the formula for ISI and it was the way the concept was practiced in developing countries such as Latin

America and Asia in the mid 1900's. The model was largely influenced by Keynesian thinking, and that is why the ISI notion was not as successful as it could have been. The American people are fed up with big government and big bailouts and Keynesian economic theory such as that practiced by Jimmy Carter and Barack Obama. So the Keynesian part of ISI would be a no-go and that would give ISI a better opportunity to succeed in America.

We already have enough evidence with GM and other government ventures such as Solyndra that government does not belong in any US industry. Government is the worst entity to operate a profit oriented organization. However, government can certainly choose sides so that it clearly favors all domestic-based companies over those that engage in profit by offshoring.

As you are digesting that last sentence, you probably noticed that there is one word that needs to be changed. The US government with its free trade policy and its anti-American trade agreements with 17 different countries and its being a proponent of offshore outsourcing to this day, does not have to choose sides. It has already chosen the other side. It is time for American leaders to change sides. Choose America first. It's about time.

Additionally, the ISI notion of subsidization of vital industries (including agriculture, power generation, etc.), is not needed in the US. US farmers are already the best in the world, and they cannot offshore the productivity of the breadbasket of America to foreign lands. Additionally, the US is already number one in power generation though government can help in this regard. Government can get out of the way and permit power companies to produce enough energy to support a reindustrialization effort. Moreover, government can help expedite approvals for new energy sources and stop the nonsense of backing only energy ideas that are unproven.

From my perspective, a good start in this regard would be the disbanding of the Department of Energy. Nixon created the Department when the Arabs cut off our oil supply because we sided with Israel in 1973. It sobjective was American oil independence. Instead, we import 50% more foreign oil than we did in 1973. The DOE has failed and they should be run out of town.

In my new book, Kill the EPA, I recommend removing the EPA as an economic obstacle. Capitalism works when capital can be applied to the markets in which it is needed. Government regulations have destroyed the true market balance necessary for capitalism to thrive in America. It is time to change that.

So in our modified ISI, the United States would again be fostering infant industries, such as a steel industry perhaps, and a semiconductor industry, a rail industry, a shipbuilding industry, an electronics industry, and a reinvigorated energy industry, and others. Government would not be the prime mover nor would it provide subsidies. It would permit any country to build in the United States and all takers, American and foreign would be given most favored status and lots of positive press on government websites and on any government sponsored medium simply by operating in America with a preponderance of American employees.

Until the Wilson presidency (2013-2021), our protectionist systems (systems that those who hate America also hate) had brought in up to 50% or more US revenue in tariffs and kept all other taxes relatively low. One of the first events of Wilson's presidency was the passage of the Underwood Tariff as part of the Revenue Act of 1913. This reduced tariff rates from 41 to 25%. It also created the first federal income tax after the passage of the 16th Amendment. The income tax was a means to compensate for anticipated lost revenue because of the reduction of tariff duties. Tariffs had been the largest source of federal revenue from the 1790s to the eve of World War I, until it was surpassed by income taxes.

During the industrial heyday, America prospered and the best industrial complex of any country in the history of the world was formed right here. It is time to return to those days of prosperity and this time the people, not the corporations are # 1.

The profit motive, along with protectionism through large tariffs built the backbone of America. Likewise, the profit motive and corporations protecting their profits while giving the full hand to nose salute to the American people dismantled the most successful industrial complex of all time.

It is the purpose of the reindustrialization to reestablish America first and foremost as a self sustaining and highly successful country.

As a plus for the environmentalists, while we are building back our country, we can design all of the necessary clean industry equipment into the blueprints for new plants and to existing plants as they are being refurbished.

We can do it if we choose to do it!

Chapter 12   Raise Tariffs

Protection and more revenue

Why are we talking about free trade and jobs and tariffs and things that normal Americans do not typically care about? You would not be reading this book if you were not interested in what happens to America. Our leaders have mishandled our country and they continue to do so. It is time this stops and America comes back in a way that restores our former greatness as an industrial power. The more we all know about the options to handle the devastating economic effects of offshoring, the better our chances are to get the right solution in place. One of the best solutions is to relax free trade and raise tariffs. It worked before and it will work again.

America first!

Many economists, who are interested more in how businesses can succeed, than in how the people can succeed, do not like the idea of protectionism and an America-first policy. They think free trade is the best approach for American corporations and surely they are right. I have stopped caring about what is good for American corporations as they care nothing about what is good for we the people. This chapter is about what is good for Americans, not what is good for corporations. How about leaving the jobs in America for starters! Corporations already have it too good and that is what I hope to help change.

The Reason for the RRR plan in the first place is because American corporations, who are fictional citizens by law, are very poor American citizens. For their greed and profit, they have turned their fictional backs on the reason for their success—the American people. They fictionally spit on Americans every day but it sure feels real. They have chosen to forget about America and Americans and so in our America-first platform, we suggest that all Americans do the same for corporations that were once American.

The notion of reduced redistribution and reduced progressivism is explored in the next chapter. In Chapter 14, we go through the dangers of progressivism and all the other isms that can change our America into something we want nothing to do with. Why the leaders of both parties are pro-corporate free-trade and pro illegal and pro massive legal immigration is a position that does not help the American people and does not help jobs. So, before you vote for anybody in 2012, make sure they are for America-first and if they are incumbents, make sure their voting record reflects it.

An America-first platform on redistribution demands that we applaud all charitable acts but it also demands that the government should not be a charity. Americans are out of work and becoming more broke as the government encourages people not to work. This government strategy is out of synch with a real recovery strategy. Only those who really need help should receive it.

Those out of work should receive unemployment compensation to keep them going. Their employers paid into it on their behalf. Those who have reached the proper age should be able to collect Medicare and Social Security since they paid for it. Everybody else who is not helpless should work to toughen themselves up for the many jobs that will be coming back to America by our adoption of the RRR plan.

I know you care about America or you would not be reading this book. You know that if you and I do not care what happens to America; America is done? It is through! We are the only ones who can and must stop the continual demise of our country at our government leaders' hands, at corporate leaders' hands, and at union leaders' hands. The solution, is in our hands. It is imperative that our hands are lifted to form the universal hand stop sign so that nobody and nothing can continue to work against America.

Who can stop the bad guys? It is you. It is me. It is your kids. It is my kids. It is our neighbors. It is our fellow bus riders. It is the person in line with us at the Post Office and anybody else who loves America. Whatever we do, we should not let progressives talk us into giving up our freedoms and our God to worship the state, corporations, or unions.

That is our first concern. Once we get past that, then we can all take on corporations without taking on capitalism as we move back to a mercantilist approach for the next twenty or more years. For this chapter, corporations are the entities in play. However, the state, and unions also will play a big role in the overall solution to the jobs problem. We cannot afford a situation in which we know what to do and our politicians are too worried about themselves to move forward. Additionally, we cannot afford a jobs package in which unions become an obstacle for a real solution. But, Unions may be one of the ways that we get to bring back America so let's not write them off yet. We may need them.

Not all experts are high on free trade!

Paul Craig Roberts, A WSJ Editor and former Assistant Secretary of the U.S. Treasury sees most politicians on the D and the R side as either missing the point or purposely not representing their American constituencies on the dangers of free trade and offshoring. Roberts sees many economists in his field of expertise as having sold out to the globalists for personal gain, and they no longer can look at offshoring objectively.

He characterizes them as "bought and paid for" in the mainstream of economic thought. In other words, they are frauds and charlatans and the American people know way more about economics than they do. [69% say free trade is bad] Yet, these corrupt economists are the only ones cited when citations are needed.

We all know that the American public is suffering with a form of unemployment that will never come back without an overwhelming realization that it must, and then major action by powerful forces to cause it to be righted. Presidents wishing to get reelected will tell you the unemployment rate is going down while the average wage is also going down but at a faster rate. The switch from project engineer to hamburger flipper after six months unemployment compensation tells Obama's unemployment statistics that you got your job back, but did you really? Roberts' piece in Counterpunch is right on target and deserves a gander. http://www.counterpunch.org/2011/05/31/how-offshoring-has-destroyed-the-economy/

Permit me to quote Paul Craig Roberts so that we all get the essence of his brilliance on free trade and offshoring and then we can get into the details about raising tariffs as the best approach to a solution.

"These are discouraging times, but once in a blue moon a bit of hope appears. I am pleased to report on the bit of hope delivered in March of 2011 by Michael Spence, a Nobel prize-winning economist, assisted by Sandile Hlatshwayo, a researcher at New York University. The two economists have taken a careful empirical look at jobs offshoring and concluded that it has ruined the income and employment prospects for most Americans.

"To add to the amazement, their research report, "The Evolving Structure of the American Economy and the

Employment Challenge," was published by the very establishment Council on Foreign Relations.

"For a decade I have warned that US corporations, pressed by Wall Street and large retailers such as Wal-Mart, to move offshore their production for US consumer markets, were simultaneously moving offshore US GDP, US tax base, US consumer income, and irreplaceable career opportunities for American citizens."

It surely is tough out there folks!

Our esteemed representatives are listening to the "bought and paid for" economists to know which way to go. More free trade and shipping more high paying jobs overseas will crush our America. Pick up the phone today and tell your representatives "no more free trade and no more offshoring." Tell them to check out the RRR plan as it is the best way out of our dilemma. Free trade is only free to the country to which American workers give their jobs. Nobody gives up a good job willingly.

Corporations are tough to fight and we are well aware that through their lobbyists, they have bought off our representatives, and now we know from Roberts' report, they have also bought off some economists. It is tough to get the truth because the media sides with the liars. Yet, for some strange reason, we continue to elect these traitors. Let's say "no more to that," for when we do not pay attention, we always get the government we deserve.

There is hope as long as you can spend some time for America. There is always hope if we think of America as a good place and from our motley backgrounds, we can do exceptional things. There will always be bad people but it is time that we learn to identify who they are and no longer place them in positions of trust.

Tariffs have many purposes

You may recall as we discussed the Wilson years, in Chapter 11, that the nefarious United States Income Tax and the IRS were not here just 100 years ago. In fact, the income tax would never have been passed if it were not that there was pressure by the Democrats to stop protecting American businesses. In the pre-roaring twenty-years, businesses were mostly run by Republicans so there was a political connotation to the passage of the 16th amendment.

Would you have ever thought that the Democrats, my party, would want an income tax to plague all the people—even those who make just a few bucks? Woodrow Wilson was a big-time progressive in the nature of Barack H. Obama. He brought in the income tax and ever since that day, the government has been in the handout and redistribution business. In these tough economic times, most Americans are hoping that the new American Dream is something a lot more substantive than just a "handout."

Progressives were defamed back after the turn of the 20th century but they recently have begun feeling safe to come out in public again. The leaders of the Democratic Party, like communist leaders, do not necessarily reflect the views of the people in the Party. So, again the leaders are talking about "progressive ideas."

These are not "advanced ideas." They are the same socialist / communist ideas that carry the barebones label, "progressive." When you heard Barack Obama tell Joe the plumber that as President he would like to redistribute income, you probably thought you heard it wrong. Obama now admits, he is a progressive and he loves the notion of taking from those who earn it and giving it to those who have sat on their duffs and not earned a dime.

In this earlier era of our history, Wilson and the Democrats were progressives. They loved the notion of the income tax so much that they pushed through the 16th amendment for without the amendment, an income tax would be unconstitutional. Then they passed the income tax legislation and began to reduce tariffs. Some think the income tax was a great social tool for progressives to redistribute income even if the recipient had chose not to work? Is this really a great and noble notion? Many Americans see huge taxes as wealth confiscation by government and in fact it is stealing.

For Catholics and Protestants, it is not noble at all. You may recall that stealing is against the seventh commandment of God and Moses. Even government is not permitted by God to confiscate the property of the people. People may give willingly to churches and charities. Confiscation and Constitution are not synonyms.

As sure as corporations have no soul, governments also have no soul and thus in both of these fictional entities, evil spreads rapidly when there is money involved. Taking more and more bucks from the people became easy once the income tax was permitted. Even before the US entered World War I, the income tax, just several years old, was bringing in more revenue to the government than any other source—including the tariffs.

Parkinson's Rule

Parkinson's rule, which describes the notion of humanness in the workplace, is as follows: "Work expands so as to fill the time available for its completion." Kelly's spending rule is a corollary to Parkinson's as follows: "Spending expands so as to fill the difference between no spending and the maximum amount in the treasury." Obama's rule is not at all similar. It is as follows: "Spend other people's money as long as nobody is telling you not to spend it and when they do tell you not to spend, simply ignore them."

The 16ᵗʰ Amendment came first

The irony of the income tax is that our government in 1909 came to the people and asked us to permit our trustworthy government to be able to levy a tax on income. The Democratic Party had been begging for this for many years and in many ways. They felt tariffs, which had made the US a formidable power after less than 100 years of existence, were regressive. Since they were consumption taxes, they were believed by the Democrats to impose a heavier burden on the poor who consume a higher proportion of their income than do the rich. As a point of note, I think this is claptrap.

So, the progressives defamed tariffs as a regressive tax, and they clearly do not like regressive because it is backward and theoretically just the opposite of progressive. The worst part of the term "regressive tax," is the word regressive itself which is simply an ugly sounding word meaning the opposite of progressive. Yet, a regressive tax is a tax that is imposed equally and that means fairly, on every taxpayer. Regression means that every proponent of the tax will pay the same percentage as the next guy. It keeps voters a bit more honest.

Americans do not need free-trade

Our competitors do but Americans do not benefit from free-trade. Once a trader, a manufacturer, or a seller of any kind is inside the United States, not on the outside looking in, they have access to the richest free trade zone on the planet with well over a quarter of the world's purchases being made here each year. Though China and Russia may be larger geographically, they are smaller economically. One could readily conclude as fact that Americans would prosper more than any other people in a tariff-only tax system. And, in fact, until Wilson and the Federal Income Tax, we were doing just that and we were doing just fine. Everybody wants to do business in America, including faux American corporations who build their products elsewhere.

Everybody, rich and poor, benefited from the tariffs that kept America prosperous until the 1920's. Tariffs incent American industry to expand. Additionally, more workers are needed when industry expands, and so there are more jobs available and the people earn real incomes. All of the work is done in America so there are lots of jobs for lots of Americans.

By voting for the 16th amendment, the people actually asked our honest and truthful government to take more and more of our daily toil. Yet, it is fascinating at how trusting Americans are of Americans if it is for the apparent common good. So, the 16th Amendment was placed in front of the people. The patriotic and trusting people of this country voted for it as it appeared like a good idea. Their representatives at the time advised them to do so, and Americans trusted that their representatives were working for their well-being. Without this implicit trust in government, we would have no income tax today.

The irony at the time of Wilson is that Republicans were always looking for barriers against free trade. As the producers of goods, the Republicans wanted protection so that their products from the mills, the farms and the factories—those made by Americans, were priced better than those coming in from foreign lands. High tariffs on imported goods assured this. Because of the tariff protections, by 1910, America had become the most industrialized nation on the face of the earth. Let us repeat this sentence for effect:

Because of the tariff protections, [not in spite of the tariffs] by 1910, America had become the most industrialized nation on the face of the earth.

Today, the bad guys are our own corporations. Protection-ism is anathema to the notion of free trade and of course free trade is in vogue with all of the globalists, a number of whom have been and one who continues to be president(s) of the United States. How has free trade helped you today?

For countries that need help like the US right now, the infant-industry argument is a valid economic justification for trade protectionism. The basic argument is that budding industries most often do not enjoy the economies of scale that their more established competitors from other countries may have. Thus, they need to be nurtured and protected until they can attain similar cost advantages that a business obtains due to expansion.

The US again needs to be protected but this time it is from its own faux American industries such as Apple, Microsoft, and even IBM. Today the corporations that run the "American" industries no longer choose to stay and build their products in the home country. In many ways domestic corporations who build their products overseas have given up on America and when they ship products back to America, companies that build in America and who hire American workers to do so, need protection from them.

The argument to protect new businesses was brought forth as far back as 1790 by Alexander Hamilton, the 1st US Secretary of the Treasury. Obviously, protectionism worked for the United States until the Income Tax assured politicians of revenue without taxing neighbor countries.

England, the major US competitor of old, the mother ship that had, by its successful trading practices convinced American Presidents to employ mercantilism to build US industry, eventually got lost in the grand notion of free trade. After all, at the time, in the days leading up to the revolution, England literally ruled the world and America was looking for a way to become large and successful as England had always been.

Unfortunately for England, by the time the US had determined that the mercantilist strategy as deployed by England, was the best approach to expand the infant industries in America, the British had chosen a different course. Since they were so powerful, the British decided to be fairer. One of England's swings *like a pendulum* found it so consumed in the notion of free trade, rather than the mercantilism that had kept it strong for hundreds of years, resulted in its losing its zip as a country. In the process, of espousing free trade, England denigrated to less than half of its former GDP. The moral of the story is that free trade is not good for the country that owns the game. Free trade is not good for the country that is giving up the business. It does help all the other countries. The verdict is in. It has not helped the US.

At the end of what I would like to call England's unintentional "downsizing by dumbness," the former world ruler was made weak by its own free-trade practices. Germany was in the process of picking apart England in World War I. England would have been a German isle if a former colony (the United States) had not emulated the great Brits in the practice of mercantilism. Nobody on earth had the industrial might of the US at the beginning of World War I, and to the best of my knowledge nobody has yet to eclipse us, though the piranha are circling.

The US was not involved in the war until 1917 but England was almost finished when President Wilson answered the call for help. If it were not for the resources of the US, England would have fallen to Bismarck and become a German nation. Ironically, Germany had gained its power using the same style of mercantilism which had enabled England to rule the world. England had forgotten what had made it successful just as the US has today. The US at the time of World War I had been a practitioner of the creed of mercantilism from the late 1700's. During WWI, the US was even better at it than the Germans. The free trading British would have been goners had they not been such great teachers.

In the 1980—2012 era, the free-traders are now a mix of
Republicans and Democrats going back from Ronald Reagan
forwards. So we have Bush / Clinton Bush / Bush / almost
Clinton – whoops, that last one is for sure Obama. During the
Reagan years, but growing rapidly afterwards, American
businesses for profit reasons, decided it was OK to separate
from America and Americans. Reagan was convinced that the
US was so powerful that free trade could not hurt us. He also
thought globalization was a good idea because it brought in
small countries that would always be left out in the past.

Reagan did not foresee the issues that came with knocking
down the trade barriers and tariffs leaving America unprotected
from within. Reagan certainly knew the evils in government but
he had yet to meet the real face of evil until he embraced
corporatism as if it would remain loyal to America in a global
trade environment.

Obama, just as those presidents from the mid 1970's on, loves
globalism. However, Obama pretends to hate all corporations
while he aligns himself with specific corporations. For example,
some Obama friends include: GE, Honeywell International,
Intel, Dow Chemical, Boeing, Coca Cola, JP Morgan Chase,
Microsoft, Goldman Sachs, and of course GM and Chrysler.
These allegiances help Obama in getting reelected and they
have helped him grow the government to an unprecedented
size.

I am convinced that this President does not wish to know what
will succeed in moving the economy forward and creating real
private sector jobs. Rather than being prepared to succeed,
Obama has his team ready for mop up operations. As soon as
his regulations, policies, edicts, and executive orders
overwhelm American business and the public at large, and all
of this triggers a market response that says, "We're done;" we
probably will be done. Obama has enough patience to get us all

through just one more election cycle, after which he will figure out how to own the whole game by executive fiat.

If I wake up three decades from now still alive, I will recall hearing of this globalist ideology in this way: "It seemed to be everywhere. No matter who you were, you could not escape it. If you were a national politician, you were either destroyed by it or it is why you prospered. The idea had certainly captured the attention of both national parties. These progressives were products of the same universities that had elected Roosevelt and the New Dealers."

No matter how prevalent globalist thinking may be today, it is the wrong approach for the sovereign nation of the United States of America.

Democrats claimed not to be progressives or socialists or Marxists at the time of Roosevelt, because they had received a big haircut after the Wilson days. But, in their hearts, they all knew that the ideology at the top of the Party had not changed. The regular people, like my dad, did not know about their big plans. He was a regular guy as were most Democrats. He was a pretty tough guy as were most Democrats. Perhaps because of guys like my dad and your dad and a lot of other pretty tough dads, it took progressives to the turn of the millennium to actually begin to show themselves brazenly in public again.

Many Americans grew up as nothing and then learned how to be something. We were assisted by the great principles of this country. Whether our parents were Democrat, Republican, Green or Libertarian, we continue to be eternally grateful to an America that not only permits us to dream but helps us achieve the dream. Americans are not accustomed to being slammed back to the pavement earth as a proletariat or a peasant but unless we change direction, the end of the middle class is on the horizon. It will be a precursor to the end of the United States.

I never had a thought growing up that I was poor because I grew up in America. While I was poor, there was never a

handout that came our way as my dad worked for a living. I
think that is why I felt American and not like a person who was
helped by Americans. Either way, like many baby boomers, I
am most grateful for the help I received in achieving a college
degree. I for one are glad there are rich people, and I believe
that with mercantilism and protective tariffs, protecting our jobs
from our own corporations, more and more Americans can
partake of the American dream. More and more Americans can
shoot for the moon, become rich and then help other
Americans. That is what America is all about.

Poor leadership can be replaced

Let us go back to why we are here in this book about recovery
using the RRR plan, and why we are in this chapter. The
potential for the American dream is being limited by our poor
leadership. America has been neutered by our representatives
and a President who cannot seem to grasp the full meaning of
our great heritage.

Our economy is in the toilet and our industry captains caused it
by deciding to be the captains of ships sailing towards distant
waters. I am here to tell you all today that it is OK to complain
and if any of our industry captains decide to turn their vessels
on us and punish us by the curse of "deprivation of product,"
we will punish them by a major deprivation of market.

Let's deprive faux American corporations of our market

If the great "American" corporations whose products are built
overseas by non-Americans in the Otherlands or other well
known places, will not ship iPods or iPads or Blackberry's or
BMW's, or Wolverine pull-on flat bottom boots, or Barbie
Dolls, or Xbox 360's, or Dell PC's to the USA, then the people

of the USA can invite their competition into the US to build these items and any other item for us. We can all say good-by to faux American corporations.

Isn't it time we all got a pair? They tell me women ask this of other women today and perhaps it is a perfectly valid and no longer inappropriate question. Should the United States be the little guy in the world or should we regain our domination through obvious strength, not Obama diplomacy. Ask the Soviet Union how they came to the decision to break-up if you think Reagan-level strength is not necessary to solve real problems. That was the last time the US was strong in deed and in perception.

Does it not make you wonder why Apple, as wonderful as the late Steve Jobs was, and IBM, a company that would never turn its back on America unless it was necessary, and Microsoft, whose Bill Gates would give you a billion as long as he got two back, and of course HP, who learned that being the biggest in revenue no matter who gets hurts is worth giving up the company credo, "The HP Way!"—one and all—they have abandoned America.

None of these companies give a rat's mcduff about America. They all moved out and our government promised not to tell us! Our government promised not to defend us in any way. Our government, not another government, permitted the fruits of American ingenuity to be manufactured overseas by non-Americans.

Moreover, many other of our other "finest" corporations packed their bags and on departure provided a muted middle finger solute to America and Americans as they chose to gain profits overseas.

They believed in American exceptionalism. They just chose to end it in their day.

So, we ask ourselves, why in the days in which they could have lobbied the Congress and the President for protectionism, did corporations not do so? Could it be that corporations felt they had opportunities elsewhere and were better off pretending that they were forced to leave the United States, the country in which they had been originally chartered?

Corporate deceit with government help

Why did corporate America, with its privileged access to the greatest market on earth, our United States, go along with sharing that market with its manufacturing rivals from all over the world? One who studies psychology would suggest corporations, thriving in America at the time would have been insane to upset the market. So, they did not. It was like they had a deal with the devil and the devil would not tell. Was the devil of the day, the US government?

Why did they agree to take their share overseas? Why did they choose to strip America of the royalty on the corporations' very existences, which Americans had nourished and assured from inception? Why would American corporations go ahead and turn the profit on that hard-fought innovation that had occurred in America from our sweat labor over to foreigners, who had contributed nothing?

Surely, the corporations, in their wake, left nothing for America but their paltry unemployment compensation insurance. In fact, I have such little regard for these faux American entities that I would bet that more than likely the nasty corporations contested unemployment for their laid-off workers. I would not be surprised if they forced their former loyal workers through a nasty appeal process from a reluctant government that appeared to believe the blessed corporation and not the newly impoverished employee.

If I were a lawyer, and I thank God often that I am not, I would conclude with just a sense of reasonable logic that the government and corporations are in cahoots, as it seems that everybody else gained--record corporate profits, and free trade agreements. Yet, the American people lost jobs, income, and spirit.

Protectionism through trade tariffs is a country's means of becoming a mercantilist nation, protecting its industries and its jobs. Nowhere in recorded history did a home country's corporate industries ask to not be protected. But with faux American corporations importing the work of foreigners into America, the protective tariffs would have been against themselves, and damn well they should be still.
So, there was a wink and a nod with government and industry colluding, and somehow there was a trade-off that corporate America got a laissez-faire policy while it gave up American workers. Tough as it is to accept; that is what they did. It was intentional. Corporations claimed huge cost savings and government bragged about free-trade while Americans were wondering what hit them and why?

How about a profit motive? The U.S. corporate market was already well established in America. It was not going away any anytime soon. Corporate America could very easily risk sharing that market if, in return, it could shift its own production out of the United States to countries where the wages were low and regulations were light. Bingo! The world was at the beck and call of those American corporations that had consciously decided to not stay American at heart.

IBM became a champion for offshoring

I worked for IBM for 23 years of a promised 30-year career. The beauty of IBM was that though it chose an inglorious way to rid itself of people, who in any other system would have simply been laid off with nothing, once an employee accepted the deal, the deal itself was a good deal. Hard as it is to believe I was not on the first list of those who were deemed expendable. You see, I had this thing about speaking my mind to management and so I was surprised that after round one, I was still with the company.

In 1993, IBM was looking for body counts to reduce its expenditures and they tapped the lowest ranked employees for discharge. Others were offered the opportunity to get the package even if not selected by management. Eventually I agreed to a sweeter deal than the first offer that I had seen. As a Senior Systems Engineer, I was able to sneak out with the best package IBM had ever offered to the "technical field force." I thank God and I thank IBM to this day. Those who were more unaware than I—who chose not to leave with the package offered to us all, did not fare as well as I as time went by.

Management actually honored me by telling me, at 43 years old that the company had many uses for me and would prefer that I not take the optional package. They did not force me to stay with IBM, however, and I credit them with that. I got out and I love IBM to this day because the company was as good as it could have been under the economic circumstances of the times. Many companies today are not as nice, Perhaps IBM today, though I cannot offer commentary either way is not that way anymore. I hope IBM is still OK! Yet, I do not delude myself. The only real driver for corporations is corporate profits, even within IBM. I do still own my IBM stock.

I believe IBM would have liked to have remained as good a company as it could possibly be. Many global corporations over the years, including IBM have been very successful being US based with major foreign operating units. IBM did what it did to its "leftover" employees because it had to, not because it ever wanted to be Mr. Bad. I knew I had to get out. I would suspect that companies that were not IBM that actually would bring out a "Mr. Bad" image at the drop of a hat had no problem taking every single job that was possible overseas!

Many of us who know what a gracious company IBM was even when it was almost decimated in the early 1990's by chairman John Akers' gross incompetence recoil just thinking how bad it would have been working for a man with a ruthless creed like Jack Welch.

Welch was GE's CEO from 1981 to 2001. Whereas IBM's both Thomas Watsons' (Senior and Junior) pined for employee loyalty, GE's Welch showed his disregard for employee loyalty when he opined: "Ideally you'd have every plant you own on a barge" By that, he meant a readiness to seek out at a moment's notice the lowest possible wages and most pliable governments (weak regulations, low taxes, hostile to unions, etc.) anywhere on the globe.

Trump says 25% tariff

I am writing this book in the USA and I surely do not think that it would be better if I wrote this in China. Most Chinese I know or have met are fine people and are almost all exceptionally bright. But, China, the country is not a place for me. It is at odds with the USA in many ways, including trade, and our government should do something about it. Trade tariffs are appropriate as long as they are not excessive.

Donald Trump says 25% on China and OPEC nations is a good tariff rate. Maybe he is right. Trump in his own way is for the reindustrialization of America and a return to mercantilism. He also advocates a 20 percent tax on all domestic companies that outsource their jobs overseas. I think it should be higher but I think Donald Trump and I are on the same page.

There are a lot of issues for American corporations to deal with in relations with the Chinese. The US government with its wimpy Congress must think that Chinese trade is OK the way it is, even though Chinese products dominate the landscape in America.

American corporations might not be as pleased with the Chinese government as they once were as the Chinese now demand that our corporations give it all up to make a buck in China. American corporations are concerned about themselves—not about China or America. The Chinese demand they give up their secrets to gain China's business. But, American companies are not suicidal. They are profit oriented.

In the US intellectual property is protected, and corporations would be willing to bet that they would still be able to sell to China's growing markets. If not, just like Google, they need to be ready to pack it up and let the Chinese wonder what their next move will be.

Is capitalism or mercantilism right for the USA?

There is this notion today that capitalism is not doing it for Americans. This deal suggests that those Americans who should be top tier employees, who have either been fired or laid off and are nonetheless unemployed right now, are simply victims of capitalism. Maybe that is true but that says that capitalism, when it hurts the home country, such as when the corporations choose to offshore, needs to be reevaluated.

Let's take a look at the proof that pure capitalism as a market philosophy, including the elitist notion of free trade, has not helped average Americans at all.

If we could hire "The COUNT" from Sesame Street, he would be able to quickly add it up. Eight million jobs have been lost in manufacturing over the last 30 years while 5 million white collar jobs have been lost at the same time. While capitalism became more pure and government continued to think that the notion of global capitalism was more important than American capitalism, the result was ordinary Americans were not COUNTED by the COUNT.

Somehow, American legislators and in many cases regular Americans who felt they would be employed forever, no matter what the circumstances might be, thought the "pig" would never stop producing pork. Well that is until they too began to lose their jobs; then from their eyes, they finally recognized that the "pig" had died. Then, many more American jobs also died. Many had already bit the offshore dust but the government had never complained because the tax revenue sources were still producing. With a 1.65 trillion dollar deficit and climbing, it is time to complain. It was actually time twenty years ago.

Government always appears to be more concerned about the effects of its policies on jobs than it actually is. Nobody expects a government lament, and unfortunately, there is none. But, there could have been some action before it got this bad. Where were they?

Government offshores jobs

Back to the future! Government is so immune to how the people feel about offshoring that agencies in 40 states as well as Washington, DC today are using foreign workers instead of American workers. One of our governments' favorite positions to offshore is the help desk to handle customer service for food stamp inquiries. How ironic that they take away American jobs in the public sector to help people on welfare.

Surely we should penalize companies that forget they are America-based and we should deny them government contracts. What should we do about governments that choose to use foreign workers in foreign countries rather than Americans?

A 2003 NetworkWorldFusion article quotes industry consultant
Jack Heacock, who wonders whether the U.S. should impose
tariffs on overseas call centers, "to better balance the playing
field and the U.S. economy and information privacy." Stop
thinking about it! Of course we should!

Free trade—a worldwide wealth distribution scheme

It began in the Wilson days but the notion of free trade was
always a worldwide wealth distribution scheme. The English
gave up world domination for free trade. Was that really fair?
Was it worth it? The dissolution of tariff protection has forced
US workers to compete against employees in other countries,
who will work for a small percentage of what Americans need
to survive. American businesses that offshore jobs love the fact
that the overseas societies have little or no regulations and there
are no unions with which to grapple.

When I first thought of this large body of information available
for the topic of the reindustrializing America, just as with the
other sets of 3-R's, I was looking more at a solution
methodology, rather than the solution. On the way to the
solution involving the reindustrialization of America, we must
do at least one other thing that starts with R. There is no
choice. We must **R**aise tariffs on American corporations and if
that is not enough, then all foreign corporations must pay a
tariff. I like to call this: "tariff induced re-industrialization."
You can bet American companies will be back if they are put in
a position in which to sell their goods in America, they will pay
a nice sized tariff.

Essential and non-essential industries

Offshoring of jobs did not happen overnight. Essential
industries, along with their jobs, have been off-shored, while the
non-essential industries have stayed home. By not producing
the essentials of course, America is made vulnerable.

After World War II, the English began its own watch-making industry. Prior to the war, the English and other European countries were happy letting the skilled Swiss watchmakers provide their time pieces. During the war, they learned that the skills of the watchmaker were needed for perfecting armaments. England paid more attention to assure vital industries were supported in the country after the war. America needs to do the same thing now.

Can you see a bunker buster bomb being assembled in Iran? I know it sounds silly so use another country and it is just as silly. Now, if the US were building the bombs, surely we would put a GPS in them and assure the bombs would not detonate anywhere within the 50 states. Do you see how non-silly it is to suppose that any country might add a little more technology to the mix?

So if a diverse industrial base is necessary for defense, why has the President and Congress permitted so much of America's industrial base to be exported overseas? Should the US not take an inventory of its vital industries and its craft skills to assure that like the English, we are never left short of what is needed to survive and conquer. Then when we know what industries must be built, let's get the job done.

We all know why corporations offshore. They see it as helping their bottom line. Even though finished goods as well as raw materials must be shipped at considerable expense across vast oceans to find their way to America's store shelves, corporations believe that it beats paying the high price of American labor to make products here. The biggest expense for many businesses is labor. They find cheap labor overseas and they can make what they want with no red tape. When they have to pay a nice tariff to sell their products, the game will be tilted more in America's favor.

Do American corporations have a beef?

Scott Hodge, president of the Tax Foundation, a think tank in
Washington D.C. thinks corporations have more than labor as
a beef: "By keeping our corporate tax rate so high, we're
creating an economic Berlin Wall around the United States."

Hodges also suggests readjusting American attitudes towards
work. Though not as popular as blaming the government,
Hodge thinks that unions add a drag on productivity since the
corporations must go through the unions to motivate the
employees. They don't have to do this overseas.

He also cites all the government mandates and regulations that
have made America an unattractive place to do business. But
even if government did all the right things to bring industry
home, there would still be another formidable roadblock from
Hodges' perspective. That roadblock according to Hodge, even
if the union issue were settled, another problem for business is
the individual potential employee.

Hodges suggests that that the American laborer more and more
resembles his European brother; he expects high pay and
generous benefits for very little work. And now America has
entered a new stage of European-style unemployment. So the
American worker must ask himself what he is willing to give up
so that he can have the dignity and security of a job. It is tough
to want to give up nice unemployment benefits for example to
take a job when the job does not pay as much. In fact, if an
American would do that, he or she would be thought of as a
fool by his peers. Yet, we all know that everybody cannot be on
unemployment indefinitely.

Nobody is really working on the problem

Even if the American worker were willing to give up higher
wages for a job, the current administration in Washington is

unwilling to give up its plans for the perfect workplace. There are no real plans to end federal mandates or relax regulations or slash corporate tax rates. There is a lot of lip service.

Here we are with real problems and we have nobody but politicians working on them. It is no wonder that things are still not right! The thinking from the White House indicates just the opposite. Though things are not right, rather than making them right, this President wants to talk people into believing all is well. He is the master spin artist.

Moreover, for the President of the United States, and the Congress, ideology comes before practicality and as long as we are stuck with such leaders, America will be the poor house. Look how stubbornly the ideologues cling to Obamacare as a solution when they know it has already exacerbated the problem for businesses that still have an option to leave America. It is yet another reason to pack up the jobs and leave. When faced with that reality, our President digs in on the idea of repealing Obamacare. Obama recently said: "We're not going back. I refuse to go back."

So the reindustrialization of America, the shift to mercantilism and tariffs, along with regaining the jobs, remains on the distant horizon. It is not even a flicker on the teleprompter of this Administration's agenda. Vice President Biden recently said: "there's no possibility to restore 8 million jobs lost in the Great Recession." What a goof! Why not VP Biden? Have you given your brain the year off?

Biden is probably correct but only if the government, which he influences, refuses to do what it must to attract business and make it profitable for US corporations to create their products and provide in-house services (call center, accounting, IT) in the United States rather than someplace else. Even still there is hope if Americans show Mr. Biden and Mr. Obama the way home at the end of their first term. What's acceptable for government isn't necessarily good for the individual.

The only way America can be great is to escape from our post-industrial malaise and again become the brains of the world's economy and a major industrial force. To do this, our industry must first be successful in our own economy. We need tariffs to reindustrialize. We have a lot of smart people in this country and when we bring our educational institutions up to the level they should be—America will again be a fountain of ideas and inventions. But we have no monopoly on brains.

Indeed, due to our inadequate K-12 public education industry, we now have experts telling us that American workers are not knowledgeable enough and we must import brains from other countries. Add to that our long-idled workforce, which is losing its skills. Once we regain the will to be the best, we will again be the best in the world in all we do. We have little choices – reindustrialize, raise tariffs, or melt into oblivion. If only the left and the right understood this fully, we could call a 20-year truce to our everyday ideological battles.

It's appalling to discover the things that we find often by accident. For example, I just learned that the berets for one of our elite military units were contracted to be manufactured abroad. It is just too easy to buy foreign products. Don't we have anybody here today who can sew?. Will we all have to go naked if China gets upset with us?

John N. Hall, a programmer/analyst from Kansas City with a nice American sized brain; writing for *American Thinker* in July 2010 sums this all up perfectly: "When China contracts to build our Nimitz-class aircraft carriers for us, it'll be a good time to learn Mandarin. The longer America postpones her reindustrialization, the weaker she'll become. A nation of burger flippers cannot stand."

Amen!

The bottom line is to bring on the tariffs so that American corporations find it far less expensive to produce in America than to import from their plants overseas. Prosperity is within reach.

Insights on some important corporations

Reading the blogs about the IBM and Apple worker carnage from offshoring, and those writing about the issues, I quickly got the idea that those who have lost their jobs are convinced it was a Democrat / Republican / US Corporation partnership that enabled companies to pull it off with minimal negative press coverage. It was not an accident, and all parties knew that Americans would suffer. It just did not matter.

Obama & Google Town Hall wife of engineer

Darin Wedel, of Fort Worth Texas, whose wife Jennifer in early February, 2012, engaged President Obama about H-1B visas in a live town-hall meeting on Google thanked the President for helping him get a job but also said the president's view on the job prospects for engineers in his field "is definitely not what's happening in the real world."

The fact is that engineers are losing their jobs faster than people in a lot of other professions. Graduates from the finest and the not so finest are being eliminated as companies dismantle whole plants and ship the jobs overseas. Ironically, when folks like Wedel go looking for a job, they may find that the jobs available even in their own company are scheduled to be filled by non-Maricans who have been sponsored by their company with an H-1B visa, giving them six years in an American job and then more than likely a green card and permanent residence. So, what is it that America has to offer for smart people nowadays?

There is another story about a Stanford graduate who is a Robot Designer. He was hired for four months before his job was outsourced. His words are as follows: "I didn't think that after four months of employment at my first job out of grad school I would be laid off with 900 other people in the semiconductor industry."

The IEEE organization of engineers, notes that all types of engineers are losing their jobs at a noticeably faster rate than other professionals. Big time perpetrators are HO, Microsoft, IBM, Apple, and many tech companies. Forget about a tech career unless Congress implements the RRR plan. These companies have shed thousands and thousands of jobs just this year. An IBM Civil engineer got tapped recently and he says: "My manager called me into his office. Um, I expected him to say, 'You're safe.' But he surprised me and said, 'You're included in the layoff.' "

The old IBM, from the top down, always tried to do the right thing for employees. It seems the new IBM always does the right thing for the shareholders. IBM's deal for this poor engineer was that he could go work in India or China since no more engineering opportunities existed in the US. Engineers there can count on making about 1/3 or less than what they make in the US. He chose not to take the generous offer: "I considered it an insult. You know it's pretty common knowledge that IBM has been offshoring jobs, so this is sort of like a cold slap in the face"

There is a Union at IBM now but most don't join, fearing for their jobs. It is called Alliance@IBM "It's clear IBM is moving work offshore at a record rate," said Lee Conrad, national field coordinator for the Alliance. Shareholders may like today's results since the cuts appear to literally be paying dividends. Last year IBM put up about $13.4 billion in profit, which was a substantial increase from the year before.

IBM is not the only faux American corporation out there. There is lots of data that permits analysts to infer that multinationals overall cut 2.9 million jobs in the United States and added 2.4 million overseas between 2000 and 2009. Who does that really help?

Ironically, IBM and others have issues dealing with the host countries for their successes. Some of IBM's dirty work is done at the White House level. For example, in early 2012, **India has been voicing concerns that visas [such as H-1B] for tech workers are becoming too hard to obtain. Now trade talks are postponed indefinitely. Maybe IBM or Apple or HP will have to talk turkey directly to [you're not going to say Turkey, are you?]**

Ironically, billionaire capitalist Mayor Michael Bloomberg argues feverishly that the H-1B program also benefits the US economy by adding to the pool of skilled workers. I suspect that Bloomberg has not been swimming in this pool recently or his tummy would be suffering scraping brush burns.

Are we reentering the labor arbitrage days of the Robber Barons? For jobs, it is a surely a buyers market as it was as immigrants flooded our shores as early 1900 capitalists tried to become the richest persons in town.

The country is broke and the income Americans make today cause them to go broke not too far from payday. No wonder why there is no middle class to buy up even the cheap homes in foreclosure. Here is a good non-IBM story to demonstrate this: In 2008, EDS, a company originally founded by Ross Perot was acquired by corporate IT giant, HP. Since that time, with a surplus of IT people in the US as jobs have gone overseas, life has not been very good for former EDS employees. Perhaps HP bought the company merely to eliminate competition for their IT services. They surely have not endeared themselves to the former EDS employees.

The star of this coming story is a reasonably new HP employee after the acquisition. He had about 20 years experience at EDS. This guy readily confessed what is now happening at HP to former EDS employees. He may not have used the word,

"Hell" but that is apparently where he landed. He is still alive and strange as it may seem to HP followers, Carly Forina was not the perpetrator.

This poor soul from 2008, had been getting matter of fact correspondence over the years at specific times that would immediately reduce his base salary. EDS employees apparently were prepared for salary cuts between 2 1/2 percent to 5 percent in total upon arrival at HP. But, HP had other plans.

When the first cut came, it was 2.5% in February 2009. Then in April, another 10 percent cut. After other cuts the addition began as the cuts kept coming. The employee writes:

"My pay is being reduced a total of 29 percent, 20 percent effected Sept. 1, the additional 9 percent effective Sept. 1, 2010," the man said. That's nearly a 32 percent salary cut for one employee." Other former EDS employees said that they have received salary cuts as much as 47 percent. Sounds like HP has been talking to some late 19th century Robber Barons.

Apple Makes Great Machines (not in America) – picture credit - Apple

Why should IBM and HP take all the heat? All corpor-ations are doing it. "Should we still call them American?" is perhaps a better question. It is not good for America or Americans, though it is good for corporations—at least for now.

Apple has been showing off its Chinese plants (see picture on prior page) and how great it is to have such phenomenal technology. So, a wise journalist asked the spokesman at the photo shoot, "Why isn't more manufacturing taking place in the U.S.?" The Apple spokesperson answered: in a way most evasive US companies would answer.

They said that it appears to be that it's simply no longer possible to compete by relying on domestic factories and the ecosystem that surrounds them. In other words, they can't do business in America. My source did not give all the reasons why and none were political. Apple noted how great it was that they were able to move to China and launch great products but they dodge being implicated in offshoring. Americans need to call them out on it every chance we get.

That last Apple statement there leaves one feeling almost impressed by the no-holds-barred capabilities of these new Apple manufacturing plants. Did Apple say their products could not be built in America? Just about!

Here is a boastful quote from Jennifer Rigoni, Apple's worldwide supply demand manager until 2010: "They could hire 3,000 people overnight," she says, speaking of Foxconn City's complex of factories in China. In other words, America simply cannot compete. Is that not annoying to hear? I do not see it that way. This is a big cover-up. Blame Americans or else Apple will get blamed.

She continued: "What U.S. plant can find 3,000 people overnight and convince them to live in dorms?" Jennifer, why would anybody want to live in a dorm when they already have a home? She did not talk much about the suicide strike their prized contractor Foxconn had settled with about fifty of its workers. Conditions at the plants were so bad, Workers were putting together a massive suicide pact in case working conditions were not improved. Apple forgot to mention that. Is that what Apple meant by the ecosystem not being right in the US?

Apple admits that cheap and willing labor was a major factor in its decision to farm work out to China, but it avers that its supply chain management, production speed, and flexibility were bigger incentives. Hah! They might be able to get parts sooner there because other US companies are right next door. How about if the US did not give incentives for companies to offshore, and now, how about if the US is big enough to demand that US corporations take the homeland into consideration in all of their decisions? When we begin to tax imports from American corporations, they will be seen as the impresarios that they are. Let the jobs begin!

Unfortunately, a great innovator from Apple died last year. From my perspective, Mr. Jobs, as fine a man as he was, had little loyalty to America. He would not have brought manufacturing back to the US though his company expects to sell tons of items to American consumers who flip hamburgers for a living. America is 25% of the world market. Companies can be really successful merely careering to America and Americans. It was not enough for Jobs and it is not enough for IBM or HP or Cisco or others. So, the American people, in charge of our own markets, must make it worth the while of the corporate entity to think American.

It has been documented that at a dinner with Silicon Valley bigwigs, Obama asked Steve Jobs what it would take for him to decide to produce the iPhone in the states. I give the President credit for this one [but not many others]. He asked why that work couldn't return. The word on the street is that Steven Jobs told the president in no uncertain terms that, "Those jobs aren't coming back. I think when it costs Apple a huge tariff to get those devices shipped back into this country to sell, we will see Apple's attitude change. Maybe manufacturing will be back in the US. Maybe not! Am I simply an optimist or is everything cost / profit based in life?

Pardon my use of words that would never be heard in public in the 1960's. Here goes a little rebuttal.

Perhaps with tampons and condoms being advertised on TV, progressive thinkers have been convinced that they can sneak anything by the dumb buying US public. In its annual report, Apple publicized that its overseas suppliers stuck to its maximum 60-hour work week just 38 percent of the time. Is that an admission or a statement that Apple will do better? I do not know! Does it mean that if US workers are not prepared to work 60+ hour weeks, they should not ever expect to get hired by Apple? What PR person would make that statement if they had not gotten the OK. It is not OK, Apple, sorry! There's more to this but this is enough!

The media notion and the notion brought forth by Obama in the state of the Union and repeated by Apple and a lot of corporations is that Americans are just not qualified because we are simply untrained. We're not even good enough to haul out the trash if you listen closely! We're lucky that we are being fed. Over 1800 engineers are unemployed and the President tells kids to get a degree in a great field such as engineering. I think by now he knows he is wrong so somebody will be blamed shortly. Maybe it was Bush who did it!

Despite how dumb Americans are according to Obama, Sallie Mae has not given up on collecting the loans that supposedly made Americans smart. If all that expense on college did not make us smart then maybe we should start shutting down some universities.

Somehow, China can grab a few good hands from the rice patties and miraculously, they are better than US trained engineers? Do any of us believe that? I don't think so.

Apple and others are not poor (financially) companies but they are poor in spirit and American loyalty. After my four years of high tech at King's College, when I graduated in 1969, and joined IBM as a as a Systems Engineer, IBM would still not permit me alone with an important customer until I finished a rigorous internal training program that took 1.1/2 years.

If I were the only one in the class, I would have felt inadequate but I was typically in the top 10% of class of size 40 and each week at IBM Education Centers, a new class began for new employees. College, no matter how good, does not fully prepare any new hire for the job market. Who are we kidding? Every employee needs some degree of training, even the Chinese.

Is America's education system at fault?

The American education system is no reason for Apple or any other company to offshore production. Considering that American colleges and graduate schools are filled with foreign students on visas, one might conclude they would not come here if it were a waste of time.

So, let me say it is rubbish that America "has stopped training enough people in the mid-level skills that factories need" and that's why so many companies have moved their plants overseas. It is bull claptrap. Just as the Chinese can come in from the farm and be productive, so can Americans, regardless of their HS education. Our people stock, from tough and resilient individuals migrating here, is the best in the world. Nobody is better than an American.

Let's tell the truth about the Chinese and the Americans. China's super-low wages and nonexistent labor, environmental and human rights protections are the driving force behind American corporate offshoring. Apple has begun to look at a

30+ percent compliance rate to a 60-hour work week as a good thing. It is a lousy record, Apple! Do not flaunt 30% compliance in attempt to make Americans guilty that we have real lives. Americans struggled to make the 40-hour week the norm in this country and we do not plan to go back.

What are American corporations doing to countries across the globe? Is it our military or our corporations that are really getting foreigners sour on America? Sixty plus hour weeks, poor working conditions, and suicide pacts! What an Apple legacy. Though it can clearly be better and it is not as good as many foreign systems, the problem is not the American education system.

I found this as a commentary on the web: " Sadly, Obama, is also courting the richy-rich business groups who are benefitting from offshore outsourcing American jobs and importing lower-wage "guest workers". Yea, his campaign was stupid, rude and irresponsible in the Hillary Clinton (D-Punjab) comments but it's unfortunate that Obama felt compelled to drop the whole issue of Hillary and Bill's ties to the elites benefiting from American job losses."

This is not about Obama but clearly he is not even aware that we have sold out our college graduates to American Corporations and foreign interests. Maybe he was the grand orchestrator and now feigns ignorance for campaign purposes or maybe he knows little about little. I do not know. I am a conservative.

I know I am conservative because there is nothing I have yet seen from the progressives that give me an "A hah" moment. No "A hah's" on Obama's Seven Deadly Sins. No "A hah's" at all. If Obama stopped outsourcing and stopped the ills of free trade tomorrow, I would give him credit. Yes, I would!

The thing I worry about the most on offshoring and free trade and reindustrialization is that it is not even a top ten notion for the TEA Party. What that means is that if we take really conservative people who we may love, and we superimpose on them the fact that they are Republican, does that change our desire to support them. I admit, Republican today is a better second label for a TEA partier than Democrat as I am one of those. Being a D is not good for regular people. Being a real R may be impossibility.

How do Americans see free trade?

My definition of an R has always been someone who has at least $50 million in the bank. This is one reason why why conservatives and Republicans sometimes part ways. TEA Party conservatives cannot get Republicans to vote on all matters in a conservative fashion. Yet, Republicans have sure been trying to co-opt the TEA Party like we are all the same. I am OK with that as long as they really think like us. My concern is that if real Republicans are making so much dough on offshoring and free trade that they cannot be real Americans first, as well as conservatives, then they are not what I am looking for as an option to run the country.

As a Democrat and TEA party member, I have been endorsed twice by the Independence Hall TEA Party—once when I ran for Congress and lost and the next time when I ran for US Senate and was forced to withdraw for lack of funding. A D being endorsed by the TEA Party. You bet I am a conservative, and I am more conservative than most R's.

Is the TEA party being duped by real Republicans that offshoring and free trade are not important issues for John Q. Public? If you are an R, and a conservative, do you have $50,000,000 in the bank in any form right now? Do 80% conservative R's cut the mustard in the TEA Party? Is 80% acceptable to you as a TEA Party member?

So, what do Americans think about free trade and offshoring, regardless of D or R affiliationi? Here are the stats:

- 69 percent of Americans think that free trade is bad for jobs
- 18 percent believe free trade has created jobs
- 61 percent of self-described TEA Party supporters say they think free trade has harmed the United States, just four percent less than union members:

TEA Party folk are pretty smart!

What's ironic about most TEA Partiers opposing free trade is that as I caution above, according to some of my sources, numerous high-profile TEA Party-endorsed candidates are ardent backers of the free trade policy. Perhaps they are real R's more than conservative TEA Party advocates.

I have the names but I am not quite sure of whether they are really pro free trade and pro-outsourcing so I will give them all a chance to comment on the notion.

Just like most conservatives who like to tell a candidate how they feel. I have tried to reach many people such as these in this esteemed category and I found that either their emails are not listed or they do not have an easy way for John Q. Public to reach them in any form. For their own reasons, they choose not to hire even one American to check out their emails and decide whether they are worthy of a non-automated response. I know since I get no responses and I try.

So, pardon me if I list their names here as the information I read declared these TEA Party people guilty of being pro free trade and pro-outsourcing while 61% of the TEA party are not for free trade one iota. Let them contact me to reconcile this at my still open campaign email campaign@kellyforussenate.com, and then I will publish their responses to this hopefully unfounded charge and give them exoneration if it is deserved.

My fear of course is that politicians who have co-opted the TEA Party movement do not share its conservative view on free trade. I actually cannot stand myself for putting these names in front of you but here they are. Let them contact me to tell me I am wrong.

- **Rand Paul:**
- **Joe Miller AK**
- **Sen. Jim DeMint SC:**
- **Rep. Tom Price GA**
- **Marco Rubio FL**
- **Mike Lee: UT**
- **Pat Toomey, PA**

I have seen that Ron Paul is against all American weakening trade agreements and I admire him for that.

I would ask the TEA Party leaders to assure that any person backed by the TEA Party is against free trade which means the offshoring of American Jobs and it also means that H-1B and other visas take the jobs of the displaced Americans. That is a double whammy!

One major financier of the TEA Party movement, Americans for Prosperity (AFP), also supports free trade agreements. On its congressional scorecard, support for further free trade agreements is a major category, and AFP gives legislators who are critical of these agreements worse ratings. This lends merit to the idea that AFP is a corporate-backed astroturf front group, not a group of grassroots Americans claiming to represent average Americans who are sympathetic to the TEA Parties.

I have never met the Koch Brothers, but they are probably fine guys, at least a bit better than George Soros who appears to be anti-American. Soros has a lot of front groups. The Koch Brothers, who I probably agree with on everything else in life but free trade, are for free trade.

Why would the brothers be for free trade? It is simply because it brings billions more into their treasury each year. They are definitely real Republicans. Yes, they are conservatives also but not where the money meets the road.

I sent the Koch brothers a copy of RRR in its first printing. I received no response. Even Donald Trump responded. I think they know what is in the book and they can sniff a no-free-trader type guy with one nostril closed. I think that as older guys who are actually older than me, that they might consider making their peace with God, rather the next billion. I admire them for how tey are stalwarts against Obama and company and the hard left progressives. But, free trade hurts Americans and so here we part company. I know that I am neither God nor close, but I represent regular people who call themselves American. I am not a globalist and I do care about people in other nations. I also do not care about Americans who are billionaires who choose not to help Americans. But, everybody is welcome to forgiveness from somebody sometime.

Like they say on the airlines when the oxygen masks fall, put yours on first, and then you can save your kids and others around you. So, the Koch Brothers may very well be big TEA Party backers, but they are Republicans (over $50M in the bank) and so they see things differently than regular human beings. As a regular human being, my mask is on, and I will help all who need help, even the Koch Brothers. I am not sure about helping George Soros unless I am the last man available!

The brothers chose not to invite me or my brother Joe to the Koch Bat Cave to talk about RRR. My RRR book is a populist book, written by a conservative for conservatives, and so I know why I was not invited to HQ/BC. If you are a person with another notion, such as the $50M GOP gold standard, you do not want to mingle with paupers. That is my perspective on the difference between conservatives and Republicans. It is OK for the TEA Party to take donations from Republicans who are real conservatives but we should not take anything from a co-opting force that wants to use their 80 to 95% TEA Party conservativism, to change the TEA Party into Republican agents.

Why is there a TEA Party? We must never forget! If Republicans were doing the right job, we would not have needed a TEA Party. Let's not sell out to the R's for any reason! Conservatives need to look at free trade as anathema to protecting America, Amen!

Bring on the Tariffs. They will help reindustrialize America and that will be good for the American people.

Chapter 13   Revitalize Energy

Obama hates the energy industry

What a shame that when we need him the most, our President is on the other team. Just this week [2012], I turned over to the printers my new book titled, Kill the EPA! I now have a new updated and refined edition available on Amazon and Kindle!

I was motivated to write this EPA book for many reasons. The first reason is that regulations are pummeling US businesses to the point that they are motivated more than ever to move out of the US. Nobody will hire a new employee when with each step they take, in which to improve, the government slams them down. The EPA is the worst oppressor but many other government agencies contribute to the morass in our economy.

There are other industries that are forced to stay in the US because, as an example, they can't take their acreage and their farm to another country and they can't take their barns and herds of cattle to another country. Yet, those businesses with options in countries close by may be considering them. Canada and Mexico may look pretty good right now for any company in those businesses who would consider the trek.

One force that would motivate farmers and anybody else that endures their harassment to go north or south of the border is the EPA. They are on farmers with a vendetta and the latest EPA annoyance is that they are preparing dust regulations for animals that kick up dust on the range. They already require manure to be weighed so that the government knows how much methane cows and other animals are producing. The unnecessary work is having an impact on the price of food while Obama fiddles. If it were not real, it would be funny.

Additionally, and this is the worst of it. Obama hates coal fired power plants. Actually, the president hates all fossil fuel produced energy of all kinds—including oil and gas, and he seems to not like nuclear as well. He does like geothermal, and wind, and solar, and though many think he has enough power himself, he would probably not want to plug himself into all the transformers to assure America has enough watts to last until he is bounced out of office in a huge waft of voter energy.

As we all know, the EPA is Obama's weapon of choice and the EPA's weapon of choice, in the battle to destroy the American economy, is regulation. Obama is preparing to wipe out 40% of the coal plants in the power grid. New EPA enforcement of long-time rules regarding mercury and sulfur to coal ash and water intake which cool equipment is now being aggressively pursued by Obama's pals in the EPA. The pace of new regulations is simply unprecedented and impossible with which to comply.

Some coal fired plants can retrofit with scrubbers, but Credit Suisse, an international financial services group estimated that compliance will cost as much as $150 billion in capital investment by the end of the decade. For what value? The only value I see is if you are a progressive president and you are not interested in people having jobs or living well. More and more people will have to be on welfare with energy subsidies if they can even get power, because they will not be able to afford heat, light, and electric appliances. That is the Obama way.

Either the $150 billion is paid or 40% less coal power is on the grid. Welfare or not, nobody will be able to buy enough power. How, in an already collapsed economy, can a President be serious about punishing the population to this extent?

The increase in electricity costs is simply another tax on consumers and businesses, and besides cold toes in the winter, and sweaty feet in the summer, it means more lost jobs. Replacing so much so fast would require shut downs of as much as 40% of the coal plants and lead to brownouts and shortages, but the White House will be unaffected because Obama has his own power. Of course I jest on that last point.

This chapter, however, is not about reducing regulations. We've been there already in Chapter 5, as that is the third R of the original RRR plan. I can't see America getting to energy self-sufficiency or an adequate energy plan until this President reaches end of term in 2012(please) or 2016. In reality, none of the RRR plan has a chance to happen while this uncaring ideologue is still in office.

But, there is always real hope, not the false hope promised by Obama. That hope is that the EPA will be dismantled by the next Administration and that the RRR plan will be adopted to help save America from Obama and his forty czars.

Make energy a really big industry

This part of the RRR plan is to revitalize energy as an industry in the US. I see no reason, with all of the gas and oil reserves we have that we cannot satisfy our own energy needs and become a major exporter of energy to other countries. Can you imagine the many energy jobs that will come to America when that happens? Let's just spend a bit more time discussing the energy problems in the US right now before we end with the promise of a productive and bountiful energy industry beginning hopefully in 2013.

The Obama team has an energy strangulation strategy!

The rest of the world is not letting any grass grow under its energy loving feet. While Obama is continuing to pretend that the rest of the world as we know it has already ended, he is hard at work trying to end it for America. The world outside Obama is very busy drilling for oil. The action is going full speed in the Mediterranean, the Turkish Black Sea, and even the Gulf of Guinea.

We know that In Brazil, the state-run Petroleo Brasileiro SA, known as Petrobras; to which our President donated $2 billion from the US treasury loan bank, is working on one of the largest oil fields discovered in the Western Hemisphere in 30 years. Another field nearby is expected to deliver another 15 billion barrels of oil. This one pool is supposedly two-thirds of the total proven deposits of crude in the United States. But, Obama conveniently lies about that number so that he can fund solar boondoggles for his campaign cronies such as Solyndra.

Obama has decreed that rather drill baby drill, he will regulate baby regulate. One of his regulations is that the US will not attempt to get any oil from the eastern Gulf of Mexico and the Atlantic and Pacific coasts at least until sometime after 2017. The Outer Continental Shelf program effectively bans drilling in those areas for the next five years. That decision canceled four lease sales in Alaska, a major crude oil opportunity.

One would believe that the EPA is now running the Energy Department but it probably doesn't matter which is running which as both should be eliminated. Nobody in the Obama Administration cares that a major source of high paying jobs and an increase in energy supplies without cost to the taxpayer would come with more permits being granted. Oil companies cannot drill without permits and the Obama Regulation Company is literally holding the permits.

While Obama is not willing to budge to help the US harvest known fossil fuel reserves by drilling, he has no problem providing vast subsidies to speculators, almost all of whom have campaign ties to the White House, for useless wind farms and solar projects. Exploiting our own massive energy reserves would create revenues for financially strapped state governments and increase revenue to the federal government. Maybe we could use some of it to reduce the deficit and if we are lucky, it can be used for the debt.

Rather than rely on science or economics, the Obama team sees an energy strangulation strategy as its best option. They plan to make other sources of energy unavailable. It is no accident. The pattern is obvious. You will have to figure out why yourself. I think the answer is simple. Obama hates fossil fuels and nuclear power and perhaps he is not too keen on America or Americans.

It is economically infeasible and right now it is technically infeasible to use wind and solar or geothermal energy though they all have huge subsidies. Would we not be better off buying scrubbers for coal plants than to go to the casino every day and bet on wind, solar, and geothermal? All the payoffs are negative, and the corruption is thick.

Renewable fuels not ready for prime time

The US is not the first to take the renewable fuels route. We are the first to not learn by anybody else's mistakes, however. Heck, we still think creating a food shortage by brewing ethanol is a good deal though it has been proven to be more harmful to the environment than fossil fuels and it is less efficient. What have other countries found?

Germany has a little deal going on in their first pilot offshore wind farm called "Alpha Ventus" in the North Sea. Unfortunately in recent tests, all six of the wind turbines were completely idle due to gearbox damage. Due to the intermittent and highly variable nature of wind, Germans relying on the puff of the wind must prepare for significantly higher electricity costs, and more frequent blackouts, and of course major backups.

The National Grid in Scotland was forced to ask wind farms to shut down for the second time in a month—because it was too windy. Shall I say that again? No, I think you got it. Can you believe it? In late October 2011, seven wind farm operators switched off their turbines because they were generating too much power as storms ripped across Scotland. Since the wind was not producing, the backup had to be deployed to produce the needed power and this left Scottish taxpayers with yet another bill. Additionally, they must pay wind farm operators compensation when asking them to stop their turbines. Time is money as they say.

The legislators and bureaucrats in Washington should spend a few bucks to gussy up the front of the buildings where they meet with the lobbyists to make it reflect the jockeying and gambling that goes on. Lobbyists are continually investing their dollars in perquisites that might motivate our esteemed representatives to make the "right" move every now and then. Just as the casinos in Las Vegas have facades outside, such as Venice, New York, or Paris, a nice façade that reflects the gaming going on inside Washington buildings would better reflect the actual action on the tables. The somber look of stone structures for representatives trying to convince the Nation they are addressing the needs of their constituents, while they are gambling away the treasury, does not seem appropriate. .

This Administration is not shy when it comes to talking with anybody who tomorrow may become a campaign donor. They talk to environmental activists, and renewable energy lobbyists, and venture capitalists hoping to benefit from government subsidies. They listen to the enthusiasm of corporations trying to improve their bottom line with a juicy grant. Despite their willingness to speak with those who can also help on the campaign trail, the Administration has no time for geologists and engineers and they don't have time to research the results of various approaches tried by other countries.

Well, they listen sometimes when the song is familiar. For example, the Administration listened in Spanish when Spain was excited about their green plans. However, when economist Dr. Gabriel Calzada, a professor at King Juan Carlos University in Spain showed that for every "green job" created by wind and solar investments, 2.2 jobs were lost in the regular economy, there was no excitement to be had. The listening stopped. The truth comes with pain sometimes. The joke in conservative circles was that the Administration ignored her pleas and went off to talk to the Danes to get their ideas on green.

Is Raul Castro smarter than Barack Obama? Castro plans to bring in a huge Chinese built oil rig (Why don't we build those?), which in mid-November as the first printing of this book was preparing for the press, was on its way across the oceans to Cuba. The Castro brothers will be harvesting oil in shared US waters in the very near future. One must ask, "Does it make it any safer if the Cubans are drilling and pumping oil off our coast than if the US oil industry is doing it?" Perhaps we can make some prisoners from Guantanamo available for work release duty on the new Cuban rig?

Over the last ten years, Russia has pulled itself up by its bootstraps and because of oil; it is becoming a world power again. Just what we needed! Ironically, Russia is also into timber, which one might argue is oil about a million or so years away from harvest. The Russians have learned how to make a buck on everything. It is almost like they have become a mercantilist country.

They surely give no other countries a break. For example, the Russians just raised the export duties of felled timber so high that countries like Finland may not be able to import it economically anymore. Why would Russia do that? They are using their customs and duty policy to force countries to build pulp and paper factories in Russia. Finland is very upset about it but the Russians care about Russia first. There is a lesson there for America.

Finland's Minister of Foreign Trade Paula Lehtomäki complained that Russia's move violates the World Trade Organization treaty that Russia signed three years ago. Maybe Russia was only kidding. One thing for sure; Russia will not hurt Russia to help any other country. Why does the Obama Administration think it is OK to hurt America to please the world?

Oh, and when the Russians are not cutting down trees to spite Finland, their major miffintiff at the controls, the man whose soul George Bush was able to peer into, Vladimir V. Putin, a leader who has developed an uncanny mastery of the politics and a deep understanding of the economics of oil, is taking a backseat to nobody on the energy stage.

While Putin was making oil a priority, things kept getting better. While he was president and prime minister, his favorite country, Russia moved up to the top of the global oil business, surpassing Saudi Arabia as the world's largest oil producer. Which country is our President's favorite? Many are convinced it is not the US!

Why can't the US become # 1? We passed the Russians in space exploration years ago though under Obama we have recently given them back the cup. Why can't the US become the # 1 oil country in the world in oil exploration? It's got to be easier than space exploration. Don't you think? My conclusion is bad management.

As a person who at least tries to be a patriot, I do feel guilty citing Vladimir Putin as a person from whom Barack Obama, our President can learn. But, that is the case. Here is another

Russian example. The Russians know they can no longer put people who can help them in prison and expect the help will still come. Recently, there is a consensus, from Putin on down, that unless the Russian oil companies are given proper incentives in not only raising recovery in the brown oil fields, but also to move more aggressively into onshore frontiers, and offshore, the future consequences may be dire.

Now, if our own Barack Obama was briefed about the consequences being dire as surely he has been about energy, what would he do? I would say he is already doing it. He is getting in the way of the opportunities that may come to America. He has an energy policy that is directed against whatever is good for America. That is Obama's ideology. Obama is why America cannot be successful. Putin is why Russia is successful and why their businesses are motivated to do the right thing for the country. Besides, Putin uses American consulting companies and auditors to assure things are going his way. Who does Obama use, the GAO?

Petroleum exports account for 40 percent of Russia's budget revenues. Our deficit is about 40% in total. To me, if we could get to the moon, our geologists and our famed oil companies ought to be able to get us to the point that we can make a lot of money and become prosperous again if we were to invest again in a national oil industry. Yes, that means more refineries also. The US is best at that.

In May 2011, with oil at $124 a barrel, progressives on the Senate Appropriations Committee voted to block environmentally sound development of oil shale in Colorado. That gives you an idea that it is not just Obama but it is Obama and friends—such as his corrupt Senator friends like Bob Casey Jr. from Pennsylvania. Casey has come out publicly against drilling. He mails out well-rehearsed, yet highly inaccurate responses to constituents who ask about US support for energy drilling, such as in the Bakken fields. Casey says no! This excerpt is from Casey's letter:

"According to the U.S. Department of the Interior, 79% of all known oil reserves on public lands are open for drilling right now. In fact, drilling activity in the United States has increased 361% over the past 7 years. Unfortunately, because we consume 24% of the world's oil while we have only 3% of the world's oil reserves, further increases in domestic drilling alone will not produce enough oil to lower oil prices that are set on a world market. "

"For these reasons, I do not believe that increased drilling will provide a long-term solution to this serious problem, nor will it provide short-term price relief by itself."

Now, that is the response of a hopeless pessimist. America has no chance until the blame America first crowd are sent home. The Senate must be replaced and Obama must be replaced for any plan such as RRR to be able to help America. How uninformed and ideologically slanted can a Senator be?

For more than thirty years, our Congress would not authorize aggressive exploration though they have no problem paying campaign cronies to start bogus solar businesses. The argument that we will not get oil overnight is the most stupid argument anybody can make about anything. Why build that bridge? We won't be able to get across the river tomorrow even if we start building it immediately! My father had a word for people who think like that. I will spare you the word until we meet in person.

The Hope and change man must have looked in the mirror a while back and he must have seen Jimmy Carter looking back. While on the campaign trail in 2011, he told his fellow Americans that more pain—not more production—is the answer. I am not sure if he was mimicking Casey or it was the other way around. Neither appears to be ready to help Americans. "No we can't" appears to be the new energy mantra for the progressives. I do not agree.

We've got the right stuff.

We need good leaders but there are none. The US can certainly run a fine gas, oil, and coal business and we should not feel depressed because we are so well endowed with natural gifts. By some estimates, for example, we have about 850 trillion cubic feet of natural gas ready to eliminate our energy dependence for a at least a century.

Our current government administration unfortunately does not want America to lead in anything, especially fossil fuels. Obama will provide sufficient obstacles to the success of any valid energy plan. Our *current* leadership is bent on improving the world by lowering the status of the US to that of second class nations and "making us all equal" accordingly, instead of providing the opportunity for all to achieve and for all to be successful.

A lot of Americans are seeing right through the Obama ideology and are directly blaming him for the non-recovery. They are 100% right. He is not a cure. Obama is a cause of the recession and until he pulls a Snagglepuss and exits, stage left, we'll be stuck in the quicksand.

GreenGo, a blogger offers a few thoughts on Obama and Green and Obama and oil. This is from 10/28/2011.

"With Obama clones running the country our fate is a nation of Detroit's. [Apologies to Detroit] We are set at the brink of being energy independent if we can get a leader who loves this country. Our manufacturing can make a giant comeback as well if we start the process by flushing out the illegals that are parasites on our economy. Who will save us? I see no one in the ranks that will change our current path. We need another Andrew Jackson, but all we have is Obama clones."

The Financial Times in the Christian Science Monitor offers the following:

"The oil industry and environmentalists are nervously awaiting a decision from President Obama on whether he'll allow construction of the controversial, 1,700-mile Keystone XL pipeline. Snaking through the Midwest, the pipeline would carry Canadian oil-sands crude to Texas refineries. The project comes as many new technologies have already helped revive declining domestic oil fields, reducing imports from a record 60 percent of U.S. consumption in 2005 to about 47 percent now. Many people once considered energy independence to be an unrealistic dream. Is it now reasonable to think that the U.S. could wean itself off of oil from the volatile Middle East?

Absolutely! America's energy future has changed: "There's a new U.S. oil boom underway," says Ed Crooks at Financial Times. New techniques such as hydraulic fracturing (to break up underground rock and free trapped reserves) and long-reach horizontal drilling have uncorked what could be a 100-year supply of natural gas. And with oil-sands crude coming, too, North American energy independence is no longer a distant dream—it's really within reach."

Unfortunately, in late 2011, Obama's boys put a big X through the notion of a pipeline any time soon. As a result the Canadians who have the oil and are ready to ship it are now looking for other customers since the US apparently doesn't want it. Again, we see reason after reason why this administration needs to go and an energy friendly, jobs friendly, economy friendly, business friendly administration needs to be in charge.

American Petroleum Institute (API) study

"What could the oil industry achieve if restrictions on oil drilling in the United States were lessened? The American

Petroleum Industry commissioned a study that assumed oil drilling would be allowed off the currently prohibited areas of the East and West Coasts, in waters off Florida's Gulf Coast, in Alaska's Arctic National Wildlife Refuge, and on most federal public land not designated as a national park. It also assumed that it would get approval to build pipelines to accommodate a doubling of Canadian oil sands production and the continuation of the tax policies currently in place for the oil industry.

"The API commissioned the study from energy consultants. Wood Mackenzie, found that domestic production of petroleum liquids would increase from 7.8 million barrels per day in 2010 to 9 million barrels per day in 2030 under current policies due to increased production from shale oil and deep-water drilling. However, if the industry could meet the assumptions of the study, domestic liquids production could reach 15.4 million barrels per day close to the 19 million barrels a day that we currently consume.

"That would create 1 million new jobs over the next seven years and 1.4 million by 2030. The industry already supports more than 9 million jobs throughout the economy. The study indicates that the United States can come close to producing enough new oil and natural gas to displace all non-North American imports within 15 years. More than $800 billion in cumulative new government revenue could be generated by 2030 and $127 billion by 2020, equal to about two and a half years' worth of current federal spending on roads. Most importantly, no new taxes or increased government spending is needed to accomplish the results of the study.

Their conclusion

"Around the globe, countries are drilling for oil onshore, offshore, and in oil shale deposits. But the United States is hampered by government rules and restrictions to developing its vast resources. Without increasing taxes and without increasing government spending, the oil industry in the United States could make us independent of non-North American oil imports. And in doing so, they could create jobs and add billions of dollars to government revenues. Why don't we take the challenge?"

According to a Pew Research Center Poll, a couple of months before the BP Oil spill, 63 percent of adults favored more offshore drilling in U.S. waters. By March of 2011, the proponents of offshore drilling in U.S. waters rose back up to 57 percent.

The Hill reports: "'The government is doing what it can to ensure that the first full-scale oil exploration in Cuba's part of the Gulf of Mexico will not endanger Florida's pristine beaches that lie only miles away,' the top drilling regulator told lawmakers on Tuesday (October 18). But the assurances did not completely convince senators at a Capitol Hill hearing that the United States would be prepared to respond to a worst-case oil spill scenario in waters controlled by its long-time Communist foe."

The Cuban oil technology is sparse. The Cuban technology is primitive and unprofessional without the help of the United States. In short, Cuba cannot safely drill without the United States' assistance!

An Obama administration source told the New York Post: "People are crazy over this. It's a very big problem. They're talking about drilling off Cuba, but the way currents flow, the oil would hit Florida." The source failed to say that due to Mr. Obama policies, the number of drilling rigs off American shores has drastically decreased!

Barack Obama is timid when it comes to doing something about this Cuban oil rig. He is trying to please both the drilling expansionists while politically placating Florida's voter-rich, influential Cuban-exile community which strongly opposes additional economic interaction with Cuba! Yes, politics comes into play once again!

GOP presidential candidates like oil

Most GOP candidates say YES to push for more oil drilling areas to be opened up by the Obama administration. It's like every GOP candidate is using Sarah Palin's "Drill, baby, drill" remark from 2008 as a springboard for political fodder.

For instance:

Herman Cain, former candidate - "The idea that high energy consumption and conservation are at odds is a myth peddled by liberals."

Rick Perry - "The quickest way to give our economy a shot in the arm is to deploy American ingenuity to tap American energy."

Michele Bachman - "I would consider drilling in the Florida Everglades, if it could be done responsibly."

Mitt Romney - "We're an energy-rich nation that's acting like an energy-poor nation."

Newt Gingrich - wrote the book entitled "Drill Here, Drill Now, Pay Less."

Rick Santorum - In relationship to opening up Arctic drilling, he has accused Barack Obama of putting caribou ahead of "something good for our country and our economy."

There is a clear line of distinction in the next presidential elections. Obama has taken a more "cautious approach" to expanding oil and gas production. Some GOP critics accuse him of intentionally locking up resources.

Then Interior Secretary Ken Salazar defended the administration's slow energy approach. He explained: "I don't think we should be drilling anywhere and everywhere, and I think those who propose it are wrong. Drilling for oil in Everglades is not going to resolve the energy challenges we face as a country. What we need to do is to have a broad energy portfolio...that does include oil and gas, but it has to be done in the right places and it has to be done with the right kind of review and the right kind of regulatory oversight." Did Salazar have a heart to heart with Bob Casey Jr.?

The United States has a wealth of oil resources though the Obama Administration likes to only tout the proven oil reserves of this country, which are about 2 percent of world reserves. But, proven reserves are always growing and world oil reserves are the highest they have ever been: 1.47 trillion barrels. Reserves grow because of continuing exploration and development, new technological development, and higher oil prices that make previously uneconomic sources of oil economic to develop. For instance, if North Dakota had not continued to drill, it would not have increased its reserve level that has grown over 150 percent between 2006 and 2009 while oil is being extracted. That is a neat deal. Oil comes out and as it comes out, the amount of oil available to come out increases.

Point in time conclusion

The US is facing higher oil and gasoline prices that have become sustained this year and record heating oil prices for this winter. Even though the United States has a wealth of oil resources that can be developed to increase domestic oil production, create jobs, and increase government revenues, all of which would eventually wean us off overseas oil, our government controlled by BHO will not provide those resources for energy development. How can this President suggest that he is pro-jobs and pro energy? Does he plan to talk to the fast-food industry to see if they can engage in a huge hiring plan? Oil jobs make Americans cash rich.

Have you ever seen this Heritage Foundation email?
"Dear Fellow American, "When President Obama took office, gas prices averaged $1.80 a gallon. Back in 2012 it was over $4.00 in much of the country. Now, because of American exploration, it is down to about $2.25 per gallon, Bravo US!

"Why the increase in 2012? The Obama administration's irrational drilling moratoriums, restrictions, and mountains of regulations are squeezing off oil supplies. That's why gas prices were giving us all a shock every time we fill up our cars . . . and it was raising the costs of other goods, killing jobs, and weakening our already shaky economy. Notice the prices of other items are not coming down! "What do you think about the Obama policies? ...

"We need to use America's vast oil resources that the Obama policies are keeping in the ground instead of making them available for cars, trucks and industries. America has –

✓ "Tens of billions of barrels of oil in restricted areas offshore.

✓ "Tens of billions of barrels under American soil, barred from being extracted.

✓ "And 800 billion barrels of recoverable oil from oil shale in western states.

This is three times greater than the proven oil reserves of Saudi Arabia.

"The Heritage Foundation—America's leading conservative policy organization—understands that a strong drilling policy that makes good use of America's oil resources is critical to lowering gas prices for you, your family and the entire economy.

"We need Congress to take action to reverse the Obama restrictions and make our vast resources available for our use. We need to drill now.

"Sincerely,

Edwin J. Feulner, Ph.D.
President
The Heritage Foundation"

"P.S. The Obama administration is killing American jobs and keeping gas prices high by choking off oil drilling in our country. Instead, he told the people of Brazil that they should drill for oil and that "we want to be one of your best customers."

I think that sums the issue with Obama and energy quite well. Check out the appendix at the end of this chapter and remember that never before has a president worked so hard to make the American people vulnerable to our enemies. – Reprinted from personalliberty.com.

America is ready to have a huge oil industry with a huge number of high paying jobs required to sustain it. Let's vote to get government off the backs of the oil producers so they can help create an America in which all of us can prosper!

Chapter Appendix

Is Obama An Agent For OPEC?

http://www.personalliberty.com/conservative-politics/government/is-obama-an-agent-for-opec/?eiid=

December 7, 2011 by John Myers

TransCanada Corporation wants to build a pipeline that would transport tar sands crude oil from Alberta through Montana, South Dakota and Nebraska on its way to refineries on the Gulf Coast.

We are staring into the face of $180-per-barrel oil. Under President Barack Obama, the Nation is not producing enough oil and is importing far too much of it from potential enemies. This is a reckless game engineered by the President, because oil is America's economic lifeblood.

It recently become apparent that Obama either does not understand the danger the country is facing or, worse, is willing to ignore it because he has conspired with Arab oil exporters to give them dictatorial powers over America's energy needs and economic future.

The United States is critically dependent on imported oil, consuming almost 10 million barrels of foreign crude every day. That is about three times more oil than the United States imported 25 years ago. With Obama's restrictions on further oil exploration, especially offshore, the United States may import 18 million barrels per day by 2020.

Gang Green

"Gangrene" is a medical term used to describe the death of one part of the body. It happens when the blood supply is cut off to the affected area.

I witnessed gangrene overtake my dad's legs after he underwent surgery on a bulging abdominal aorta at the Loma Linda University Medical Center many years ago.

I never studied medicine, but I have spent my lifetime studying economics. It isn't a stretch to use the analogy that petroleum is the lifeblood to the U.S. economy.

Keystone Kops Or An Agent For Saudi Arabia?

Petroleum is essential for the United States. With so many hostile governments selling it to us, it would be easy to think that Canada would be America's energy oasis. The two countries haven't had so much as a skirmish in 200 years, and more than any other nation, Canada has stood shoulder to shoulder with the United States. So close are the two peoples that I can't tell the difference between being in Montana or Alberta.

Both Nations have Judeo-Christian values and common law borne from the Magna Carta. American and Canadian men fought and died together during the two world wars.

On the surface it seems like a pretty simple equation: Canada has 180 billion barrels of reserves, second only to Saudi Arabia, the kingpin petroleum producer and de facto leader of the Organization of Petroleum Exporting Countries.

Canada has a democratically elected parliament. The House of Saud is a desert fiefdom run by a few dozen billionaire princes. Whereas Canada has combat troops stationed in Afghanistan killing Muslim militants, Saudi Arabia provides tens of millions of dollars to Islamic terrorists bent on killing Westerners.

Beyond this, Canada has been a rock-solid energy supplier to the United States. In fact, thousands of Americans work in the Canadian petroleum industry, and there are hundreds of U.S. corporations that have a large stake in further developing Canadian petroleum. Scores of Canadian corporations are traded on the New York Stock Exchange. Conversely, Saudi Arabia has nationalized its oil properties, and it implemented two oil embargoes against the United States in the 1970s.

It only makes sense that the United States would sign on to buy more Canadian crude. But with Obama, common sense is not at all common.

TransCanada Corporation is seeking Presidential authorization to build its $7.5 billion Keystone XL pipeline. The line would transport tar sands crude oil from Alberta through Montana, South Dakota and Nebraska on its way to refineries on the Gulf Coast.

A number of groups, comprised mostly of environmentalists and liberals, have banded together to oppose its construction. Obama is leading the crusade against Canadian crude.

The President said last month: "Because this permit decision could affect the health and safety of the American people as well as the environment, and because a number of concerns have been raised through a public process, we should take the time to ensure that all questions are properly addressed and all the potential impacts are properly understood."

The President doesn't seem concerned that 1,661-mile pipeline would deliver 700,000 barrels per day of crude from the oil sands to the United States.

The Hawaii Reporter recently ran this headline on an opinion piece: "Obama's Catastrophic Pipeline Copout."

David H. Wilkins, U.S. ambassador to Canada from 2005-2009, wrote:

   The proposed Keystone XL Pipeline offers nothing but promise: tens of thousands of desperately needed jobs, and a big step toward ensuring North American energy security. But in mid-November, promise gave way to politics when President Obama punted on the pipeline permitting decision, delaying it until after the 2012 election. The Wall Street Journal called the decision a "Keystone Cop-Out."

   I call it a catastrophic cop-out, one with certain economic and diplomatic consequences. The decision on the KXL permit was expected before the end of this year and elected officials in both Canada and the United States rightly called it a "no-brainer."

The project would reduce dependency on petroleum from the Middle East, a region that is rife with civil war. And what of the economic recovery that Obama promised three years ago? You would have to have been in a coma to see that things are no better and that, overall, the U.S. economy might be in worse shape than when he took office.

This gets me back to why the United States should be begging to sign this pipeline deal. It is estimated that the project would create a minimum of 20,000 well-paying U.S. jobs. That economic bonus would span far beyond all those families that could again have a wage earner and would spill over to every part of the economy, from Wal-Mart to mom-and-pop shops.

In fact, the pipeline deal will add more than $20 billion to the U.S. economy. An extra $5.2 billion in State property taxes would be collected.

Crude Consequences

The United States will have to deal with the consequences of turning its back on Canadian crude. First and foremost, Ottawa is building closer trade ties with Beijing with a great deal of emphasis on a possible blueprint that would deliver Alberta's oil sands to the West Coast, where it could be delivered via tankers.

Last month, Canadian Prime Minister Stephen Harper met with Chinese President Hu Jintao about future Canadian oil exports to China.

Harper said: "This does underscore the necessity of Canada making sure that we are able to access Asia markets for our energy products."

Canada is counting on China to be a key investor in Alberta's oil sands projects and a big buyer of crude which would flow through a proposed Northern Gateway Pipeline if Canada encounters further opposition from the Obama Administration. This will make the United States all the more dependent on Arab oil. You would think Obama would understand this. The truth might be that he understands it all too well.

Yours in good times and bad,

–John Myers
Editor, Myers' Energy & Gold Report

Chapter 14 Reduce Redistribution

Government redistribution is not charity.

As we look at all the R's that are necessary to bring back jobs to America, we have to take a hard look at the notion of reduced redistribution of wealth. Many of my cohorts in the Democratic Party, especially the leadership, are filthy rich. They literally have money coming out of their ears. That's probably why they don't like flat taxes and the like because they too might have to pay their fair share of taxes if they had not structured the system to provide them with such rich deductions, which if other people got them, they would call them subsidies.

What I also find about my fellow Democrats is that, as a rule, they do not give much to charity. When I wrote my first political book, _Taxation Without Representation_, I was amazed at the paucity of giving by some of America's most notable free-spending Democrats. They want charities to get a lot of money; they just don't like to give. Check out some tax returns from some of your favorite Democratic politicians and you will see. Feel free to check out the recent returns of Vice Miser Biden if you don't have a favorite.

Filthy rich Democrats are not at all against giving to the poor. In fact, they are pro-poor for sure. The catch is they want to give your money to the poor. You see, it would not be redistribution if they simply gave half of their holdings to the poor. That would be real charity. The rich Democratic leaders structure their redistribution schemes after they make sure their personal fortunes cannot be touched by too much altruism in the tax code.

The rationale for a Reduced Redistribution "R" in the RRR plan is because nobody is stupid enough to work day in and day out to be successful if the government is going to come by and poof—take their earnings and give it to somebody else. So, all of the R's are predicated on businesses and shareholders and CEOs and entrepreneurs and all of the worker bees from the knowledge category to the manual category, being able to realize the gain from their work efforts.

For the corporate officers and others from the faux American corporations who offshored, reduced redistribution means they too, if they are enticed to come back to America and help our country reindustrialize, can keep the bulk of their earnings. God never intended for government to be the biggest thief in town.

If redistribution of their efforts is still a bullet on the government's calling card, then that will signal that more and more businesses should offshore. Eventually, when we take redistribution ad absurdum, welfare checks will be paid for by the government by taxing welfare checks. You can bet that won't work for too long. But, then again, perhaps it is best if we check with Vice Miser Biden to see how far the redistribution phenomenon can actually go. I suspect it was founded in Delaware because real Scrantonians work hard for their money.

There is a lot to this chapter but before we go there, please indulge me so I can present for your reading pleasure and edification, the modernized story of the ant and the grasshopper: It is a classic.

Ant and Grasshopper – the most modern version; it names names!

It is amazing the things that come in email. Buried here in the middle of this chapter is the three-version story of the Ant and the Grasshopper. Some might call this the story of saving for a rainy day or simply saving to get through the winter.

There are more and more people who think our President is positioning himself to be President for life unless we stop him by voting him out early. They advise looking up FDR's second bill of rights to know how close we came to total ruin after the depression. The big war actually saved America from itself. Obama knows how close we came and he thinks it can happen again. Some suggest it is part of his plan and he is not planning to stop it because he is counting on it.

How long can Obama continue if he is the high and mighty exalted ruler of a *once-great* country? Does it matter if America comes to nothing under his watch as long as he still is the executive in charge? The first ant and grasshopper fable addresses this potentiality.

The answer to "how long," is until the "rich" who pay 80% of the taxes, get fed up when they cannot get ahead in life, and in frustration they say, "Screw it, Mr. Obama, pay me too!"

You know the story of the grasshopper and the ant. It is easier to be a grasshopper if the ants must pay for your lack of industriousness.

But, one day, when the government forces the ants (those who put their surplus aside for the winter) to take care of the grasshoppers, so that they too can live through the winter, there is not enough for both the ants and the grasshoppers as the grasshoppers choose not to work for the times ahead and contributed zero, and with a body size about 10x and ant, they are big consumers.

Grasshoppers, because of their gene pool, have always viewed ants as silly for working hard preparing for the winter. No grasshopper has ever seen a winter. Grasshoppers are accustomed to a debauchery summer in which the females lay eggs for their offspring to be born the next warming season.

With no knowledge of how to survive a winter, grasshoppers had never been known for foresight. Therefore, they are by apparent destiny, one season critters. They have never been there to see their offspring the next warming season. They starve to death every winter while the eggs stay ready to continue their species the following spring.

Grasshoppers always perish during the winter because they do not prepare. Once the government forces the ants to do all the work for the ants and grasshoppers, to get the grasshoppers through the winter, eventually even the ants run out of victuals and no longer have enough to survive. So, both the ants and the grasshoppers perish under the big grasshopper (Obama's) rule.

Prologue/postlogue from the future

Obama, the King, Emperor, the highest and most exalted ruler, and overall richest "American" ever, lasted until his seventieth birthday in 2031, eating off the surplus the ants had left behind for the year 2032. But at seventy years old, and having reached 650 pounds from getting around in an ethanol / Sears Die Hard powered Jazzy, Obama's feeding needs became intense, and so he satiated himself on the last one-year supply provided by the ants. He polished it off single-handedly in just three months.

Nobody else got any as all Americans, including his own czars starved to death a month before the great one. But, it eventually caught up to even the lord, Obama, as the great one succumbed in his sixth term of natural causes about ten days after consuming the last bit of grain in the small US owned portion of the country known as Washington DC. His eminence probably could have lasted longer on corn alone but the great one demanded that it be made into ethanol for the all-ethanol Chinese cars and his own souped-up ethanol-powered Jazzy.

Meanwhile the Chinese, who were deemed exempt from the American Ant/Grasshopper law, continued to thrive in the remaining 50 states.

The Chinese then boasted that the melting pot had in fact, melted.

The ant and the grasshopper: two more versions--no names

This one is a little different than the very, very modern version above. There are two different versions with two different morals. Here they are:

Old version:

The ant works hard in the withering heat all summer long, building his house and laying up supplies for the winter.

The grasshopper thinks the ant is a fool and laughs and dances and plays the summer away. Come winter, the ant is warm and well fed.

The grasshopper has no food or shelter, so he dies out in the cold.

Moral of the old story:

Be responsible for yourself!

MODERN VERSION:

The ant works hard in the withering heat and the rain all summer long, building and laying up supplies for the winter.

The grasshopper thinks the ant is a fool and laughs and dances and plays the summer away.

Come winter, the shivering grasshopper calls a press conference and demands to know why the ant should be allowed to be warm and well fed while he is cold and starving.

CBS, NBC , PBS, CNN and ABC show up to provide pictures of the shivering grasshopper next to a video of the ant in his comfortable home with a table filled with food. America is stunned by the sharp contrast. How can this be, that in a country of such wealth, this poor grasshopper is allowed to suffer so? Kermit the Frog appears on Oprah with the grasshopper and everybody cries when they sing, 'It's Not Easy Being Green.'

ACORN stages a demonstration in front of the ants' house where the news stations film the group singing we shall overcome. Then Rev. Jeremiah Wright has the group kneel down to pray for the grasshopper's sake.

President Obama condemns the ant and blames President Bush, President Reagan, Christopher Columbus, Genghis Khan, Michael Cain, Herman Cain, Newt Gingrich, Michele Bachman, Ron Paul, Rick Santorum, Brit Hume, Charles Krauthammer, Mitt Romney, the Ants, and the Pope for the grasshopper's plight. Obama, influenced by the Screen Actors Guild, later, for political reasons, retracts his blame from Michael Cain.

Nancy Pelosi and Harry Reid exclaim in an interview with Larry King that the ant has gotten rich off the back of the grasshopper, and both call for an immediate tax hike on the ant to make him pay his fair share. Finally, the EEOC drafts the Economic Equity and Anti-Grasshopper Act, retroactive to the beginning of the summer. The ant is fined for failing to hire a proportionate number of green bugs and, having nothing left to pay his retroactive taxes, his (ant) home is confiscated by the Government Green Czar and given to the grasshopper.

The story ends as we see the grasshopper and his free-loading friends finishing up the last bits of the ants' food while the government house he is in, which, as you recall, just happens to be the ant's old house, crumbles around them because the grasshopper chose not to maintain it.

The ant then disappears in the snow, never to be seen again. The grasshopper is found dead in a drug related incident, and the house, now abandoned, is taken over by a gang of spiders who terrorize and ramshackle the once prosperous and peaceful neighborhood.

The entire nation collapses, bringing the rest of the free world with it.

Moral of the new story:

Be careful how you vote in 2012.

I've placed this in this book because I believe that readers of this book are ants!

You may wish to pass this on to other ants, but don't bother sending it on to any grasshoppers because they wouldn't understand it anyway.

Protectionism, not progressivism from the Founders

Though we think mostly of wars in the formation of our country, it was really the government policy of the Founders that permitted us to be so successful. Protectionism and tariffs played a substantial role in building America's industrial base and it also sustained the government as there was no need for an income tax until tariffs were reduced by the progressive Wilson Administration.

President Wilson as we all know by now, was a first class progressive / socialist and he was happy that the 16th amendment had just been ratified by ¾ of the states when he took office. That permitted him to wield great power to move his social programs forward immediately.

Like Obama, Wilson liked the notion of redistribution of wealth to a fault. Once the income tax became law, there was always pressure in the United States for more social welfare and more income redistribution. With the income tax, tariff reductions, and the socialism introduced by Wilson, the US made a subtle change during Wilson's second term from a mercantilist country to a purely capitalist country. As a reminder, mercantilists do what is necessary for the business and the country and capitalists do what is necessary for the business. Mercantilists are thus capitalists that consider the native country in their decision making.

By the way, if you are very looking for a bona fide racist, look no further than President Wilson. He had such a problem with "negroes," that he segregated his cabinet offices. Look it up! Wilson is the hero of modern day progressives who unfortunately have become the heroes of African-Americans. I do not understand that connection.

Throughout its history, the United States had resisted all notions of tipping into communism, socialism, and progressivism every time the ideas were well explained. The purveyors of these notions were eventually looked upon as kooks and goofs and otherwise social outcasts by the typical American. But, in all cases, this was not until they had made their mark.

The many varieties of socialism evolved in part from the disagreement on the means by which a more equitable distribution of wealth in society is to be achieved. This is a point on which no two socialist philosophies seemed to agree. Marxist socialism proposed the forceful establishment of a workers' dictatorship; conservative social democrats advocated parliamentary reform and trade unions; other factions saw it even differently.

http://www.referenceforbusiness.com/encyclopedia/Sel-Str/Socialism-and-Communism.html#ixzz1cJygsIdv

Is communism ready for a comeback?

So, this time around in 2012, when most Americans think that the jobs dilemma and the poor economy have nothing to do with socialism or communism; think again. When things are not going so well economically, these very alive orthodoxies have been known to make a comeback.

You may know that when communism broke out across the world in the early 20th century it was a thought revolt against the notion that people could sustain themselves without government and its contrivances. The communists believe that you need a commune to survive. The wannabe communist government leaders in many real countries other than the US and most European countries had convinced their people that they were being persecuted. Moreover, they were powerless against the rich bourgeoisie intelligentsia and they needed to act against the oppressive government in order to survive.

Perhaps they all began as innocently as "Occupy Wall Street" but soon all "socialist" revolutions become co-opted by somebody more powerful, like maybe George Soros, waiting in the darkness for the right time. The key attribute of the co-opters is that they can provide the proper direction for the movement.

In Russia, it was the Bolsheviks and some others, who were just waiting for an opportunity to move. And, so, the Russian revolution is the best 20th century example of a communist takeover. It eventually became an extremely bloody revolution as designed by its organizers. It was not an accident since communism can never come into being without the kind of revolution that the Beatle's John Lennon wrote about:

"You say you want a revolution
Well, you know
We all want to change the world
You tell me that it's evolution
Well, you know
We all want to change the world
But when you talk about destruction
Don't you know that you can count me out? "...

Destruction is a key to a revolution or there is no real revolution. The rest of Lennon's lyrics are on the Internet for you to simply use your favorite search engine. There are two very interesting interpretations of Lennon's "Revolution," that I found at the URL site below. I include them to help demonstrate that not everybody thinks social change through revolution, the communist way, is acceptable.

http://www.lyricinterpretations.com/Beatles/Revolution

On April 4, 2008 at 5:00 PM, Anonymous wrote the following comment:

"This song [Revolution by the Beatles] is about the radicals protesting the war [in the late 1960's and 1970's]. They are talking about the protesters becoming too radical and almost as bad as the government. A lot of people asked them [the Beatles] to contribute to causes to protest the war, but protests were becoming very extreme, hence "but when you want money for people with minds that hate you'll have to wait."

Also they spoke of protesters wanting to change the world with a revolution but they started being destructive and it's not about Mao in the physical sense, but more of an example of how extreme they were becoming. That they weren't going to have followers if they were so radical so basically it's about closed minded radicals opposing closed minded government. At least that's what I think."

On April 2, 2009 at 08:32 AM, TOP RATEDTheSeeker wrote the following comment:

"The song takes a look at those who vehemently criticize the government and questions whether the alternatives they propose (if they actually have any) are truly any better than what they are criticizing. This especially rings true about the 60's "revolutionary" period, but can still ring true with some people today (think: those politically-active activist college students you know/knew and who are always going to rallies and protests, who apparently think that the government can do no right, and honestly think that they hold all the answers to their society's problems).

"It seems like John is acknowledging that the world no doubt has a lot of problems, and that there is always some need for change and progress to fix them. And it's okay to be passionate about such things, as long as you maintain perspective and stay true to what you preach (i.e. actually living up to your stated ideals of peace, nonviolence, tolerance, open-mindedness, etc.) But when you become radical and intolerant, and begin advocating violence as a solution, then you become just as bad as the system you're protesting against.

"What's more, if you become radical, you're also a hypocrite. Protestors preach the virtues of love and harmony, and then go on to advocate violence against their fellow man (those in the government). They speak highly of peace and freedom, and then go on to fly the banners of murderous, totalitarian tyrants like Mao Zedong or Che Guevara. How do such contradictions make any sense? They don't.

"There is no such thing as violence in the name of peace. As soon as you let your righteous indignation over legitimate grievances degenerate into blind hatred of your opponents, you lose all credibility. A "revolution" driven by such a mentality does not improve society, as it was supposedly intended to do. It simply replaces one tyranny with another."

Aren't both of those comments extremely insightful? Neither are incite-ful and that is good.

Are communist revolutions peaceful?

We hear a lot about the people rising up but in almost all situations, it really is agitators on behalf of major ideologies that push the revolts forward. During a fully communist revolution, rich families are not very happy that they are "asked" to give up their houses and all their possessions by the working class known in communism as the proletariat. Maybe in the next revolution, in order to increase the supply of nice homes for the proletariat, the revolution will expand the notion of the bourgeoisie to include the middle class.

Regardless, whether rich or middle class, people are prone to prefer to keep their nice homes or mansions and live in them rather than give them up. They are especially not happy that they would be led off to a "rich prison." But, once the revolution is for real and the destruction begins to occur, there are really no rich prisons. The rich (and perhaps the middle class this time) are simply killed in less humane ways than cattle would be slaughtered.

The people in the "revolutions" are so agitated by organizers that they are uncompromising. Anybody who looks like they might actually support peace and kindness and a nice world in which to live can easily become martyrs to the wild acts of the agitated proletariat.

So, a new communist government, while being formed for the takeover, would first convince the peasants to grab more and more from those nasty property owners. "Why should the rich own the land?" Why should the rich have life savings? Communist leaders would turn the people against the people in class warfare. That is why in 2011, many see this notion as practiced by the American President as very dangerous.

Eventually in many communist regimes only the government is organized, and the new government, out of the shadows, quickly takes control. People who become a part of the inner government are secure and they remain safe as they help the leaders continue to operate as their loyal comrades (subjects).

Meanwhile, the regular people—the proletariat as they liked to be called before the revolution, are the ones who would have prosecuted the revolt at the behest of the same leaders. One would not expect that the rich would give up their property without some resistance and so it was up to the proletariat to get the gristle work done. At the end of the revolution, the proletariat had lots of blood on their hands from killing the rich.

From http://www.hawaii.edu/powerkills/COM.ART.HTM:

"What made this secular religion [communism] so utterly lethal was its seizure of all the state's instrument of force and coercion and their immediate use to destroy or control all independent sources of power, such as the church, the professions, private businesses, schools, and, of course, the family."

No matter which communist government you examine from Mao to Pol Pot, the new government would prove to be at least as repressive as the one it replaced. In Russia for example, the country's new rulers were drawn largely from the intellectual and working classes rather than from the aristocracy—which meant there was a considerable change in direction for Russia. In the communist notion in the end a commune forms and is leaderless—well; the leaders ultimately had to declare the final stage of the revolution, and it never came. Thus the fallacy of communism is that in the second last stage, those in power never give it up to the people at large.

To review, in communism, the proletariat does the bidding of the leaders in achieving the objectives of the revolution. And, mysteriously, even at the point when all communists are to become equal, there are still leaders. The cream is separate from the milk; the country never homogenizes, and those left behind see a situation that is even worse than the one in which they were motivated to join.

It is impossible for all the revolutionaries to have it good after the revolution. Though all are equal on the theoretical plain, as in Steinbeck's classic, Of Mice and Men, some are always "more equal." In the end, the proletariat is equal to the miserable mess at the bottom of the scale and they do not receive much from the powers in the Communist Party or the communist government.

In essence under communism, an individual by definition becomes subjugated to the will of the commune (masses). The trick, of course is since the millions cannot talk in one voice, though this is the promise, the leaders, who are a distinct minority—not the commune en masse, make the decisions. Eventually the proletariat members who are good thinkers recognize that they have been snookered by the leaders but it is way too late. They either try to join the inner circle or accept that nothing has gotten better or at worst, they are disposed of.

Few can ever understand how their "successful revolution" had brought on a dictatorship. Yet, it is inevitable.

After being permitted to kill whoever they wished with impunity, in the name of the state during the revolution, the proletariat, who doubled as the workers and as the soldiers of the revolution had to begin to mind their p's and q's as they too might become a danger to the state as rogue individuals. So, they are inevitably forced to behave or they too are killed as unwanted insurgents.

Many of these once regular people, who would subsume themselves into the message and who would assure the success of the revolution, cannot conceive of having to quickly yield to a new "government." So, as an ongoing part of the cleansing of the revolutionaries after the revolution, the stubborn proletariats are killed off as needed. Once the killing begins, it is easy to continue. This is how post revolution harmony is achieved in actuality.

The reality is not as Karl Marx had hoped: "Between capitalist and communist society lies the period of the revolutionary transformation of the one into the other. Corresponding to this is also a political transition period in which the state can be nothing but the revolutionary dictatorship of the proletariat." But, the reality is it never happens because it cannot happen because once humans get power, they do not give it up easily.

Before we summarize, Marx and Engels were often of common mind on their thinking that somehow humans can live in a peaceful community with no leadership in perfect harmony. In practice it never came, and as a pragmatist, I don't think it ever can... ever.

For those who see Barack Obama as a modern day leader of people willing to form into a progressive collective, it helps to see that this ideology simply does not work. As bad as the before scenario may be, once the blood begins to spill, it will get worse. Moreover, the unwritten part of the manifest is that once the rich bourgeois are killed off, a new group of rich, different from the last, will take their places. As you can see below, the thinking of the two masters of communism is different but it is the same nonetheless:

Marx thinking: the dictatorship of the proletariat imposes a series of restrictions on the freedom of the oppressors, the exploiters, the capitalists. We must suppress them in order to free humanity from wage slavery, their resistance must be crushed by force; it is clear that there is no freedom and no democracy where there is suppression and where there is violence.

Engels thinking: Only in communist society, when the resistance of the capitalists have disappeared, when there are no classes (i.e., when there is no distinction between the members of society as regards their relation to the social means of production), only then "the state... ceases to exist", and "it becomes possible to speak of freedom". Only then will a truly complete democracy become possible and be realized, a democracy without any exceptions whatever. And only then will democracy begin to wither away, owing to the simple fact that, freed from capitalist slavery, from the untold horrors, savagery, absurdities, and infamies of capitalist exploitation, people will gradually become accustomed to observing the elementary rules of social intercourse that have been known for centuries and repeated for thousands of years in all copy-book maxims. They will become accustomed to observing them without force, without coercion, without subordination, without the special apparatus for coercion called the state. Communism alone is capable of providing really complete democracy, and the more complete it is, the sooner it will become unnecessary and wither away of its own accord.

Can communism / socialism work?

I can see how zealots who believe things can be other than they actually can be, can get "sucked in" by the potential for the most bountiful goodness possible; only to eventually learn, with disbelief that they cannot. Deductive reasoning proves communism cannot work. Inductive reasoning always has room for hope.

As a pragmatist, and a computer logician, I see no practical opportunity for any of the mumbo-jumbo, from Marx or Engels, as nice as it may sound, to be accepted by real human beings with real functional minds, as a life credo. Yet, I have seen it happen.

Knowing that inductive reasoning permits the illogical to be in fact possible, since there is no country experience in history proving that such giving up of one's liberty and freedom for a communal cause can ever work, my conclusion remains the same. I find it impossible for communism to work as intended by Marx and Engels. I am also aware that just because it cannot work does not mean that somebody will not try it again.

Progressivism / socialism / communism summary

The objectives of the progressives, who run America today is to move away from our capitalist society and onto something in which the state is paramount. Unlike communism, the progressives believe the state is a god and is necessary for the proper functioning of the good of government. Since the state is the god, there is not room for God in the life of a progressive.

They know that mercantilism, a more country-first notion of capitalism is still capitalism and so they look to shed those bonds completely. Communism denies that the state is necessary and thus, communism cannot ever work as intended.

So, the idea is to sneak in this intermediate notion of a state so that communism ultimately will come forth as all of the people in power give up their power. That just about describes why it can never work. Which leader is longing to go back to being *one of the boys*?

Progressives seek a redistributive harmony to embrace the land. Many of us have seen its results in our own time in communist Russia, communist China, and other communist lands. Yet, many in America are still clamoring to bring this scourge to America. Somebody always gets hurt, and sometimes, as in China and Russia, and Cambodia, the death toll is in the millions. For what?

Can you tell me why the US did not go communist before Obama? Could it be the Constitution? As we fully explained above, all forms of communism are ideologies that subsume the individual to the collective. Americans sing about wanting to be free and being free. Americans have been here for just a bit over 200 years and almost all people—from the colonists to the foreign national who escaped his country's repressive regimes to the illegal immigrant who escaped American authorities and finds a way to become a citizen—none are looking to give up an ounce of their "freedom."

Most Americans who travelled great distances to become Americans found their origins to be repressive and they are not interested in living under repressive regimes in America or anywhere else. The seeds of discontent for collectivism are bred into American loins. Americans are for individualism, freedom, and full liberty. When led well, Americans are for America first! And when not, eventually, like now, we thirst for freedom from the oppression which we brought upon ourselves. The answer, however, is never more of the same.

The black experience in America is both tragic and wonderful. A preponderance of whites cry when we hear the stories of blacks losing their freedom and worse during the slavery period.

We cry for the pain the African village felt as children were swept away and other children lost their freedom. The blacks who love history today know how important freedom really is. "Free at last!" is such a memorable phrase that it is indelibly etched in my mind. Communism, progressivism, socialism, Marxism, are not forms of freedom. They merely are a means of changing masters—white or black. It is merely changing masters for a people who want no masters.

The United States is narcissistic in a good way. We do like to boast about being American. We love our country. Americans love America. Americans are also trusting of other Americans for the most part. Unless there is a perpetrator rocking the car outside and the dog starts barking, Americans are prone to trust other Americans and we also do our best to be trustworthy.

If the dog is barking, however, Americans are not stupid. Whether the perpetrator is American or not, Americans feel no obligation to trust the folks that are rocking the car. They can be white, black, or brown, red, or yellow, and it does not matter. If the preachers of love preached love for all, then we could move on from the "race" thing to something that can unite us all. We are all Americans. I love saying, "I am an American," even more than saying "I am Irish!" You bet I love America. Don't you?

The United States has become a highly socialized nation because there is a wing of the Democratic Party and a smaller wing of the Republican Party who are progressive liberals. Just as I am a conservative Democrat, there are progressive Republicans. George Bush I, George Bush II, Jeb Bush I, and many other Republicans hide behind their business-friendly façade and work the country as liberals.

Progressivism is all caught up with the redistribution of other people's money. The Bush's showed their true colors and they are not as American as they would like you to think. They were not for Americans as they directed all of their resources for the benefit of the illegal alien community, without considering the impact on John Q. Public. If progressives like the Bushes and the Obama's and the Biden's spent their own money, I might even think they were noble. But, they are not.

The Founders were interested in freedom

The founders never intended this country to be in any way socialist / progressive. The precepts of this country reflect the Founders' intentions. The Constitution does not permit wealth redistribution or health insurance redistribution or any kind of redistribution of the gains of one to make up for the losses of another. Real charity, religion, and churches fill that gap in this country—not government!

These precepts permit us all to live in a land where we have enough freedom and enough liberty to be able to work hard and enjoy the fruits of the initial revolution and the spirit of '76. They are enumerated as life, liberty and the pursuit of happiness. I am so pleased to be an American, and I offer no apologies.

That is where it ends but we forget often as some politician someplace gives us something and we feel beholden to her. When a representative does her job, they should receive accolades and that is about it. When their term expires, they should be freed of the burden of representation so they can be normal people and return to their former jobs.

Otherwise they will inevitably become pandering politicians, and they will make the people be beggars for their apparent bounty. Americans must be brave enough to end this and vote in people like themselves to assure that America prospers and the government is not permitted to pick winners and losers in any aspect of society.

The founders did not wish there to ever be a ginormous central government to take huge amounts of money from one group of people and give it to any other group of people. History is replete with instances of large scale redistribution and in all cases; the incentive to work diminishes for the people as the desire for handouts increases.

At the same time, as the rewards of giving handouts increases for the politicians. The inevitable is that the countries end up with an entire class of people that have learned how to "make a living" by being a sponge of government beneficence, and that can easily bring upon the ruin of any country. Right now, for example, the United States is in a stage of ruin. Will we survive? Not by expecting handouts, that is for sure!

Thomas Jefferson and Benjamin Franklin were indisputably brilliant. In 1816, Thomas Jefferson wrote the following:

"To take from one, because it is thought his own industry and that of his fathers has acquired too much, in order to spare to others, who, or whose fathers, have not exercised equal industry and skill, is to violate arbitrarily the first principle of association, the guarantee to everyone the free exercise of his industry and the fruits acquired by it."

In other words, if you want something, go earn it!

The end of a republic occurs when people start realizing that they can vote themselves money out of the national treasury. In Benjamin Franklin's own words this sounds like: "When the people find that they can vote themselves money that will herald the end of the republic."

Our republic as it exists today may be seen 100 years from now when the failure of the United States can be clearly viewed in hindsight, as the last period in which the people could unite together to save America. With nobody trusting anybody, and class warfare being promoted by the President himself, it is likely that it may already be too late. If the current President is reelected, people will have voted to clear out the storehouses and the bins of the collective wealth and foodstuffs accumulated by past industrious generations and like the ant and the grasshopper. Then, regrettably, one spring neither ants nor grasshoppers will have survived.

Politics in America is dirty and repugnant and when politicians show their true colors, it is like taking a fishing trip to the Gehenna Underworld. If only we had leaders instead of politicians, America would have more of a chance.

You see politicians constantly promise what they are "going to do" for various groups of people, and many people see it as if their ship has come in. Well, the ship is now empty and it has a huge hole in it. Are you ready to hop aboard to benefit, or will you try to fix the ship so the country can prosper?

It is good to help helpless people and that should be a charity and not a function of government. But, it is not good to make people helpless. That is the most unkind act of all.

Our founding fathers were 100% for charitable acts to help those stumbling along until they got on their feet. Our progressive government suggests that people down on their luck should simply cut off their feet since in the progressive world; they won't need their feet again. Somebody will be there to take care of them. I hope many do not feel that way.

The founders did not believe in excessive taxation and in fact they liked less the notion of repressive taxation by a huge national government. The problem the founders faced in their time was England, and once the colonists broke free from England, none were ready to sign up for large scale redistributions of wealth. The founders saw it simply as stealing.

Has the US become England of old?

I regret from what I see, our country, because of its exceptionally poor leadership, has become the England the colonists hated. China and Russia and those countries that are coming out from under dominant socialist or communist regimes are in many ways the new American beachhead and their people are the new colonists laboring to make their reworked governments function.

They know how bad it can be. It will not be too long before they realize their mettle is more than our mettle, and if we don't choose to become a real country again instead of a bunch of puffballs waiting for a handout, they will kick our butts in the same fashion as we kicked England's butt.

Nobody is for the welfare programs that make people helpless. Yet, welfare programs are necessary in limited scope. To survive with government charity, a country can only help out people who are in the direst of circumstances. When everybody, including those receiving subsistence have a nice TV in every room with cable connections, and a new to mid-life automobile, and their teeth get cleaned by real dentists, and there is little difference in the ability of the givers and the takers in terms of possessions and the ability to possess, welfare has already gone over the top. Why should one pay for another? It is not natural and it is unsustainable.

The US cannot cut off all welfare programs today even though we have carried it too far. We have permitted a very large percentage of Americans to become helpless. Worse than that, government has encouraged many to become helpless. Many simply do not know how to take care of themselves. If they were tested, they would fail. If we stopped all government support all of a sudden, people would begin to suffer immediately.

But, if we do not announce the withdrawal of full support to anybody who chooses not to be productive, even though they can be productive, we will no longer have any support structures to help those who we caused to become apparently helpless. Soon after the Chinese or the Russians take over, they may offer more charity than the former US; but do not hold your breath on that one.

Where we are today is that many people have become what some cynics might call "pets of the government." If our government chose to no longer require elections and no longer was docile, what do we think might happen to these "pets?" If the people want the US to survive, we must all engage. You don't think any of the original colonists or the first few rounds of immigrants felt they could live on handouts? Nor can we! Our government must work for us by making sure the people, more than the corporations or the unions are # 1.

Can we become self-sufficient?

We know what is wrong. Our society—that's you and I and those who we awaken every day—must begin teaching all citizens to be self-sufficient, while we ask all non-citizens to kindly leave or sign up for some non-special treatment.

But, do we do that? No, we teach our citizens that it is perfectly OK to permit the government to take care of them from the cradle all the way to the grave. And we provide bounty for non-citizens. Whose resources can possibly support so many people for so long a time? That is why the US is broke—$15 trillion in debt. It is as if we are preparing to permit the country which conquers us to have an easy time of it.

So would our founding fathers be in favor of the corporate greed that we witness today with once proud American corporations trading in labor arbitrage in America and outside in the offshore markets? You know that such good and intelligent people would not permit that. Then why do our leaders permit it? Our "leaders" are not leaders. They did not study Franklin or Madison or Jefferson and they know not how to run America. That is the only answer. They have instead become the lowliest of people—politicians.

Corporations, unions, and government

For their own greed, they have been bending the Constitution for so many years, that in many ways, they have broken it already by ignoring it. We must repair the Constitution by removing every suspicious politician from office and replacing them with real leaders. They are out there in America someplace. We just have to find them.

Corporations should not have the power that they have gained from illegitimate Supreme Court Decisions. These decisions must be reargued in a new government.

Government should not have the power it has gained and unions should not have the power on the national stage they have gained. Of all three groups, which represents all the people? To that question, I would answer that as "none." Nobody represents the people. Instead there is some natural countervailing power in play that inhibits one of the three legs from toppling the others, and that is why Americans must regain control of the government so that we have at least one of the major legs of power in this country.

If government represented the people as intended, instead of itself, the mess could be kept in check. Government has become an entity unto itself and it too has desired to survive and prosper independently of the people who pay the salaries of its employees.

Government today is the big switch hitter. One time it aligns with unions, and one time it aligns with corporations so that in the end, government gets its way and the people always lose. This government of ours must be replaced by peaceful means. For those not paying attention and I know it is none of us either by reading or by writing this book, this happens at the polls about every two years. Americans are in control of their own destiny. Vote for new government. Implore your favorite citizens to run for office for one or two terms, and then help them win.

Union thugs should not be permitted to trample on the people's property that is owned by the government nor should they be permitted to trample on individuals' property. If corporations, unions, and government people were armed and operated in groups, they could slaughter whatever singular people they chose. That is the ultimate chaos and we must be concerned about it because one at a time, a lot of damage can be done. Most Americans, who are armed with second amendment privileges, know that they will never give up their arms for this very reason.

There is hope. With normal people getting together in groups and labeling themselves, such as the TEA Party people in the spirit of the Boston uprising, a lot can be accomplished. The growing dissatisfaction with the size of government is being manifest and it is being taken seriously. Just as in the final stage of communism, those holding the power, as nasty and undeserving as they are; are not about to simply give it up.

Polls suggest that at least two-thirds of Americans are now dissatisfied with the size and influence of major corporations in America today. I would bet a similar number feel the same about government and unions.

Eventually, unless the people continue to operate together in bands such as the TEA Party, and Occupy Wall Street, our entire system will crumble, especially if there are too few people still willing to work hard!

The real intent in this book, of course is not to present Americans with a conundrum that is unsolvable. The Constitution is actually the best guide to turn things around. Our tax system has become entirely unfair and it simply does not work. I have outlined this as a big problem in Chapter 2, and the whole thing does need to be scrapped.

Of the three big problems, corporations, unions, and government, corporations are the biggest culprits in the current demise of the country. Making the tax system better will actually help corporations behave better naturally. That is not enough however. Corporations need to have their citizenship revoked and they need to be held truly accountable by the people for being either American in behavior or anti-American in behavior.

Why don't you ever hear about the things I have brought forth in this book on mainstream TV or in the newspapers? It is an easy answer. Look who owns them.

Media bias is bad for Americans

About five years ago I can recall thanking God for Fox News but now even Fox News has bit the dust. There is no real conservative voice on TV anymore so I am turning to radio. I think it is government's role to assure that rules are put in place that do not permit a company like GE, which coincidentally paid no taxes on huge earnings last year, is able to own NBC, MSNBC, and CNBC.

No wonder Obama likes them and mysteriously, they pay no taxes, and have you ever heard one of their personalities suggest a conservative may have even stumbled on a good idea. That's why you know GE's media slop are lying all the time, trying to persuade Americans that things are not as they seem. But, of course despite GE, they are!

The U.S. media scenario is dominated by ginormous corporations that, through a history of mergers and acquisitions, have concentrated their control over what we Americans see, hear and read. In many cases, these giant companies are vertically integrated. That means they control everything from initial production to final distribution. Are you satisfied that the aggregate news media is sufficiently independent enough to broadcast or print the facts, or are they influenced by self-interests for their parent corporations or sibling corporations or their child corporations?

Though GE/NBC may be the biggest violator of the people's right to know, Fox is owned by NewsCorp; ABC is owned by Disney; and CBS, surreptitiously I would say, is owned by a company that sounds a lot like CBS. Yes, it is the CBS Corporation. They own the CBS Network. CBSCorp is also a media conglomerate.

When Fox fired Glenn Beck, I began to become suspicious that there would no longer be a source of conservative news on mainstream TV. I was right. Just when you think Fox is going to get it right, you find there is an oil money connection or a Rupert Murdock (a liberal and NewsCorp's most significant owner) connection in that he needs Obama to save his own skin in the scandals. So, is there really an independent voice on TV anywhere? I do not think so but there is radio, and that is pretty fine.

Lots of factories closing

Was it progressivism that caused, since 2001, over 42,000 U.S. factories to be closed down for good? Do the progressives have jobs or shall we say compensation for those who lost jobs? Were any jobs lost before 2001, and have more been lost since and will more be lost in the future or will somebody stand up for America?

Why are all of our politicians just standing off to the side with their hands in their pockets. Answer: Because they choose not to lead but to politic instead!

Americans are in the middle of a huge economic nightmare that is absolutely unprecedented and there is no ER team on the scene trying to resuscitate the country. People on the dole are not inclined to help and people paying for the dole are so frustrated trying to make ends meet for themselves, they are ready to cry wolf! So, now is redistributing wealth the answer. Or, is this a notion that says we are going under so let's make the deck chairs look real nice before the ship goes down. Can we learn from the Titanic?

Americans are smart enough to know that redistribution and progressivism will take us to perdition. We need a comprehensive overhaul of our entire economy. Reject socialism and communism and embrace the Constitution. Let's get a divorce from progressivism and get it right the second time around.

Let me end with a comment I saw on a blog: "Give a man a fish; you have fed him for today. Teach a man to fish; and you have fed him for a lifetime."

Chapter 15   Reduce / Eliminate Lying

Is there a right to lie?

Government believes it has a right to lie. Some religions believe they have the right to lie to defend their faith. When I went to grade school, I can recall my teacher specifically telling me there was no such thing as a white lie. All lies are lies. There are no white lies. What about institutional lying by corporations, by unions, by government, and by their puppets in the media?

Back in late 2001 in the US, an office that had to be designed by George Orwell came into being. It was called the Office of Strategic Influence. It was to become a new layer of federal bureaucracy within the Pentagon. Its purpose was to place false news items with foreign news organizations.

Former Defense Secretary Donald Rumsfeld has since claimed, "Government officials, the Department of Defense, this secretary and the people that work with me tell the American people and the people of the world the truth." After taking an awful lot of heat, Rumsfeld announced that he had closed down the office in 2002.

Yet, sometime after that, there was a big rumor that cited Rumsfeld as having backed out of "his" closure comment. The rumor suggested that Rumsfeld said they merely got rid of the name while the function still exists. Can both a flip and a flop be true? You make the call.

Ben Franklin gives us the following powerful quote: "They that can give up essential liberty to purchase a little temporary safety

deserve neither liberty nor safety." Can we expect our
government to tell the truth?

In late 2011, you may have heard that there was a proposed
rule change to the Freedom of Information Act (FOIA) that
would allow federal agencies to tell those requesting certain
law-enforcement or national security documents that the
records do not exist—even when they do exist.

Under current (previous perhaps) FOIA practice, the
government may withhold information and issue what's known
as a *Glomar* denial that says it can "neither confirm nor deny"
the existence of records. The new proposal, which is part of a
lengthy rule revision by the Department of Justice, would direct
government agencies to "respond to the request as if the
excluded records did not exist." Many groups have objected to
this proposal. It gives government the right to lie. Do you think
the Founders would have gone along with such nonsense?

Open-government groups object.

"We don't believe the statute allows the government to lie to
FOIA requesters," said Mike German, senior policy counsel for
the American Civil Liberties Union, which opposes the
provision.

Another Lie

President Obama is on record as grossly underselling America's
oil supply. The President is quoted as saying that we only have
2% of the world's supply. Was this an under-sell; or did the
President simply lie big time?

The President chose to leave out the 10 billion barrels available
in the Arctic National Wildlife Refuge and the 86 billion barrels
available offshore in the Outer Continental Shelf. The President
has a drilling ban on this oil. It also does not include the 800

billion barrels of oil discovered and locked in the shale of Wyoming, Utah, and Colorado.

As a point of fact, the oil shale alone is estimated at three times larger than the proven reserves of Saudi Arabia. So, one can rightfully conclude that the claim that the U.S. only has 2% of the world's oil is definitely false.

Did Obama officials lie about amnesty scheme?

All government agencies report to the Executive Branch. For his own reasons, President Obama is for giving full amnesty to illegal aliens. He has tried the open door of Congress several times but Congress has closed the door each time when the President admits he has no respect for immigration laws.

So, since he cannot get amnesty through Congress, Obama is trying the back door. His minions in the U.S. Citizenship and Immigration Services sent out a memo outlining ways the administration could bypass Congress to enact amnesty for millions of illegal aliens through "administrative means."

Is this a lie, a deception, a failure to follow the Constitution or something else? It sure isn't honest government.

Figure 15-1 Caution Illegal Immigrants Prohibited

Is Obama really the master deporter?

The Houston Chronicle uncovered an effort by the Obama administration to suspend the deportations of illegal aliens that, according to them, have not been convicted of any "serious" crimes. Who can be trusted? Yet, countless incidents are reported across the states of illegal immigrants committing second, third, and many more crimes, each of which are serious!

Medicare will cost just $3Billion

In 1966 at a projected cost of $3 billion, the Congress debated Medicare and passed the bill. Looking forward to the future from 1966, government accountants and the Congress and President Johnson estimated that Medicare would reach $12 billion by 1990 using inflation-adjusted numbers. They were way off. By 1990, the tab was $107 billion. Today Medicare is approaching $485 billion with no signs of leveling off. How much confidence should we have in any cost estimates by the

White House or Congress? Are such estimates simply lies, or are they the result of incompetence?

Medicare will not affect healthcare – just kidding!

If you like reading legislation, feel free to go to Section 1801 of the 1965 Medicare Act. It reads: "Nothing in this title shall be construed to authorize any federal officer or employee to exercise any supervision or control over the practice of medicine, or the manner in which medical services are provided, or over the selection, tenure, or compensation of any officer, or employee, or any institution, agency or person providing health care services."

Is this how Medicare is actually implemented in practice? Your doctor or hospital can tell you there is hardly one little gram of truth in the whole statement. Is this institutional lying? If so, there clearly is no defense reason for doing so.

Only the rich will pay income taxes!

Here is a real good one. Republican President Howard Taft was in office when he was beseeched by Congressional supporters to set the 16th amendment into process. He was told that only the rich would ever pay federal income taxes. The amendment was ratified and the tax bill passed and in 1913 when real revenue began to come into the treasury (after the protective tariffs had been reduced) only one half of 1 percent of income earners were affected.

Congress then adopted a 1 percent tax on net personal income of more than $3,000 with a surtax of 6 percent on incomes of more than $500,000. Those earning $250,000 a year in today's dollars paid 1 percent, and those earning $6 million in today's dollars paid 7 percent. Soon afterwards, the top rate was upped to 15%. In other words, once the rich were sucked into the system, the Congress assured that all Americans, rich and poor, would be burdened forever to pay a tax on their meager income.

By 1917, the goose was just too golden for Congress and they sent the top rate all the way up to 67%, but all the while they added things to the code so that the really rich had enough exemptions that the whole thing was a charade and only the poor were in the audience for the performance.

Though President Taft was promised that only the rich would pay, it was clearly a lie and it was the beginning of the politics of envy as Americans were duped by their own representatives into ratifying the Sixteenth Amendment. As soon as Democrat Woodrow Wilson took office, the income tax took effect and government spending as we now know it began in earnest.

The Social Security Lie

Another big Congressional lie is Social Security. Here's what _a 1936 government Social Security pamphlet_ said: "After the first 3 years—that is to say, beginning in 1940—you will pay, and your employer will pay, 1.5 cents for each dollar you earn, up to $3,000 a year. . . . . .in 1943, you will pay 2 cents, and so will your employer, for every dollar you earn for the next 3 years. . . . And. . . beginning in 1949, twelve years from now, you and your employer will each pay 3 cents on each dollar you earn, up to $3,000 a year".

The maximum payment was $90.00. So, OK was this a lie? Congress could not handle the truth so they ended the pamphlet with this big whopper: "That is the most you will ever pay." Today's reality has us paying 6.2 cents on each dollar that we earn up to nearly $107,000, which comes to $6,621. If we were working in 1936 dollars that would be $432 not including the employers share of the tax. Was that a lie?

Why We Believe

Walter Williams, writing for www.thefreemanonline.org in October 2010 answers the question of why we believe this crap in such a clear fashion and so much in synch with my views that before I saw the citation, I thought I had written it myself. Williams does such a perfect job of summing up why we believe in Congressional and Presidential balderdash that I present his paragraph to you now for your edification and enjoyment:

"Here's my question: Why are so many Americans taken in by Washington's lies? I think there are several likely answers. Man is tempted by what looks like a free lunch. He is also tempted by government's promise to permit him to live at the expense of someone else. Some people are totally ignorant of the effects of government programs on the socioeconomic fabric of our country.

There are many Americans who do understand the problem but what do they care?... Any politician, who endeavors to eliminate the massive spending programs, in an effort to forestall the calamity, will be run out of office by the program's beneficiaries. That means the status quo rules. People might ask: What can be done to preserve American exceptionalism and greatness? My answer to such a question is a question: How do Americans systematically differ from citizens of past great nations who supported political actions that ultimately drove their nations into the ground?"

How fast can I make you furious?

In the fall 2011, Attorney General Eric Holder found himself on the Congressional firing line about the "Fast and Furious" (F&F) initiative / fiasco. It seems the AG while in front of the Congress suffered from one or more misstatements of fact. This F&F initiative helped funnel illegal guns to Mexico in a botched attempt to learn more about the participants in the illegal weapons trade.

It was a fishy deal to begin with. The blogs run rampant with speculation that the anti-gun faction of our government was trying to use the program to shut down the second amendment. The JD reportedly hoped to show just how bad guns are by putting them in the hands of really, really bad people. The bloggers see the gunrunner project as a big ruse for even bigger goals. Either way, it was poorly implemented.

In May, 2011, pretending like he heard his first cuss word, Holder spoke to the congressional committee on oversight run by Rep. Darrell Issa, R-Calif. When asked when he first heard about the F & F project, he offered that he had been briefed only a few weeks prior to his testimony. The facts and Holder are not in synch and some brave members of Congress such as Senator Grassley are taking Holder to task on the lie.

The facts show that Holder was informed about "Fast and Furious" at least as early as July 2010. Is this a white lie or a regular lie? Does the government think it no longer must tell Americans the truth?

Will the media ever tell the people the truth?

While Congress and the President are part of the institutional lying deal and have been from time immemorial, I give you this quote from John Swainton, who was the chief of staff of the NY Times at the time he made the remarks below. He offers a scourge against his fellow journalists who are manipulated often for business and agenda purposes. Swainton shows remorse in his statement but does not say he is sorry. This September 2011 quote is very telling

"There is not one of you who would dare to write his honest opinion,.... The business of a journalist now is to destroy the truth, to lie outright, to pervert, to vilify, fall at the feet of

Mammon and sell himself for his daily bread. We are tools, vessels of rich men behind the scenes, we are jumping jacks. They pull the strings; we dance. Our talents, our possibilities and our lives are the properties of these men. We are intellectual prostitutes."

So, are journalists today motivated to deliver to the public the truth or something else?

Lies and major bias by the press are surely making the news as institutional lying is being called out more than the usual lately. CNSNews.com reported that four billboard trucks bearing the message "Stop the Liberal Bias, Tell the Truth!" began circling the Manhattan headquarters of ABC, CBS, NBC, and the New York Times on September 30, 2010. The trucks were scheduled to do so for eight hours every weekday for four weeks as part of an awareness campaign run by the Media Research Center, a watchdog group that analyzes the media for liberal bias. Similar trucks also operated in the Washington, D.C. area.

L. Brent Bozell III, president of the Media Research Center (MRC), the parent organization of CNSNews.com, said the "goal of the 2010 Tell the Truth! Campaign is simple: 'to force the liberals in the media to stop pushing an agenda and just tell the truth... Liberal media news networks' need to report the facts about massive growth in government and its control over our lives, and about spending, deficits and debt'...they also need to tell the truth about the efforts to turn our country into a European-style Socialist state."

Thank you Mr. Bozell

Nobody likes a liar. Deceit is another form of lie that not only involves a lie; it involves a cover-up right within the lie itself. Americans want their government and their elected officials to tell the truth in all matters by policy. Only when there would be a serious security issue would Americans agree to see their government lying to them but we would expect that there

would be enough real Americans with the proper security
clearances as part of the permission set so that the people might
relax. But, quite frankly, even this is spooky because who is it
that carries the real truth and why should anybody believe
them?

Lying for political purposes is about as loved as the stuff at the
bottom of the ocean. I am sure you do not want me in this book
at least to find all of the many lies told by government to the
people. I think I have sufficiently convinced all that lying is
rampant and it is not new. From my perspective, I am
convinced that to have a real country that tends to the needs of
its people, lying cannot be condoned.

Liar Quotes:

Here are a few famous quotes about lies. They help us put the
lying issue in perspective and in many ways, these quotes are
enjoyable and thought provoking to read. As edifying as this
section is, and as cute as some of this is done, please let us not
be liars, everyone.   Enjoy!

If you tell the truth you don't have to remember anything.
Mark Twain

Who lies for you will lie against you.
Bosnian Proverb

No man has a good enough memory to make a successful liar.
Abraham Lincoln

A half truth is a whole lie.
Yiddish Proverb

Those who think it is permissible to tell white lies soon grow
color-blind.

Austin O'Malley

The least initial deviation from the truth is multiplied later a thousandfold.
Aristotle

When you stretch the truth, watch out for the snapback.
Bill Copeland

A lie may take care of the present, but it has no future. **Author Unknown**

I never lie because I don't fear anyone. You only lie when you're afraid.
John Gotti

We tell lies when we are afraid... afraid of what we don't know, afraid of what others will think, afraid of what will be found out about us. But every time we tell a lie, the thing that we fear grows stronger.
Tad Williams

Honesty is the first chapter of the book of wisdom.
Thomas Jefferson

Men occasionally stumble over the truth, but most of them pick themselves up and hurry off as if nothing had happened.
Winston Churchill

The truth is more important than the facts.
Frank Lloyd Wright

A lie gets halfway around the world before the truth has a chance to put its pants on.
Winston Churchill

It is not without good reason said, that he who has not a good memory should never take upon him the trade of lying.
Michel de Montaigne, translated

If we were all given by magic the power to read each other's thoughts, I suppose the first effect would be to dissolve all friendships.
Bertrand Russell

It is impossible to calculate the moral mischief, if I may so express it, that mental lying has produced in society. When a man has so far corrupted and prostituted the chastity of his mind as to subscribe his professional belief to things he does not believe he has prepared himself for the commission of every other crime.

Thomas Paine, The Age of Reason

When truth is divided, errors multiply.
Eli Siegel, Damned Welcome

Truth is such a rare thing, it is delightful to tell it.
Emily Dickinson

Cherish the friend who tells you a harsh truth, wanting ten times more to tell you a loving lie.
Robert Brault, www.robertbrault.com

It is not difficult to deceive the first time, for the deceived possesses no antibodies; unvaccinated by suspicion, she overlooks lateness, accepts absurd excuses, permits the flimsiest patching to repair great rents in the quotidian.
John Updike

Speak the truth, but leave immediately after.
Slovenian Proverb

The highest compact we can make with our fellow is - "Let there be truth between us two forevermore."
Ralph Waldo Emerson

Man is least himself when he talks in his own person. Give him a mask, and he will tell you the truth.
Oscar Wilde

Today I bent the truth to be kind, and I have no regret, for I am far surer of what is kind than I am of what is true.
Robert Brault, www.robertbrault.com

The truth needs so little rehearsal.
Barbara Kingsolver, Animal Dreams

Society can exist only on the basis that there is some amount of polished lying and that no one says exactly what he thinks.
Lin Yutang

Some people will not tolerate such emotional honesty in communication. They would rather defend their dishonesty on the grounds that it might hurt others. Therefore, having rationalized their phoniness into nobility, they settle for superficial relationships.
Author Unknown

It takes two to lie. One to lie and one to listen.
"Homer Simpson," from the TV show The Simpsons

There's one way to find out if a man is honest - ask him. If he says, "Yes," you know he is a crook.
Groucho Marx

I am different from Washington; I have a higher, grander standard of principle. Washington could not lie. I can lie, but I won't.
Mark Twain

These quotes are sometimes humorous but they also show the power and predominant nature of the lie. Now that you are relaxed, consider this series of quotes from Joseph Goebbels, who served in official title as chief propagandist of Nazi Germany. You may never think the same about lying or socialism for that matter again. Think about whether the Obama administration or any other appears to be practicing this stuff.

If you tell a lie big enough and keep repeating it, people will eventually come to believe it. The lie can be maintained only for such time as the State can shield the people from the political, economic and/or military consequences of the lie. It thus becomes vitally important for the State to use all of its powers to repress dissent, for the truth is the mortal enemy of the lie, and thus by extension, the truth is the greatest enemy of the State.
Joseph Goebbels

The most brilliant propagandist technique will yield no success unless one fundamental principle is borne in mind constantly - it must confine itself to a few points and repeat them over and over.
Joseph Goebbels

Think of the press as a great keyboard on which the government can play.
Joseph Goebbels

Whoever can conquer the street will one day conquer the state, for every form of power politics and any dictatorship-run state has its roots in the street.
Joseph Goebbels

Chapter 16   Reduce Government

The era of big government is back

Liberals and conservatives do agree on some basic things. Truly!

The era of big government has returned with a vengeance. We now have the largest federal work force in modern history. The expectation by the end of 2011 is that government will have grown to about 2.2 million employees.

You may recall back when President Clinton declared that "the era of big government is over" and he joined forces with a Republican-led Congress that took on a "contract with America," in the 1990s to peel back the huge federal work force. The Obama employee increases have moved the total employee figure past 2 million for the first time since even before the Clinton era.

Over the last three years since President Obama has taken office, according to John Boehner's office, the federal government has added 200,000 new federal jobs. Perhaps the President has not gotten the word that the country is broke. What business hires 200,000 workers when it is running at a loss and it has no cash-flow? The answer is a business with an unlimited line of credit led by incompetent management. Any such business is destined to soon be out of business. And, so the Obama led US government!

Government today is simply too big and it should be substantially smaller. The cost of government, which is the factor which controls the national debt, is too high. It has been stifling the economy since 2009. Clearly, making government smaller would help.

The Bureau of Labor statistics suggests that the typical federal worker is paid 20% more than a private-sector worker in the same occupation. We have statistics that would call this a gross understatement. According to this government agency, median annual salary for a federal worker (that means the most common) is $66,591 v. $55,500 for a private industry worker. As you can see, that is an $11,091 difference. I regret to say that I don't buy that as the difference.

Think of the unemployment rate, for example. More and more private industry employees are losing their jobs while more federal employees are being hired and while the federal government has provided stimulus dollars to cities and states and school districts to prop up their employee's earnings to assure no government anywhere would feel the need for any of their employees to take even a modest pay cut.

The Constitution does not suggest that huge sums of national dollars should be redistributed from the non-working to the working or from private sector employees to public sector. However, big government is so big that it thinks it can do anything. But, just because it can, does not mean that it should. It is up to you and me and our leaders to stop big government from destroying America.

We will now tell the whole story and more accurately than it was told by the prevaricators in the labor department. The Bureau of Labor Statistics is not the only game in town. USA Today has done some analysis about the lack of parity between the wages paid in the private and the public sector. Their analysis is a lot more aggressive in showing the disparity between private and public sector jobs. It also appears to be much more accurate.

USA Today published a 100% differential between the two. Public sector employees make twice as much as those in private sector. Maybe the US Bureau of Labor Statistics had another agenda for their reporting or their data was ten years old.

USA Today provided their results in the following words:

"At a time when workers' pay and benefits have stagnated, federal employees' average compensation has grown to more than double what private sector workers earn, a USA TODAY analysis finds.

"Federal workers have been awarded bigger average pay and benefit increases than private employees for nine years in a row. The compensation gap between federal and private workers has doubled in the past decade.

"Federal civil servants earned average pay and benefits of [a whopping] $123,049 in 2009 while private workers made $61,051 in total compensation, according to the Bureau of Economic Analysis. The data are the latest available".

What should government do and what should it not be doing?

Agencies such as the FBI and the CIA, and the Department of Defense are vitally important for the safety of Americans. The Department of Homeland Security does a very poor job and should be rebuilt and reduced in size. We do need more border guards and a fence and we need to take the whole idea of illegal entry into the United States more seriously.

I would like to see much of this mission and funding being given to the Border States as Washington is too far away to manage this effectively. The federal government would best serve in an advisory capacity to the states in this regard.

In terms of things that the federal government should not do, first of all, it should not sue states willing to take on part of its role in anything. It should not manage healthcare for sure and it should not manage businesses.

Many of its agencies such as the U.S. Department of Education and the U.S. Environmental Protection Agency, and the U.S. Department of Energy are so costly and have performed so poorly, that there are often calls for their elimination. A lot of dollars would be saved from such eliminations. That's not all:

As we note in other chapters, reduction in the size of government can come by eliminating a lot of departments as well as reducing the headcount across the board in departments that do not directly impact national security. I share a number of positions with Ron Paul.

For example, I oppose the federalization of airport security and the TSA, and as noted above, the Homeland Security group and any increase in police state tactics for the US. I would also eliminate many federal government agencies, such as the U.S. Department of Commerce, the U.S. Department of Health and Human Services, the Federal Emergency Management Agency

(FEMA), the Interstate Commerce Commission and the Internal Revenue Service in addition to the previously mentioned Department of Education, Department of Energy, and Department of Homeland Security. Of course, as noted in other chapters of this book, all of the funding for Obamacare and the cadre of new workers brought in should be eliminated immediately.

Congress lies to keep us in our place!

Congress engages in much chicanery to give the public the idea that they are working on our behalf. Most of the time, however, they are not. So, when we see promising bills come out and they begin to go through the process, we often think these will pass and become law. It is a good sign to see good legislation but often the bills never come up for a vote and Congress uses their one-time existence to show how magnanimous they were as representatives in proposing things that are destined by design to never happen.

One such bill appears to be H.R. 2114 which is the "Reducing the Size of the Federal Government through Attrition Act of 2011." What a joke this will be next year when it is still on somebody's desk.

It was put forth by the 112th Congress: 2011-2012 with an idea to reduce the size of the Federal workforce through attrition, and they also note that it is for other purposes, which are not divulged. The sponsor is Rep. Darrell Issa [R-CA].

The bill right now, as this book is being written is in the first step in the legislative process. The next step is for the bill to go to committees that deliberate, investigate, and may revise it before going to general debate.

Unfortunately for the good bills and fortunately for the bad bills, the majority of bills and resolutions never make it out of committee.

Government is confiscatory

Democrats love big government. They do not as a rule like charities either. Instead, they like the federal government to be a big charity. As they figure out ways to increase their wealth through insider trading, they like to limit the general public's opportunity for getting rich.

They like to take as much from anybody who has become successful and they use class warfare techniques to convince those in society who have yet to become rich that it is OK to steal the wealth of anybody who begins to do well in life and redistribute it to those who are yet to become rich.

In many ways instead of permitting anybody to realize the American dream, today's' liberal / progressive / Marxist Democratic leaders want to turn the American dream into a handout for which nobody must ever work. To do this, they depend on big government to pull it off. They also depend on a tax system so complex that they can spare their own income from being taxed for redistribution. You know that Congress devises special deductions and subsidies for which only they or select cronies qualify. They love giving your money to somebody else and taking credit for handing it out. With a small, accountable government, they would not be able to do this as easily.

Though I have been a Democrat all my life, I find today's leaders of the Democratic Party to be out of touch with reality and out of touch with the original ideals of the Party of the working man. I am a proud TEA Party member and my Senate Candidacy for the Democratic nomination in Pennsylvania is endorsed by the Independence Hall Tea Party, which operates in the tristate area: Pennsylvania, New Jersey, and Delaware.

My big objective is to reduce the percentage of the GDP consumed by the federal government.

I see so much waste in government that the best thing we can do is give them less and less to spend or our own representatives will simply cheat us of our hard earned income. I therefore oppose all tax increases as a matter of principle. Our corrupt government will simply waste my contribution and your contribution.

Short of the FAIR tax, which I support, I would like the current tax code simplified so there is no IRS or an IRS about 5% of the size needed for collections. While we have a corporate income tax, the government should be prohibited from picking winners and losers. So, I am OK with a net reduction in the tax rates and the elimination of tax credits, subsidies, and other loopholes that are geared to help some people and/or corporations while others pay their full share. I am also for tariffs and protectionism so that US industries can prosper and the funds will help with the deficit and debt and in making the tax system fairer.

There is a man who Democrats associate with the TEA Party and the Republican Party's stubborn refusal to permit the Democrats to confiscate any more of your income in unjust usurious taxes. He is not a politician and so the liberal media have attacked him ferociously.

Grover Norquist has been targeted by Democrats because he wants to dramatically reduce the size of the government. He thinks in most ways like I do and I love his quip on reducing the size of government: "I don't want to abolish government. I simply want to reduce it to the size where I can drag it into the bathroom and drown it in the bathtub."

Norquist is not the head of the Conservative Party or the Republican Party or the Libertarian Party but maybe he should be. He does think Americans have a right to become successful and once they do, they should be able to live a bit of the American Dream rather than have the government steal all of the proceeds from their efforts and redistribute it to those who have chosen to sit on their duffs. This drives Democratic leaders and their cronies in the media nuts. Good!

By doing all of this, Norquist, and I believe that we can reduce the size of government and that is a very good thing.

Grover Norquist heads a group called "Americans for Tax Reform." Their mission statement is quite admirable: "The government's power to control one's life derives from its power to tax. We believe that power should be minimized"

A cavalcade of budget reductions to reduce the size of government

Republicans and TEA Party conservatives and others who are thinking clearly have asserted that the federal government doesn't have a revenue problem; it has a spending problem. Their conclusion is correct. We can translate this to fit the theme of the chapter by noting that the United States does not have a spending problem, per se; we have a big government problem. To support a big government, the problem is a country must spend, and spend, and then while waiting to be rescued from its huge size, it must spend some more.

Most Americans recall the trauma our legislators put us through during the 2011 debt ceiling debate. It exposed a deep divide between "spending cuts" and government reduction. Our politicians had sold us out by spending that which the treasury did not have. Yet, all of a sudden, these contemptible politicians, who are on a trajectory to increase the debt $5 trillion by the end of 2011, and $15 trillion by the end of 2021 somehow got religion. One camp says *ignore fiscal discipline*, and the other says, pretend that you are not ignoring fiscal discipline by *making cuts of token amounts* using subterfuge. Meanwhile neither camp is serving America.

Both camps have signed up to extend the debt to about $25 trillion over ten years while pretending that they are trying to reduce spending. Despite the charade, somehow, knocking off about $3 trillion from the bloated $25 trillion has become impossible for our inept Congress. Yet, even with that "reduction, which has all the increases in the budget already factored in," the debt will increase from $15 trillion this year to $22 trillion in ten years. How could our incompetent Congress, with that much excess already built in, not even pull off a decrease in the increase?

You see it is all smoke and mirrors with little reality. This deceitful Congress tries to achieve its spending cuts through slowing the rate of what many call "straw men" baseline projections of growth. In other words, though Congress talks spending cuts, they are really talking about slowing the growth of spending increases but not stopping them at all. Consequently, the Congress, and I mean both sides of the aisle, propose spending cuts without downsizing one iota of government, along with all its nasty effects on the private sector.

The media unfortunately joins them in not to telling the truth. Instead of spelling it out, the biased media slammed Republicans who were trying to protect your opportunity for the American Dream. Meanwhile Democrats were hoping you would go to Australia to find any dream you may feel you need to fulfill because they are not about to give it to you here.

The media has made Republican opposition to tax increases a negative, while not doing any fact checking on the notion that there will be no real cuts. The problem for Democrats and their friends in the media is that cuts in spending actually downsize

government. That is not something about which a socialist
regime and its complicit media have any interest.

Republicans unfortunately have not taken their small amount
of power that they gained in 2010 very seriously. They seem to
be happy being known as *not as bad as Democrats* instead of
being gutsy enough to do what they promised the people.
Republicans caved into the media and Democrat threats
because they feared the debt limit deadline would be enough to
sink their opportunities for reelection. In this they are as bad as
the campaigner in chief, but not really. Nobody is that bad.
Rather than try to assure that the walking and talking members
of society understood the Ryan budget blueprint, for example,
they instead hid from it so that Americans would not associate
anything truthful with the Republicans.

Republicans were not really afraid of a government shutdown
in April, or August, or October 2011, they were afraid they
could not explain it well enough to the people to avoid the
blame.

Besides the lying media, there is one really big problem in the
idea that conservatives can help get the country functioning
again. It is called the Senate. The conservatives own the House,
lock stock and barrel, but the House will not make hay with this
in the press. Though I see John Boehner as a fine man, I have
concluded he is an ineffective leader. Conservatives deserve
more than Boehner.

The conservative House has actually done an OK job, but the
media, including Fox will not give them proper coverage so the
people can actually begin to trust that it is the dark forces of the
progressive / liberal / Marxist Democrats who are working
hard to bring the country under.

Harry Reid, the Majority leader in the Senate is intentionally
impotent and he guides the impotent do-nothing Senate so that
it does nothing. It has not passed a budget in over 1100 days.

As such, with the possible exception of the MilCon/VA bill, the Senate will not pass a single appropriations bill, thereby rendering all the House bills irrelevant.

By the way, before you applaud the Senate for its one fiscal act, consider this: "Citizens against Government Waste" (CAGW) were not very pleased about this solitary act of the Senate's 2012 Military Construction Appropriations Bill. The worst Senate of all time could not resist the smell of potential success, and so, though they could not pass a real budget, they were able to insert two earmarks into this bill. It shows that they can continue indefinitely being unconcerned about the plight of America.

I found a simple solution to downsizing US government on the Internet. It is not cited. The message is that it would be easy to reduce the size of government if we really wanted to downsize government. The suggestion is to start with easy programs, which history shows not only do not work, but cause actual harm. Examples include NPR, Planned Parenthood, NLRB, etc. and just cut them out.

How can any prudent conservative disagree with that approach? The suggestion continues that after these simple cuts, it would be wise to go after wasteful giveaway programs, including food stamps to those not needy, housing allowances, all subsidies including ethanol. Nobody is talking about the people who absolutely survive on these programs because they have issues in life. But, how many people have figured out how to game the system so they can collect unearned benefits? We can eliminate them merely by de-incentivizing the workers who encourage them to sign up for the grab bags from our treasury. In Pennsylvania, the newly elected Governor has recently been praised for such actions.

Another great quote came in from Internet sources, which explains our dilemma quite well: "Democracy must be something more than two wolves and a sheep voting on what to have for dinner." — **James Bovard**

Besides the small budget reductions before the Bovard quote, I would suggest that we eliminate some of the bad agencies such as the EPA, Energy and Education. After eliminating whole departments, perhaps some by attrition and others quickly to avoid more pain, cut the whole government by some large enough percentage, effective immediately. Let's take a hard look at this James Madison quote so we know just how dangerous it is playing with this kind of fire in big government.

"If Congress can do whatever in their discretion can be done by money, and will promote the general welfare, the Government is no longer a limited one, possessing enumerated powers, but an indefinite one, subject to particular exceptions." — **James Madison**

Senator Jim DeMint of South Carolina says: "Electing Republicans who don't have the courage of their convictions may be easier in some circumstances, but it won't save our country." — **Jim DeMint**

Big Government dot com offers some great thoughts on making government smaller. We should pay attention and encourage our lawmakers to bring forth good ideas such as these:

"We can stop the debt from growing by lowering the federal budget deficit to zero. We've done it before and there's no reason that we cannot do it again. The last time we had a balanced federal budget was in 2000. The mechanism that helped achieve this was the Gramm-Rudman-Hollings Act, a law that has now been allowed to expire. Gramm-Rudman-Hollings required across-the-board cuts if the President and Congress did not reach agreement on set deficit reduction goals. In effect, it supplied the backbone needed to control spending when backbone was lacking. We need to restore Gramm-Rudman-Hollings at once.

"We also need leaders in the House, Senate, and White House who agree that the time is now, and the responsibility is ours. I [the big government.com author] propose that we not only restore Gramm-Rudman-Hollings, but that we dramatically cut the federal budget deficit proposed by the President by more than half. We not only can achieve this, we must."

Here's another way in which we can achieve this. It is an old solution but it can surely be updated for today.

"First, cap non-defense discretionary spending to fiscal year 2009 levels for a savings of $101 billion. The White House Budget caps this item at fiscal year 2010 levels of $690 billion, but this category already grew from $589 billion in fiscal year 2009—a 30 percent increase. They let it rise by 30 percent before deciding to cap it. We should cap it at once.

"To achieve this overall cap, many specific budget items in this category could be eliminated entirely including the $3 billion annual expenditure in subsidies for corn ethanol. And we should sell the portfolio of Freddie Mac and Fannie Mae, and end any future government subsidies for them.

"There is no evidence that the stimulus bill has produced the 2 million new jobs the President claims, over what the private sector would have produced if the same funds had been allowed to stay with the private sector. Yet the White House proposes increasing the amount spent from $202 billion in 2009 to $353 billion in 2010 and $232 billion in 2011. I propose cutting this increase in spending over fiscal year 2009 in half for a savings of $292 billion... More ideas are more than possible if we have the heart to get our country on the right path.'

"Taken together, these proposals would have saved an estimated $750 billion in fiscal year 2010 alone, well more than half of the entire projected deficit for that year. The time to act is now."

According to **Andrew Biggs,** resident scholar at the American Enterprise Institute, little is known about the contractor workforce and whether the government is getting good value for its money. Outsourcing (not offshoring), however, may increase both savings and flexibility not realized with a large federal workforce, he added:

"If [outsourcing] were done to cover up federal hiring, that's the wrong way," Biggs said. "But if you say a contractor provides better value for money but also the ability to recast the federal workforce according to changing needs, it may make sense."

The federal government is huge and with Obamacare if fully implemented it will increase by an additional $1/6^{th}$, which we will round to 16%. In the U.S. economy, without Obamacare, total government spending at all levels represents about 28 percent of the gross domestic product, which is the total of everything bought and sold. What is now private spending makes up the other 72 percent. If we add the 16% now included in private spending for Obamacare, we are permitting government to control over 44% of our economy.

When this number sneaks over 50%, the inmates will be running the asylum and the private sector will not be the place to be. Ironically, without a robust private sector, there will be no source of funding for government and it will capsize in much the same way as the story of the ant and the grasshopper. Unfortunately for some, somebody has to work. For all our sakes don't you think that big government must be shrunk to save the country?

Ten critical ingredients to ignite small government campaigns

Carla Howell, writing for smallgovernmentnews.com offers ten critical ingredients to downsizing government. This list is worth keeping in hand as we go about the task of bringing our government down to size. The list is a fitting way to end this chapter on *Reducing Government*, the final frontier.

Howell notes that poll after poll shows that most Americans think government is too big. Like those of us reading this book, the people want to shrink the size of government substantially. Of course it is easier said than done. So, Howell says to advance the notion of small government, we must run and support campaigns and candidates for office as well as ballot initiatives that feature bold, small government proposals. How can I not agree? In this regard, the RRR plan will help for sure. Howell's 10 critical ingredients are as follows:

1. All parts of the proposal serve to shrink the overall size, spending, taxes, and/or authority of Big Government. Unequivocally.
2. It removes a chunk of Big Government - and offers no help to give it life at another level of government.
3. It removes a chunk of Big Government - and replaces it with nothing.
4. Tax cuts include commensurate overall spending cuts, and vice versa.
5. The proposal does not in any way expand Big Government. Small government. Every issue. Every time. No exceptions. No excuses.
6. When proposed by a candidate, he promises to take specific actions to make it happen, e.g., voting or sponsoring legislation.
7. The proposal directly benefits a large portion of voters in the district for which it is offered.
8. The proposal offers huge, direct benefits to the average voter.
9. The candidate or spokesperson spells out those benefits for voters.
10. The proposal takes effect in full as soon as possible, if not immediately.

Howell concludes with "A proposal that lacks any of these ingredients risks being dead on arrival. A proposal that includes all of these ingredients will wake up voters, get them to the polls, and make small government a real possibility. "

"Isn't that what you want?"

I know it is what I want.

Chapter 17   Remember Mistakes

Remember our last big voting mistake

We all make mistakes and many of us, especially Democrats
such as me, made some big mistakes about four years ago when
we got rid of the voice of reason in government and sent a ton of
conservatives home. This left government to the mere whims of
socialist / progressive Marxist Democratic representatives, and
the most liberal President of all time.

Since Democratic leadership then and still today is against
capitalism and mercantilism, this was not a good move on our
part. Our economy and many other facets of American lives
have gone way downhill. It was a big mistake. The 111th
Congress, run by Nancy Pelosi and Harry Reid and the
presidency, run by Barack Hussein Obama let us down big-time.

What we did was give the Democratic Party free rein over our
lives. For that, they decided to have big government manage our
healthcare and take away our health choices; they took over GM
and Chrysler; they bailed out banks and they prosecuted none of
their Harvard friends who stole billions on Wall Street. The Wall
Street cronies had almost collapsed the economy with their
greed. They also rammed through other legislation such as
multiple stimuli and omnibus bills that sent almost a trillion
dollars into the hands of Democratic campaign donors for
"shovel ready projects." Hah!

By the end of the two years of the 111th Congress, in 2010, the
economy was in the toilet, the debt and deficit were out of
control, and the unemployment rate went from 4.5% in

December 2008, to between 9 and 10% in December 2010. Yes, this was a big mistake, but it was very hard to undue even after we realized how bad it was.

Some mistakes are so big that they cannot be undone overnight. So, in November 2010, we went ahead and began the process of bringing America back to the people. We bounced out a good part of the corrupt 111th Congress and gave Republicans control of the House of Representatives. We even elected a few conservative Democrats. You see, I am not alone. All of this stopped the onslaught of unbridled progressive legislation as the House now provided a countervailing force to the still democratically controlled Senate and the Democratic presidency.

Why did the voters not take over the Senate also in 2010? It would have been good if we had for many pieces of legislation that passed the House were never introduced into the Senate by Harry Reid, who still is the Majority Leader in the Senate. Barack Obama blamed Republicans but it was Harry Reid who supplied all the governmental gridlock by not even permitting legislation to come up for a vote.

How is that? The people in his home state of Nevada sent Reid back to the Senate in 2010 despite his poor record. And, because the Democrats had the majority, they elected Harry Reid as their leader again. He has been hurting Americans from day one by not putting forth conservative legislation for an up or down vote. It is his job but he does it poorly. I hope Nevadans are disappointed in their man as he continues to hurt the country.

Why were Democrats able to keep control of the Senate in 2010? Republicans picked up six seats and almost gained control of the Senate. It is more difficult to win the Senate when a lot of Republican incumbents are in the 1/3 mix. Every two years just a third of the Senate is up for reelection so a blanket expulsion was not possible and there were certain liberal states that chose to keep their Democratic Representatives.

Therefore, it is up to us voters again in 2012 to clean out another third of the Senate. It is time to rid the Capitol of the stench of the most corrupt two Senates of all time – the 111th Congress and the 112th Congress. We made a big mistake in 2008 and again in 2010 in the Senate and we can undo that mistake in 2012 by voting in a conservative Senate. Republicans in most states are the best option. In Pennsylvania, of course, I am a deep conservative Democrat and I would be pleased for Pennsylvanians to select me as their conservative Senator in 2012.

We also made a mistake in our selection of the President in 2008. Barack Obama has proven to be an incompetent leader in domestic and foreign affairs. Our debt is up by $5 trillion and unemployment is at its highest levels since the depression. Moreover, this recession is so poorly managed by the Obama Administration that even Democrats such as Robert Reich suggest we have another ten years before it will correct itself. We cannot afford Barack Obama on the domestic front for sure. We cannot afford him for the time remaining in this term but we definitely cannot afford him for another four years. A vote for Obama in 2012 is a vote for the destruction of America.

On the foreign affairs side, Obama does not represent America in a positive light. He has lost Egypt and Libya and he has not managed Iran very well. Moreover, he has alienated Israel, giving the Palestinians priority over our longtime ally. He has done many more flagrant things that make America weak in the world such as cow-towing to the Russians and reneging on our promise to set up a missile defense system in Eastern Europe. Obama's lies may be glossed over by our own corrupt media but his lies have not made us any friends across the world.

We have a great opportunity to undue this big mistake as we pick a new President in 2012. He is a clever campaigner and he will lie and promise the moon to get on our good side. We must be strong and throw him out where he belongs. I do not care who is running against Obama. I think a firewood log, a block of granite, or even a pepper shaker would do a better job.

Whichever Republican wins the primary, Americans owe it to other Americans to vote him or her in as our next President. We won't get many more chances to undo the worst presidency in American history. So we better make good use of this one. .

The Grey Haired Brigade is ready to help us all win!

Well, here we are with another "R," calling us to remember and remediate our mistakes. While I was contemplating how to end this book, I received an excellent email from the Grey-Haired Brigade, and it is how I would like to put the final touches on this book. This is a powerful email. My hair is a little grey, mostly white, and I still have a few dark hairs to remind me of how I once looked. So, I feel "entitled" to use this email as my sign off for RRR.

From: anamerican@isp.com
Sent: Monday, Oneday 28, 2011 7:27 PM
To: anotheramerican@www.com
Subject: Grey-Haired Brigade

Subject: Fwd: I'm a member, don't delete just pass it on...

Grey-Haired Brigade

They like to refer to us as senior citizens, old fogies, geezers, and in some cases dinosaurs. Some of us are "Baby Boomers" getting ready to retire. Others have been retired for some time. We walk a little slower these days and our eyes and hearing are not what they once were. We have worked hard, raised our children, worshiped our God and grown old together. Yes, we are the ones some refer to as being over the hill, and that is probably true. But before writing us off completely, there are a few things that need to be taken into consideration.

In school we studied English, history, math, and science which enabled us to lead America into the technological age. Most of us remember what outhouses were, many of us with firsthand experience. We remember the days of telephone party-lines, 25 cent gasoline, and milk and ice being delivered to our homes. For those of you who don't know what an icebox is, today they are electric and referred to as refrigerators. A few even remember when cars were started with a crank. Yes, we lived those days.

We are probably considered old fashioned and outdated by many. But there are a few things you need to remember before completely writing us off. We won World War II, fought in Korea and Viet Nam. We can quote The Pledge of Allegiance, and know where to place our hand while doing so. We wore the uniform of our country with pride and lost many friends on the battlefield. We didn't fight for the Socialist States of America; we fought for the "Land of the Free and the Home of the Brave." We wore different uniforms but carried the same flag. We know the words to the Star Spangled Banner, America, and America the Beautiful by heart and you may even see some tears running down our cheeks as we sing. We have lived what many of you have only read about in history books and we feel no obligation to apologize to anyone for America.

Yes, we are old and slow these days but rest assured, we have at least one good fight left in us. We have loved this country, fought for it, and died for it, and now we are going to save it. It is our country and nobody is going to take it away from us. We took oaths to defend America against all enemies, foreign and domestic, and that is an oath we plan to keep. There are those who want to destroy this land we love but, like our Founders, there is no way we are going to remain silent.

It was mostly the young people of this nation who elected Obama and the Democratic Congress. You fell for the "Hope and Change" which in reality was nothing but "Hype and Lies." You have tasted socialism and seen evil face to face, and have found you don't like it after all. You make a lot of noise, but most are all too interested in their careers or "Climbing the Social Ladder" to be involved in such mundane things as patriotism and voting.

Many of those who fell for the "Great Lie" in 2008 are now having buyer's remorse. With all the education we gave you, you didn't have sense enough to see through the lies and instead drank the 'Cool-Aid.' Now you're paying the price and complaining about it. No jobs, lost mortgages, higher taxes, and less freedom. This is what you voted for and this is what you got. We entrusted you with the Torch of Liberty and you traded it for a paycheck and a fancy house.

Well, don't worry youngsters, the Grey-Haired Brigade is here, and in 2012 we are going to take back our nation. We may drive a little slower than you would like but we get where we're going, and in 2012 we're going to the polls by the millions. This land does not belong to the man in the White House nor to the likes of Nancy Pelosi and Harry Reid. It belongs to "We the People" and "We the People" plan to reclaim our land and our freedom.

We hope this time you will do a better job of preserving it and passing it along to our grandchildren. So the next time you have the chance to say the Pledge of Allegiance, Stand up, put your hand over your heart, honor our country, and thank God for the old geezers of the "Grey-Haired Brigade."

Author, Anon. Grey-Haired Brigade Member

Footnote:

This is spot on. I am another Gray-Haired Geezer signing on. I will circulate this to other Gray-Haired Geezers all over this once great county. Can you feel the ground shaking??? It's not an earthquake, it is a STAMPEDE.

--- End of email—

Let us remember our mistakes so we do not repeat them. God bless you all.

LETS GO PUBLISH! Books by Brian Kelly: (Sold at www.bookhawkers.com; Amazon.com, and Kindle)

LETS GO PUBLISH! is proud to announce that more AS/400 and Power i books are becoming available to help you inexpensively address your AS/400 and Power i education and training needs: Our general titles precede specific AS/400 and other technology books. Check out these great patriotic books which precede the tech books in the list.

The Trump Plan Solves the Student Debt Crisis
Solution for new student debt and the existing $1.3 Trillion debt accumulation

101 Secrets How to be a High Information Voter
You do not have to be a low-information voter.

Why Trump?
You Already Know… But, this book will tell you anyway

Saving America The Trump Way!
A book that tells you how President Donald Trump will help Americans wind up on top

The US Immigration Fix
It's all in here. You won't want to put it down

I had a Dream IBM Could be #1 Again
The title is self-explanatory

Whatever Happened to the IBM AS/400?
The question is answered in this nee book.

Great Moments in Penn State Football Check out the particulars of this great book at bookhawkers.com.

Great Moments in Notre Dame Football Check out the particulars of this great book at bookhawkers.com or www.notredamebooks.com

WineDiets.Com Presents The Wine Diet Learn how to lose weight while having fun. Four specific diets and some great anecdotes fill this book with fun and the opportunity to lose weight in the process.

Wilkes-Barre, PA; Return to Glory Wilkes-Barre City's return to glory begins with dreams and ideas. Along with plans and actions, this equals leadership.

The Lifetime Guest Plan. This is a plan which if deployed today would immediately solve the problem of 60 million illegal aliens in the United States.

Geoffrey Parsons' Epoch… The Land of Fair Play Better than the original. The greatest re-mastering of the greatest book ever written on American Civics. It was built for all Americans as the best govt. design in the history of the world.

The Bill of Rights 4 Dummmies! This is the best book to learn about your rights. Be the first, to have a "Rights Fest" on your block. You will win for sure!

Sol Bloom's Epoch …Story of the Constitution This work by Sol Bloom was written to commemorate the Sesquicentennial celebration of the Constitution. It has been remastered by Lets Go Publish! – An excellent read!

The Constitution 4 Dummmies! This is the best book to learn about the Constitution. Learn all about the fundamental laws of America.

America for Dummmies!
All Americans should read to learn about this great country.

Just Say No to Chris Christie for President two editions – I & II
Discusses the reasons why Chris Christie is a poor choice for US President

The Federalist Papers by Hamilton, Jay, Madison w/ intro by Brian Kelly
Complete unabridged, easier to read version of the original Federalist Papers

Companion to Federalist Papers by Hamilton, Jay, Madison w/ intro by B. Kelly
This small, inexpensive book will help you navigate the Federalist Papers

Kill the Republican Party! (2013 edition and edition #2)
Demonstrates why the Republican Party must be abandoned by conservatives

Bring On the American Party!
Demonstrates how conservatives can be free from the party of wimps by starting its own national party called the American Party.

No Amnesty! No Way!
In addition to describing the issue in detail, this book also offers a real solution.

Saving America
This how-to book is about saving our country using strong mercantilist principles. These same principles that helped the country from its founding.

RRR:
A unique plan for economic recovery and job creation

Kill the EPA
The EPA seems to hate mankind and love nature. They are also making it tough for asthmatics to breathe and for those with malaria to live. It's time they go.

Obama's Seven Deadly Sins.
In the Obama Presidency, there are many concerns about the long-term prospects and sustainability of the country. We examine each of the President's seven deadliest sins in detail, offering warnings and a number of solutions. Be careful. Book may nudge you to move to Canada or Europe.

Taxation Without Representation Second Edition
At the time of the Boston Tea Party, there was no representation. Now, there is no representation again but there are "representatives."

Healthcare Accountability
Who should pay for your healthcare? Whose healthcare should you pay for? Is it a lifetime free ride on others or should those once in need of help have to pay it back when their lives improve?

Jobs! Jobs! Jobs!
Where have all the American Jobs gone and how can we get them back?

Other IBM I Technical Books

The All Everything Operating System:
Story about IBM's finest operating system; its facilities; how it came to be.

The All-Everything Machine
Story about IBM's finest computer server.

Chip Wars
The story of ongoing wars between Intel and AMD and upcoming wars between Intel and IBM. Book may cause you to buy / sell somebody's stock.

Can the AS/400 Survive IBM?
Exciting book about the AS/400 in a System i5 World.

The IBM i Pocket SQL Guide.
Complete Pocket Guide to SQL as implemented on System i5. A must have for SQL developers new to System i5. It is very compact yet very comprehensive and it is example driven. Written in a part tutorial and part reference style, Tons of SQL coding samples, from the simple to the sublime.

The IBM i Pocket Query Guide.
If you have been spending money for years educating your Query users, and you find you are still spending, or you've given up, this book is right for you. This one QuikCourse covers all Query options.

The IBM I Pocket RPG & RPG IV Guide.
Comprehensive RPG & RPGIV Textbook -- Over 900 pages. This is the one RPG book to have if you are not having more than one. All areas of the language covered smartly in a convenient sized book Annotated PowerPoint's available for self-study (extra fee for self-study package)

The IBM I RPG Tutorial and Lab Guide – Recently Revised.
Your guide to a hands-on Lab experience. Contains CD with Lab exercises and PowerPoint's. Great companion to the above textbook or can be used as a standalone for student Labs or tutorial purposes

The IBM i Pocket Developers' Guide.
Comprehensive Pocket Guide to all of the AS/400 and System i5 development tools - DFU, SDA, etc. You'll also get a big bonus with chapters on Architecture, Work Management, and Subfile Coding.

The IBM i Pocket Database Guide.
Complete Pocket Guide to System i5 integrated relational database (DB2/400) – physical and logical files and DB operations - Union, Projection, Join, etc. Written in a part tutorial and part reference style. Tons of DDS coding samples.

Getting Started with The WebSphere Development Studio Client for System i5 (WDSc). Focus is on client server and the Web. Includes CODE/400, VisualAge RPG, CGI, WebFacing, and WebSphere Studio. Case study continues from the Interactive Book.

The System i5 Pocket WebFacing Primer.
This book gets you started immediately with WebFacing. A sample case study is used as the basis for a conversion to WebFacing. Interactive 5250 application is WebFaced in a case study form before your eyes.

Getting Started with WebSphere Express Server for IBM i Step-by-Step Guide for Setting up Express Servers
A comprehensive guide to setting up and using WebSphere Express. It is filled with examples, and structured in a tutorial fashion for easy learning.

The WebFacing Application Design & Development Guide:
Step by Step Guide to designing green screen IBM i apps for the Web. Both a systems design guide and a developers guide. Book helps you understand how to design and develop Web applications using regular RPG or COBOL programs.

The System i5 Express Web Implementer's Guide. Your one stop guide to ordering, installing, fixing, configuring, and using WebSphere Express, Apache, WebFacing, System i5 Access for Web, and HATS/LE.

Joomla! Technical Books

Best Damn Joomla Tutorial Ever
Learn Joomla! By example.

Best Damn Joomla Intranet Tutorial Ever
This book is the only book that shows you how to use Joomla on a corporate intranet.

Best Damn Joomla Template Tutorial Ever
This book teaches you step-by step how to work with templates in Joomla!

Best Damn Joomla Installation Guide Ever
Teaches you how to install Joomla! On all major platforms besides IBM i.

Best Damn Blueprint for Building Your Own Corporate Intranet.
This excellent timeless book helps you design a corporate intranet for any platform while using Joomla as its basis.
4
IBM i PHP & MySQL Installation & Operations Guide
How to install and operate Joomla! on the IBM i Platform

IBM i PHP & MySQL Programmers Guide
How to write SQL programs for IBM i

www.ingramcontent.com/pod-product-compliance
Lightning Source LLC
Chambersburg PA
CBHW072115270326
41931CB00010B/1564